Hiroshima and Nagasaki: That We Never Forget

Hibakusha share their testimonies of survival

Hiroshima and Nagasaki: That We Never Forget

Hibakusha share their testimonies of survival

This edition compiled by the Soka Gakkai Youth Division

Daisanbunmei-sha, Tokyo
2017

Copyright © Soka Gakkai 2017
Second Printing, 2017

Published in Japan in 2017 by Daisanbunmei-sha, Inc.
1-23-5 Shinjuku, Shinjuku-ku, Tokyo 160-0022, Japan
http://www.daisanbunmei.co.jp/

Translated from the Japanese by Miwako Sawada, Elizabeth Baldwin and Steven Leeper
Book Design by Yuichi Kimura (ZERO MEGA Co., Ltd.)
Cover and Reference Materials Design by Michiko Kurihara (MK Studios Inc.)

All rights reserved.
No part of this text may be reproduced, transmitted,
or stored in or introduced into any information storage and retrieval system,
in any form or by any means whether electronic or mechanical, now known
or hereinafter invented, without the express written permission of the publisher.

ISBN: 978-4-476-06234-2

Printed and bound by Fujiwara Printing Co., Ltd.

Table of Contents

Editor's Note 8

Foreword 9
by Soka Gakkai Youth Division leader
Mitsushiro Takeoka

Part 1

Hiroshima August 6, 1945
For a Brilliant, Smiling Future
Testimonies of women from Hiroshima

Yoshie Oka *13*

Kazuko Kawada *21*

Setsuko Morita *31*

Emiko Yamanaka *42*

Ritsuko Seidai *53*

Emiko Okada *61*

Miyoko Matsubara *70*

Chisako Takeoka *77*

Hiroe Sato *86*

Yukie Tsuchimoto *96*

Kazuko Kamidoi *104*

Keiko Ogura *111*

Nobuko Suzuki *120*

Sachiko Yamaguchi *126*

Part 2

Hiroshima August 6, 1945
A Silence Broken

Testimonies of men from Hiroshima

Shigeru Nonoyama	*135*
Katsuyuki Shimoi	*144*
Senji Kawai	*154*
Kazunori Nishimura	*165*
Kazukuni Yamada	*174*
Tadashi Kihara	*184*
Yoshiharu Nakamura	*191*
Toshio Morimoto	*199*
Hiroatsu Taniguchi	*206*
Kaoru Hashimoto	*217*
Takanobu Hirano	*224*
Shoso Kawamoto	*234*
Kiyoshi Ito	*244*
Tadayoshi Tashima	*250*

Part 3

Nagasaki August 9, 1945
Telling the Story of Nagasaki Seventy Summers Later

Testimonies of men and women from Nagasaki

Tsugiya Umebayashi	*259*
Ryoko Iwanaga	*266*
Masahiro Tanigawa	*274*
Yasuko Nakao	*280*

Masaki Morimoto *288*

Mitsuko Iwamoto *294*

Isao Yoshida *301*

Yuriyo Hama *309*

Teruko Yamaguchi *316*

Kwon Sun-gun *322*

Nobuharu Takahira *328*

Fusae Fukushita *334*

Yasuko Tasaki *340*

Hiroshi Baba *346*

Part 4

Families Look at August 6, 1945
Ten Accounts to Pass Forward
Testimonies of families from Hiroshima

Keiko Oe / Masako Kosaka *355*

Masaichi Egawa *359*

Kozo Ikegami / Sumiyo Ikegami / Tetsuo Ikegami *365*

Tatsuko Ota *369*

Takashi Katsunori / Michiko Katsunori *374*

Sachiko Nakanishi *380*

Tokutomo Hase / Tsuchio Hase *384*

Teruo Tomita *388*

Michiaki Fujii / Kazuko Fujii *392*

Kazutoshi Nakamura *397*

Reference Materials

Editor's Note

This compilation combines the English language contents of four previously published bilingual books of testimonies by *hibakusha*—the survivors of the atomic bombings of Hiroshima and Nagasaki in August 1945. They have been re-edited for this volume.

The four previously published books (in English and Japanese) are: *Hiroshima August 6, 1945—For a Brilliant, Smiling Future* (Daisanbunmei-sha, 2016) compiled by the Soka Gakkai Hiroshima Women's Peace Committee; *Hiroshima August 6, 1945—A Silence Broken* (Daisanbunmei-sha, 2014) compiled by the Soka Gakkai Hiroshima Peace Committee; *Nagasaki August 9, 1945—Telling the Story of Nagasaki Seventy Summers Later* (Daisanbunmei-sha, 2015) compiled by the Soka Gakkai Nagasaki Peace Committee and *Families Look at August 6, 1945—Ten Accounts to Pass Forward* (Daisanbunmei-sha, 2015) compiled by the Soka Gakkai Hiroshima Youth Division.

The views expressed in these accounts are those of the individuals concerned and not of the Soka Gakkai.

Soka Gakkai Youth Division

Foreword

"Nothing is more barbarous than war. Nothing is more cruel."

These are the opening words of the book *The Human Revolution* by Daisaku Ikeda, president of the Soka Gakkai International (SGI), who experienced World War II firsthand in his youth.

How can those of us from younger generations who have not experienced the sufferings of war pass on this message to the future?

With this awareness, the Soka Gakkai Youth Division has long engaged in listening to and recording wartime experiences of war survivors. As part of our SOKA Global Action peace campaign launched in 2014, we have held meetings where atomic bomb survivors shared their testimonies on more than 50 occasions throughout Japan.

Most survivors say they do not want to talk about the atomic bombing or even think about it. Convinced by the sincere appeal of local Soka Gakkai youth members, some eventually opened up and shared their stories with young people for the first time because they do not want anyone ever to suffer what they have had to endure. It was heartrending to hear their experiences, as they slowly began to speak with deep emotion and some hesitation. Their strength as human beings enabled them to transform themselves from victims to witnesses for peace—as demonstrated by my own grandmother, Chisako Takeoka, a *hibakusha* from Hiroshima whose story is included in this volume. This touches us profoundly.

We felt that we must share the desire of the *hibakusha* for peace more widely with the young people of the world, so we have published collections of testimonies by atomic bomb survivors in both

Japanese and English in recent years. This volume is a compilation of the English language components of four books: those of the atomic bombing stories told by *hibakusha* in Hiroshima (one volume of women's experiences and one of men's) and Nagasaki, as well as one volume of interviews with *hibakusha* and their families about the bombing and their struggle against radiation-related illnesses.

The publication of this book is one of several projects marking the 60th anniversary of the Declaration Calling for the Abolition of Nuclear Weapons* issued by second Soka Gakkai president Josei Toda in 1957, which he described as the key element of his legacy for young people.

On July 7, a Treaty on the Prohibition of Nuclear Weapons, a legally binding instrument to prohibit these weapons, was adopted at the United Nations. It is noteworthy that the preamble includes a call to be mindful of the unacceptable suffering of the victims of the use of nuclear weapons (*hibakusha*) as well as of those affected by the testing of nuclear weapons. It is my heartfelt hope that this book will help the young people of the world heed the feelings and words of the *hibakusha* and stand up with the determination to be personally responsible for the abolition of nuclear weapons.

In closing, I would like to express my wholehearted gratitude to all the *hibakusha* and their families who shared their stories, those involved in the interviews, the translators and publisher Daisanbunmei-sha for their help in bringing this project to fruition.

August 2017

Mitsushiro Takeoka
Soka Gakkai Youth Division Leader

*www.joseitoda.org/vision/declaration/read.html

Part 1

Hiroshima August 6, 1945
For a Brilliant, Smiling Future

Testimonies of women from Hiroshima

Yoshie Oka
First to report the atomic bombing

Born in January 1931, Yoshie Oka was mobilized to serve in the communications command of the Chugoku Military District Headquarters during her third year at Hijiyama Girls High School. She was exposed to the atomic bomb while working there (0.7 kilometers from the hypocenter in Hiroshima). She reported the bombing to the Fukuyama Regiment from the destroyed bunker. For the sake of her classmates who perished young, she continues to tell her story.

I sense my dead classmates with me

In September 1991, I shared my atomic bomb experience for the first time. For many years I had been asked to give my testimony but steadily refused. It was painful enough to recollect the experience. I could not bear the thought of putting it into words.

"Please talk to my students! They're the same age as you were when it happened!" It was this plea by a teacher of third-year students in a public junior high school in Tokyo that moved my heart.

But I accepted the request on one condition: that I speak in the ruins of the Chugoku Military District Communications bunker on the grounds of Hiroshima Castle, where I had worked together with my fellow students.

When the time came and I tried to speak in that room steeped in painful memories, recalling my dead friends left me at times speechless. Eventually, I was weeping. "That girl used to sit here. . . That one sat over there." Their faces would rise up in front of me.

Somehow I was able to finish and get back to my home, but my distress from that one experience caused my platelets to decrease in number, and my thrombocytopenia (failure of the blood to clot) erupted again. My doctor ordered peace and quiet, and I had to lie low for two years.

When my symptoms improved, at the age of 63, I began giving my testimony again. By then, I had understood that I had lived that long because I had a mission: to tell the story accurately for the sake of my friends who died in that place.

I began to receive requests to speak at schools and other institutions as well. Even now, though, I only speak inside the ruined bunker whose square, low-ceilinged rooms of sooty, bare concrete have been cleared of transmission equipment, chairs, desks, even doors. Nothing remains but humid air lingering throughout. The students who have to listen to me in those rooms probably feel uncomfortable. But when I speak there, I sense my dead classmates speaking with me.

An injured soldier shouted, "New bomb!"

At the time, I was in my third year at Hijiyama Girls High School, mobilized to the Chugoku Military District Communications Headquarters. In the side of the embankment bordering the moat surrounding Hiroshima Castle, a semi-underground bunker was invisible to the air. It was the Strategic Command for relaying orders throughout the Chugoku region.

On April 7, 50 students of Hijiyama Girls High School had been assigned to the Student Communications Squad working in the Strategic Command, off-limits to all but selected military personnel.

After another 40 students were added to the 50, tasks were allocated among the 90 students in three groups. Thirty students worked each shift. The day shift went from 8 a.m. to 5 p.m.; the night shift was 5 p.m. to 8 a.m. and after one had done the night shift there was a period of time off. Girls who worked the night shift had to attend the 7:30 morning assembly in the open area in front of Imperial Headquarters. They did schoolwork at the nearby dormitory in the morning, then they slept in order to get up and work again at 5 p.m.

The Strategic Command comprised four rooms. In the room next to the entrance, 25 people sat with receivers to their ears to pick up information from 20-plus monitoring posts covering the Chugoku region. If they picked up a report of enemy planes spotted in a certain area, they would hit a key that would turn on the designated flashing light over a map on the wall of the innermost office.

The second office was for soldiers in the Communications Unit. In the third room, four dispatchers (students) faced the wall in two rows and delivered orders from the Strategic Command to various military stations and bases by telephone. On the opposite side of that room was a switchboard. When the Strategic Command issued an order, cords had to be inserted into jacks connecting direct lines to NHK (Nippon Hoso Kyokai, the Japan Broadcasting Corporation), the prefectural office, military plants, etc. Warnings had to be sent simultaneously. Operating the switchboard was my job.

At the bottom of the door was a little window. When an order was issued, a buzzer would sound as a memo passed through the window. The four dispatchers and I would notify the army bases and military plants using direct telephone lines. We had code words for "yellow alert" and "air-raid warning," and gave a number first to indicate the time of the alert or warning.

The innermost room was behind a very thick wooden door that could not be opened. The commanders and officers who were allowed in that room used a special door on the opposite side.

When air raids began regularly demolishing other cities, I wondered why "military city Hiroshima" and its castle grounds dense with military facilities were spared. Because bombers were leaving us alone, starting at the end of July, the long night shift was divided into an early night shift and late night shift, with each group composed of 15 students. On August 5, I was assigned to the early night shift. At 5 p.m., we took over from the day shift and worked until 1 a.m. In the middle of the night, we received the report: "Enemy aircraft sighted over Bungo Channel, heading north." I sent out an alert, then a warning, to NHK and the various military factories. As they received these notices, they turned on sirens to warn the citizens and military personnel.

Around 11 p.m., a large formation of 100 to 120 B-29s attacked Nishinomiya in Hyogo, then Imabari in Ehime; Ube in Yamaguchi was bombed at 4 a.m. "To your posts!" sounded the order.

The late night shift students were awakened. I did not go off shift at 1 a.m., but worked the night through without a wink of sleep.

At dawn, things finally quieted down; I hurried back to the dorm, poured *miso* soup on a bowl of rice, ate it, returned to the bunker and waited for the day shift to arrive.

When the hour passed 8:00 and my replacement still had not arrived, I was getting impatient when suddenly, a new report came in: "Three B-29s over Hiroshima, from the east." But neither alert nor warning had emerged from the Strategic Command.

At 8:13, finally a buzzer told us that a memo was slipping through the window at the bottom of the door. It said, "Yellow alert." Turning to the switchboard, I simultaneously inserted several cords to call the personnel at military factories. I knew the routine and felt no particular tension.

I got as far as "Yellow alert for Hiroshima, Yamaguchi..." Suddenly, a white flash furiously pierced my eyes.

"An accident!" I thought, as I lost consciousness. After perhaps four or five minutes, I gradually regained consciousness within an ash-colored fog.

Desks were toppled, chairs were broken, and I had been thrown three meters. The switchboard lay on top of me.

I saw no one else in the room. Squinting through plumes of ash and dust, I could make out Miss Itamura in the corner of the room, pressing on her eyes and ears. With only a minor cut on her eyelids, she seemed to be okay.

Comprehending nothing, we went outside. The first things we saw were remnants of the three buildings that had stood on the premises. Building 1, the headquarters; Building 2, officers' quarters; and Building 3, the auditorium—all had been blown down and destroyed. The ruins of the buildings formed mountains of wood chips and broken earthen walls. There were no flames, as we would see had we been hit by incendiary bombs.

Still uncomprehending, I scrambled alone up the embankment. The Chugoku Newspaper Building and the Fukuya Department Store were the only tall buildings in the city; the rest were low wooden buildings; now every neighborhood was transformed into rubble. But as yet, no fires. I could see Ujina Port just before me, though it was four kilometers away. I could even see Ninoshima Island, nine kilometers away. No buildings blocked my view. Below the embankment, an injured soldier groaned and shouted, "We were hit by a new bomb!"

When I came back to the communications room, Miss Itamura was on the telephone saying, "That's completely impossible!" She was talking to the Shikoku Military District Headquarters, which had called to provide information.

"Are the lines open?"

I went around the room picking up strewn telephone receivers. The first two or three were dead. But I kept trying, and finally the one connected to the Fukuyama Regiment was live.

"Hiroshima is annihilated!" I shouted into the phone.

"You said 'annihilated'?"

"Yes sir. It's annihilated."

"What do you mean, 'annihilated'?"

I was at a loss until I remembered the words of the injured soldier.

"We've been hit by a new kind of bomb, sir."

Then came the sound of wood crackling. Flames were approaching the bunker. We dashed outside and saw a soldier trapped under Building 1, writhing to get free.

We ran over to him, but the thick pillars overlaying each other on top of him were too heavy. Two of us could do nothing, but the janitor, Mr. Matsui, came up. The three of us wedged a thick pole under the pillars and used it as a lever to raise them, little by little, until the soldier was able to crawl out.

No time to rejoice. The flames were upon us.

We ran to the open area in front of Imperial Headquarters where the day shift students would have gathered for the morning assembly prior to shift change. No students there.

The flames were so powerful, the air was so dry, that my hair was on the verge of catching fire. Our faces were crimson from the heat. Our clothes were so hot, we instinctively jumped into the pond in front of the ruined headquarters. But even though we covered ourselves head to toe in muddy water, it dried immediately.

Surrounded by flames, Miss Itamura and I prepared to die.

Though it was daytime, it was as dark as dusk. As we stumbled around, pitch-black rain began to fall in large muddy drops that quickly became a torrent. We stayed in the pond, fully drenched.

After 40 minutes, the rain stopped so suddenly, it seemed it had never been. But it had stopped the fires. Unaware that it was a deadly downpour full of airborne radiation, we gave thanks for the rain. Many who were rained on fell ill with A-bomb disease.

We walked behind the destroyed castle tower to search for our friends and found three students sitting on stones. Usually, we could read each other's names on the nametags we wore, but these students' clothes were so tattered we couldn't see tags. The face of one had swollen to twice its size and forced her eyes shut. Another's neck was broken, turned backwards. She was barely conscious.

We recognized the one in the middle—it was Miss Hamaoka. Her right elbow joint was ripped apart, exposing her bone and tissue. Her hanging arm looked ready to fall off any second. She was desperate for water, but there was no water anywhere.

"We'll come back for you later, so wait here," we said, and then, "Where are the others?" Listlessly, Miss Hamaoka pointed, "Over there." In that direction lay the Army's Joto Bridge. On the other side of the moat was the Military Preparatory School.

I stood up and headed that way. As I crossed the Joto Bridge, I heard the sound of a body hitting water. "Miss Hamaoka?" Murmuring a prayer, I hurried back. There she was, floating on her stomach in the moat. In her intense thirst, she must have leaned down from the embankment and fallen in the water.

At dusk, medical rescue teams came from Yamaguchi and Okayama and carried 20 injured students and 30 injured soldiers to the temporary rescue station set up in the preparatory school.

We stayed with the injured students to help out. They all cried, "Water! Give me water!" The medics initially told us, "Burn victims die if you give them water, so don't!" When they saw the injured dying off rapidly regardless, they must have decided to offer water to those who had no chance. They told us quietly, "Give them one sip at a time." I filled a kettle with water and doled it out.

An officer was sitting down, his face blue, a piece of wooden pole thrust 20 centimeters into his back. The flesh around the skull of another soldier with an open hole in his brain quivered with each breath he took. Some were dead with their eyes wide open staring into the air. Others' abdomens were split, intestines spilling out. The rescue station was filled with people in a frightful condition.

At the end of the day, Miss Furuike, Miss Miyagawa and Miss Morita returned. Rejoicing to reunite with members of our team, they, Miss Itamura and I went to the Communications Room to get a little sleep. From the rescue station sounded the cries of young soldiers: "Mother!" In our exhaustion, even their piteous screams could not keep us awake.

The next morning, we went to the rescue station to help. Only one day after the bombing, white maggots were breeding in the burns on the bodies of students and soldiers.

Mothers appeared searching for their mobilized children. One cradled her severely wounded daughter and called her name ceaselessly. When the mother's tears fell on the face of her mortally wounded daughter, she awakened enough to smile. Her last words were, "I'm dying because I helped my country, so don't cry."

By the day the war ended, August 15, all of the 20 students taken in at the rescue station had died. From Osaka an officer and a noncommissioned officer came to take over from the dead commander.

On August 18, a demobilization ceremony was held at the destroyed headquarters. The noncommissioned officer dismissed us five students and sent us home to our parents with a simple "Thanks for your hard work."

We parted with, "See you at school in the second semester," but as soon as I got home, I came down with high fever, diarrhea and weariness profound enough to drag me to the depths of the Earth. These radiation effects kept me at home for two years.

Nonetheless, in my heart I vowed to pray the rest of my life for the repose of my dead classmates who fulfilled their responsibilities until the last moment, and to give witness that they lived. I summon my courage to continue to testify on their behalf.

Kazuko Kawada

Trapped in fear as I gave birth to a new life

Born in September 1931, Kazuko Kawada was exposed to the atomic bombing at a factory 2.5 kilometers from the hypocenter as a second-year student at First Hiroshima Prefectural Girls High School. Her father was killed at home. She and her mother survived, but she suffered continuous health problems. She got married and gave birth to two children at the risk of her own life. She avoided talking about her A-bomb experience, but shared it for the first time in 2011, when asked to give her testimony. She became a member of the Pilot Club, an international organization supporting people with mental disabilities as a volunteer, based on her motto: "Value life."

The bleeding wouldn't stop when I gave birth

"Your life will be in danger if this condition continues! I urge you to give up the child." When the doctor said this, I felt all the strength drain from my body.

It was 1960. I had conceived my second child, and my pregnancy was entering the fourth month. I can't deny I was terribly sad confronting the need for an abortion. On the other hand, to be honest, I was relieved.

Day after day, I was suffering overwhelming nausea. Nothing would go down my throat. I couldn't even take water. I was losing strength and could barely get out of bed. I was extremely thin. It was as if I had a critical illness. My days were full of hardship and suffering.

Although it was unavoidable and I was following medical advice, to this day I still feel the pain in my heart. I regret my "cruelty."

A year and six months earlier, I had given birth to my first daughter. It had been a difficult delivery. I was sick all through my pregnancy, unable to eat, as if I were seasick. My womb bloated up. If I lay down on my side, on my back or in any posture at all, I was in pain.

I endured this situation at home until four months before the due date. I was pulling weeds in the yard when I suddenly started bleeding. I was rushed to Hiroshima University Hospital and stayed there a month. Then I got sick and was hospitalized again three days before delivery.

The physical pain was severe, but I faced the birth with a calm mind because the doctor in charge was my former teacher at Hiroshima Women's Technical School.

I suffered massive bleeding, but when my daughter was born, the doctor immediately said, "You have a healthy baby!"

At that time, rumor had it that A-bomb survivors usually had deformed babies. Babies were being born with microcephaly and other problems. This was the talk around town. Because both my husband and I were *hibakusha*, we were terribly worried about our baby.

We discussed the situation and concluded, "It's useless to fear the unknown. The baby given to us will be our child. No matter what it's like, we'll cherish it." We decided never to worry again, and we haven't.

Still, I remember being relieved to hear the baby was healthy.

On the other hand, my outrageously intense sickness and massive bleeding during the delivery tormented me with fear for my daughter. "She's fine now, but what if something shows up later?" The doctor said, "We need to watch her for a while." After all, both her parents were *hibakusha*. She stayed in the hospital for a month. I stayed with her as much as I could every day, and my husband stopped by on his way home from work. We had blood and other tests every day to provide the hospital with data. We were continually tense, but I trusted my teacher completely. She and the doctor who took charge after the birth were obviously doing their best, so I never lost hope.

After a month, I left the hospital happy, holding my daughter in my arms. We were seen off by many doctors and staff.

After the distressful abortion of my second pregnancy, I gave birth to a son in 1961. I was sick all through the pregnancy, but not as severely as I had been the two previous times. Still, the bleeding after delivery was so bad my life was in danger.

Two big blocks of wood, like wooden clappers, were placed on my back and front. I was sandwiched in between. Using holes at the corners, the boards were laced together with strings. Was this a treatment? Could this stop the bleeding? Feeling nothing but the desire to protect my new son and myself, I endured this suffering as well, continually covered in greasy sweat.

I don't know for sure that my excessive bleeding is related to my exposure to the atomic bombing, but both times I gave birth, I bled so much I almost died. After the bombing, I was terrorized by bleeding from the gums. I also had excessive bleeding when a tooth was pulled.

I lost all human feelings

"That day," the morning started hot.

I saw an enemy plane, a B-29 bomber, coming through the cloudless blue sky. I could hear a low roar and see a white contrail. I had graduated from Fukuromachi Elementary School and was going to First Hiroshima Prefectural Girls High School. I was 13, just starting my second year. I had been mobilized to an aviation factory which was 2.5 kilometers from the hypocenter. I remember polishing aluminum alloy plane parts.

Everybody thought it strange when we heard a plane approaching, since the air-raid warning had just been cleared. We went to the windows to take a look. A sudden, intense, orange flash. Then, the building shook violently, as if in a powerful earthquake. I heard no boom or explosion. I threw myself on the floor, then got up and fled toward the hill with the others, none of us having any idea what was going on.

After a while, something dripped down on my cheek—black, sticky rain. Maybe a gas tank exploded, I dimly thought, imagining the black rain was fuel.

I sat in that black rain on the hill desperately wishing somebody would come and save me. My friend's family came and took her home. Another friend's family came and took her home, then another. These were families who lived far from the hypocenter.

My house was 500 meters from the hypocenter in Otemachi. No one came to get me. I crouched, trembling, watching downtown Hiroshima burn.

The fire spread like a belt across the whole city. Eventually, when another friend's father came to take her home, I went down the hill with them. We left Hiroshima burning behind us and walked all through the night, heading for our designated evacuation site in Jigozen village. My grandparents' house was in Jigozen, and my father and his brothers had agreed to go there in the event of an emergency.

I still can't forget the scenes I saw on the way. Crowds of sufferers looking completely inhuman. Their faces, backs or hands or feet were hideously burnt a blackish-red, their skin peeled off and dangling down to cover their eyes. People wandered here and there like the living dead. I joined this procession and headed for Jigozen.

"Water! Please give me water!" "Help me! Help me!" The final pleas of the dying remain in my ears.

A mother carrying her badly burnt baby on her back followed

behind the procession. Her child was obviously dead, but the mother seemed not to believe it. She kept walking, constantly turning back to look at her baby. Soon, she ran out of strength. She crouched by the side of the road, and the procession left her behind. Everybody was stunned, out of energy. Nobody tried to help her keep walking.

As we walked toward the evacuation site, some people living along the road came out of their houses and offered us some tomatoes in a colander, but none of us had the power to stretch out a hand. We simply kept walking in the darkness with no reaction.

My mother happened to be at our evacuation site in Jigozen that day. She had gone to get some belongings she had left at my grandfather's house. A yellow alert kept her from going back to Hiroshima, so she escaped death.

Arriving in Jigozen, I was reunited with my mother at last, but I was neither relieved nor happy. I had no feelings at all. It's amazing how human beings can lose all emotion as a result of shock. It was as if something in my mind was broken. I was insensitive. No feelings of any kind sprang up in me.

My father had been at home that day. He ran a business with his two brothers. The three of them got along well. They held their property jointly and trusted each other completely.

On August 6, my father was exposed to the bomb with his older brother and his brother's wife, who lived in the same house as us. In our area, less than two kilometers from the hypocenter, only a few ferroconcrete buildings were left standing. Nearly every structure was burnt to the ground. Ujina Port, south of town, could be seen all the way from Hiroshima Station in the north. My home was 500 meters from the hypocenter. It was impossible to think my father could have survived.

The next morning, my mother and I, along with some relatives, left early to search the ruins of our house in Otemachi, which were still smoldering. We dug through the rubble, then walked around the town looking for my father, uncle and aunt, who we assumed were dead.

An incredible number of dead bodies were scattered through the area. There was no space to step. Burnt corpses looked like logs, unrecognizable even as male or female. I looked at their faces one by one, turning bodies over, which caused a terrible stench to fill my nose. Yet I had no sense of fear or disgust. The half-raw, half-burnt remains were not all human beings. During the war, our military city Hiroshima temporarily housed the Imperial Headquarters, and a large number of military horses were killed.

After much searching, we failed to find the remains of my father, uncle or aunt. Three days after the bombing, when the fires had died down, soldiers gathered corpses, dug holes, placed the bodies on piles of logs and cremated them. They ignited the logs and the fire gradually grew into a huge flame. As the fire gained power, the bellies of the bodies burst open with a strange hissing sound. Pink internal organs popped out, swelling larger and larger.

My mother and I watched all this in a daze.

About one month after the bombing, the big Typhoon Makurazaki hit Hiroshima. Rivers flooded. The entire city was covered in water. We had dug up the soil all through the ruins around our house but failed to find any remains. After the flood, two bodies appeared above ground near a paving stone at the entrance of our house. We decided they were my father and uncle, so we had a funeral and cremated them. My aunt is still missing.

This came more than a month after the bombing, and I still had no emotion. But that night, with their ashes in front of our eyes, my mother and I held each other and cried for the first time.

We cried a long time, and somehow those tears melted my frozen heart. Human feelings revived in me the next day.

About the time I recovered my emotions, my body began to

break down. I had a constantly high fever, bleeding from the gums, then bleeding from the throat. My mouth was continually filled with bloody foam. Blood was also in my stools, and my hair fell out. I was later diagnosed with A-bomb disease but, at the time, the cause of my symptoms was unknown. Bleeding from gums and throat were diagnosed as diphtheria and bloody stools as typhoid fever, both legally designated infectious diseases.

With no facility to isolate me and no doctor or medicine to treat me, I had to fight the disease alone lying in a storage room in my grandparents' house in Jigozen. I was isolated in the storage room, not allowed to go out. We kept my "legally designated infectious disease" secret from the neighborhood. My mother went to the bamboo grove at the back of the house and buried my vomit and excreta late at night. Soon rumors arose in the neighborhood about a female ghost haunting the bamboo grove.

I don't know where she heard about it, but Mother said, "*Dokudami* (saururaceae) is good for your disease." She picked the *dokudami* leaves growing in a nearby field every day, roasting them in an earthenware pan and extracting the essence by boiling them in a kettle. She made *dokudami* tea for me to drink. I was forced to drink that smelly *dokudami* tea instead of water. She was so thorough she used *dokudami* extract to boil rice gruel for me.

Then, mysteriously, I recovered enough in three months to go back to school. I was rescued by my mother's absolute determination to save her daughter. I believe I was miraculously able to recover thanks to the *dokudami* tea and my mother's love. Even now, when I see the white flowers of *dokudami*, I feel I am looking at life itself.

Our house in Otemachi was burnt out, so my mother and I moved to my uncle's hut near Miyuki Bridge.

When we gathered at school for the first time after the bombing, I learned that many of my friends had perished. The students and teachers who had remained at school and all of the 280 first-year students mobilized to demolish buildings in Dohashi were exposed directly and died.

Later, I heard that schoolmates were still dying one after another. This came as a big shock. Fear pressed on me heavily. I was afraid "that day" would get me next. That fear stayed in my heart a long time.

All my classmates who survived had the same fear. As a result, we have still never talked about "that day." Each of us escaped on our own and had our own experiences, and we were all afraid to talk about it.

When asked, "What happened that day?" some still tremble and remain silent. This profound anxiety seems peculiar to atomic bomb survivors. We still have never digested our experience thoroughly. We all carry intense feelings of grief, having so abruptly lost family members, friends, our entire communities and our normal daily lives.

There were thousands of orphans. I don't like to boast, but First Girls High was one of the best girls' schools in Hiroshima. We had many students from prestigious families, and most of us studied hard to achieve our dreams for the future. However, when I returned to school, I heard countless stories of classmates who had lost their whole family. Some were left with just a sibling or were taken by a relative to live far away. Thinking about their grief at having lost access to our school and to their dreams, I felt terrible pain in my heart.

Later, I went on to Hiroshima Women's Technical School. I had a weak constitution and was very skinny. My mother was quite worried about me. Saying, "You mustn't do any hard exercise," she never allowed me to do much physically.

It was a time of severe shortages, but she did her best to prepare meals that were good for my health. I didn't have much appetite, so I could eat very little, but I received a lot of tender care. I graduated from Technical School and moved to Hamamatsu, Shizuoka Prefecture, to work as a teacher. I lived in a dormitory and ate meals provided by the school with the other students. I worked hard on club activities and got steadily stronger.

Seven years later, I returned to Hiroshima to marry. My husband was the son of a teacher I had studied under at First Girls High. My mother-in-law had a very good reputation, and my mother was enthusiastic, saying, "It's easy to find a perfect husband, but very hard to find a perfect mother-in-law."

My husband was exposed to the atomic bombing at a school in Sendamachi, about two kilometers from the hypocenter. I was exposed at the airplane factory in Koi, at about 2.5 kilometers. We knew about each other's exposure, but the effects of radiation were not well understood, so we didn't even think about what might happen. Our two children have been healthy, free of effects of their parents' exposure. We haven't told them we are survivors, but my mother-in-law was an A-bomb storyteller, so we often ended up talking about the situation after the bombing. I have a feeling they know, at some level. But I have always deliberately avoided talking about it.

I picked up the phrase "Value life" as my motto because of my experience. The nongovernmental volunteer group Pilot International was established in 1921 in the United States. In 1951 the Tokyo Pilot Club was established in Japan.

We established the Hiroshima Pilot Club in 1992. These clubs support people with mental disabilities. We support people with various natural disabilities, such as Down syndrome or developmental problems, and those with brain injuries due to accident or illness.

Specialists offer direct care to these people, of course. We organize social activities and do what we can to get society to accept them. Our volunteer activities are designed to enable people with disabilities to live in their communities. We raise funds by holding lecture meetings and other events.

The headquarters of the Pilot Club is in the US, so I have gone to the US several times to attend conferences. Some have asked, "Why are you involved in a US-based volunteer organization? You must have suffered a lot because of the atomic bomb the US dropped."

But I believe we can only create peace if we can transcend hatred. People around the world want peace to prevail. To respect all life equally, to see ourselves as human, transcending race and nationality—isn't this the path to peace?

Setsuko Morita
I speak to children who do not know war

Born in November 1932, Setsuko Morita was aged 12 when she was exposed to the atomic bombing on the Eastern Drill Ground, about 1.7 kilometers from the Hiroshima hypocenter, and sustained deep burns on both arms. After she married, she moved to Osaka, but returned to Hiroshima at the age of 56, when she began telling her story as a member of the Hiroshima Eyewitness Association and the Hiroshima Prefecture Hibakusha Association. In 2010, she began telling her story as an Atomic Bomb Witness for the Hiroshima Peace Culture Foundation in New York, Paris, China and elsewhere.

"You smell!" "Get away, it's catching!"

When I walked into the bathing room of the public bathhouse, sharp stares cut into me. Some pointedly walked away from me; those at a distance stared with frank curiosity. Faces registered astonishment and fear.

Ugly, reddish, rubbery keloid scars rose from my arms and my left thigh.

Telling myself to ignore the stares, I continued to wash my body. But then the owner came and really shocked me: "Customers are uncomfortable—they think what you have might be catching. This will hurt business, so won't you come when no one's here, just before we close?" This was not Hiroshima, but Osaka. When my husband was transferred to Osaka, I had gone with a faint hope that my life would be more peaceful in a city where no one knew that I was a *hibakusha*.

I began going to the bathhouse late at night, just before closing, but that became increasingly burdensome. In the end, I filled the kitchen sink with hot water and did a quick scrub down. It was miserable. My ugly keloids continued to cause me great suffering.

After the war ended, I entered Kokutaiji High School, a school formed under the new coeducation system. Because the school I had graduated from, Second Hiroshima Prefectural Girls School, was attached to the Women's Technical School, it would have been easy to go there instead. However, since the two schools shared a building, and since I knew many of the girls my age and older, I wanted some distance between myself and that world.

It was hard for me to look at my fellow students with burn scars on their faces and heads. They were young women, so they suffered in ways that they could not voice. And I—scarred as I was—had to hear people say, "You're lucky. You didn't get burnt on the face."

Soon after the Atomic Bomb Casualty Commission (ABCC) was established on Hijiyama Hill, American soldiers and their Japanese interpreters pulled up at my school in jeeps and called me—only me—out of my class. Sandwiched between two soldiers, I rode to the ABCC for what turned out to be cursory blood testing and strength testing, followed by countless photos of the keloids on my naked body.

As a self-conscious girl of 17, I wanted to weep with chagrin and embarrassment. When it was over, sent back to school with no diagnosis or treatment, I was left with nothing but the humiliation of being a guinea pig. From then on, I refused all calls from the ABCC for testing.

Sometimes the bullies were schoolmates who'd escaped the bombing and had whole, strong bodies. Boys would cover their faces with their combat caps and cry, "You smell! It's catching!"

(They meant my keloids.) Infuriated, I'd glare and insult them back, but when I got home, I despaired for my future. I tried to kill myself by taking sleeping pills. I tried to end it all by jumping into the sea at night.

Over and over, I lamented, "If only I didn't have these keloids!"

"Rescue messengers"

At the time of the bombing, I was 12, and a first-year student at Second Hiroshima Prefectural Girls High School. Soon after I entered the school that April, the older girls were heading off for labor service, so my first semester began in a mostly empty school. By June, the worsening war situation put an end to classes, and all students did nothing but labor service.

That day, at 8:00 a.m., my group began to weed the Eastern Drill Ground on the north side of Hiroshima Station, about 1.7 kilometers from the hypocenter. Everywhere on the drill ground grew new rows of sweet potato vines planted to increase food production.

Suddenly there was a shout. "Look! A parachute!"

Just as I lifted my face, my body was swallowed in a hot flash. Then a powerful blast threw me. I lost consciousness. When I came to, I smelled a strange smell. Ignited weeds were burning. One by one, my friends staggered to their feet, looking like ghosts. Their clothes were charred, hanging like rags, smouldering. The girl who had been weeding right next to me had been blown four or five meters away.

Some girls had been looking straight up at the sky. Their faces were already swelling with burns, their eyelids sagged and concealed their eyes. Those whose faces had been sideways on to the flash were burnt and peeling, the skin hanging down on that side as they walked.

Some girls were trying to hold in their intestines, which had burst out near their hips. Some whose eyeballs had popped out were trying to push them in with the palms of their hands. We tried to grab the hands of prostrate girls and pull them up, but the skin of their palms came off in our hands.

Though the teacher in charge was burnt from her face to her waist, she shouted, "Hurry, everyone, come here!" She led us to the shrine on the nearby hill, Toshogu Shrine. Before we students began our weeding job, we had left our bags there for safekeeping. Unable to think at all, we desperately climbed the hill. About the time we reached the shrine, I felt, "I'm hot! It hurts!"

I took my canteen out of my bag to pour cool water on my burns, but I couldn't even tell where I was burnt. We splashed water on each other to cool our burns. Some of the girls couldn't even unscrew their canteens because the skin of their hands was sloughing off.

The left sleeve of my jacket was nearly gone. When I pulled it off, I saw the skin had slipped off from the top of my arm to my fingertips, just like a long-sleeved glove. Blood was seeping down from my elbow. My right hand was swollen. From the thigh of my left leg halfway up my bottom were deep burns under my burnt *mompe* workpants.

The teacher asked, "Who can walk?"

She told the able ones to walk to our school three kilometers away in Ujina to try to get help. Four or five of us started off in a group. Enduring the pain and urging each other on, we walked for our lives.

Starting off down the stairs from Toshogu Shrine seeking help, we encountered many people climbing up, fleeing in the opposite direction.

Some had bright red peeled flesh. We passed sooty, charred, slumped people who did not look at all human. It was frightening just to look at them, so we looked away. An overpowering stench filled the air.

About 30 minutes later, I felt nauseous and vomited a large quantity of filth.

Hiroshima Station was destroyed. We climbed up on the Ujina Line platform to look over the track in the opposite direction. The city was engulfed in flames and black smoke. Most wooden bridges over the rivers had fallen. Not so Enko Bridge, which was shorn of its handrails but still standing, with a streetcar stranded in the middle.

We decided to flee southward along the tracks of the Ujina Line. In fire cisterns along the way, we saw many corpses that looked like discarded mannequins, with only the heads sticking out.

In front of the railroad bridge in Ozu, women wearing aprons called out to us. "What school do you go to? Stay strong, you can make it home!" They handed out rice balls from a large box, but we couldn't eat anything.

The rice balls were covered with ash, and, fighting nausea, I could not put one in my mouth. Gastric juices and vomit continually drooled from the sides of my mouth.

We crawled over Ozu Bridge. By that time, our burns were so painful that walking was difficult. In the river below, corpses floated by—adults, children, horses. Many got caught on bridge girders. Was this a bad dream? Was it hell? How could we believe that this was really happening? All we could think was: get back to school and find people to rescue our friends back at Toshogu Shrine. Supported only by a strong sense of mission and responsibility, we kept going.

Whenever someone passed us, we pleaded, "Please tell Second Girls School that students are waiting for rescue at Toshogu Shrine!" But they just kept going as if they couldn't be bothered. One of our group fell behind when she could no longer walk. Another split off to go in a different direction. We were scattering.

When we passed the Clothing Depot and neared our school, we saw a flooded paddy where lotus roots were growing. The fresh green leaves made us feel we had suddenly entered heaven. We all waded into the paddy. The cool water soothed our hot bodies. Of course the water must have been muddy, but we drank to our heart's content.

We learned later that two or three other "rescue messengers" were sent from the drill ground to the school to get help. However, they never made it because bridges along the way had been blown down and roads were blocked. We got to Ujina only because we detoured around the back of Hijiyama Hill.

Finally arriving at Second Girls School, we saw that the roof of the wooden building had been blown off. Our large school ground, recently converted to potato fields, was now covered by countless straw mats. Our burnt schoolmates were laid in rows. The ones with the worst burns, the ones who were about to die, and the ones who were already dead were crammed into the music room and the room reserved for special ceremonies. All in all, the girls here were in far worse condition than the friends we had left on the hill.

When we tried to touch the girls we had left behind at the shrine, their skin peeled off in our hands. These girls in the schoolyard were burnt so deep by the heat ray that when you touched them, sticking to your hands was flesh as well as skin. One of these girls said, "I have to pee." A teacher brought her a water bowl used for flower arranging and said, "Do it in this." After she was done, pieces of flesh from her bottom were stuck to the edge of the bowl. The indescribable smell of corpses permeated the classrooms. The school was in such chaos that we had no one to report to about the students waiting on the hill.

Suddenly eager to see my mother, I headed to my house 10 minutes from the school. At almost 4:00 p.m., the street was empty and quiet. As I tottered into our neighborhood dragging my left leg behind me, I was suddenly surrounded by neighbors whose faces were red with blood.

At this distance—3.7 kilometers—from the hypocenter, the blast had thrown many houses down. Flying glass had pierced faces and bodies, covering them in blood. Mothers whose children had been outside working on building demolition were fearful and waiting for them out on the street. When they saw me, they shouted with joy as one and ran to me. One cried, "If Setsuko made it back, my daughter must be all right too!" Just then, surely from relief, I passed out.

When I came to, I was in my house. The roof had been blown off, so I was looking up at the stars. My mother's face, covered in dried blood, was peering down at me. She looked scary. The neighbors had used scissors to cut off the clothing that stuck to my body. Dipping cloths in disinfectant thinned in a bucket, they carefully wiped off mud from the lotus field, blood and pus.

They brought precious rationed cooking oil and applied it to my whole body. In a room strewn with glass and other objects thrown by the blast, they cleared a section just large enough for me, rolled out a straw mat, and laid me on it.

The next day, I came down with a fever near 40 degrees that lasted a week. The doctor gave up on me. "I don't know how she's still alive!" At that time my father, who had been sure I would die, apparently made a decision. "I'm going to leave this house to Setsuko instead of her brothers off at war. No matter what, I won't let her die!" I had four brothers who were each five years apart. All were soldiers who made it home after the war.

Lacking proper medicine and equipment but using knowledge he had gained as a medic in the Sino-Japanese and Russo-Japanese wars, Father faithfully applied cooking oil to my burns, sprinkled them with baby powder and wrapped them in gauze so that the bandages would not adhere to the burns. Even so, when the gauze was removed, unbearable pain shot through the top of my head. Removing the gauze slowly did nothing to reduce the pain. My father would hold me down and tear it off all at once. Blood flew everywhere. I screamed and lost consciousness.

Afterwards, oil was reapplied, baby powder sprinkled and gauze wound around my arms and leg. This was repeated until we ran out of oil and baby powder. In the end he was painting cucumber juice on my burns.

It was a fierce battle with no assurance of success. Evidently my mother prayed, "I'm going crazy with this. Please allow our daughter to die." The ordeal must have been even worse for my father.

Day after day, my parents argued about whether he should do this treatment, but he insisted that there was no other effective way to heal my burns. Mother's hands turned purple and swollen from washing my bandages, gauze and clothing. Awful substances were oozing out of me.

In later years, we learned that the daily blood-letting that accompanied the gauze changing had helped me. A doctor said, "If your blood hadn't been constantly purged, the contaminated pus it contained would have rotted your body from the inside. It was also good that you vomited soon after the bombing, in the grove of Toshogu Shrine."

But my nephews and nieces who returned from their evacuation sites would screw up their noses and complain, "Setsuko's room smells so bad, I can't go in there." The lymphatic fluid that oozed out with the pus emitted a powerful stench.

Over and over, the scabs on my burns would come off. In the end, the thin skin would swell up into an ugly, red rubbery mass. Two or three months later, thin, reddish keloidal skin would finally form and the bleeding would stop. What I was left with were keloids under my left arm running all the way to my fingertips. On my right arm, they ran on the outside, from the elbow to the top of the arm. My left thigh was left with a bright red keloid that climbed up onto my buttocks. Because I had been bending over to weed, I was burned from behind, but for some reason my upper back escaped the flash. Even so, a third of my body was burnt—if any more of my skin had been lost to burns, I would not have survived.

Around October, I was able to return to school, where I learned about the cruel deaths of my friends. I thought my heart would break. By about the end of our third year of high school, the students who had keloid burn scars on their faces stopped coming to school.

"You're lucky, Setsuko, you don't have keloids on your face." Every time one of them said that, I felt somehow accused, wounded. What could I say? They say, "A girl's hair is her life itself." When burn scars on some girls' heads left them with a bald spot, or when all their hair fell out, what they endured I can't imagine. Girls who went through such things gradually fell silent and withdrew.

Some girls came back to school blind. One girl whose face was disfigured by burn scars collapsed at school from anemia. Her deformed mouth wouldn't open, so we had a hard time helping her breathe. Another girl whose fingers were fused together was unable even to hold a pencil. It was painful to see her show us her fingers as if it were funny. School life for most of us was miserable.

One day, a young man and his mother came to our house to ask if he could marry me. Across the street from our house was a factory that made bank safes and gate doors. An employee a year older than I had seen me commuting on the Ujina Line. When his mother first learned that I was an A-bomb survivor, she opposed his intent to propose. "She probably won't be able to help farm our fields." Later, she relented, and came with him to make the proposal to my parents. He, too, was a *hibakusha* who had been exposed.

My father's first response was, "I can't allow my only daughter to be taken far from us!" In the end, he gave in. "I'm grateful that you will take her as a bride." When we married, I was 19 and he was 20. Because we had both been exposed to the bombing, we promised to support and help each other.

In those days, ugly rumors abounded about survivors marrying each other. If a family were approached by the family of a young woman who'd been in the bombing, they were likely to reject the offer firmly. "Absolutely not! Who knows what kind of child she'd give birth to?" The question was no longer whether one had keloids or not. Now, people simply wanted to stay clear of anyone who had been exposed. This change in attitude followed the news that the new bomb dropped on Hiroshima was an atomic bomb whose radiation had long-lasting effects. When survivors understood that we wouldn't be able to marry people with normal bodies, the number of survivors marrying survivors increased. However, cruel things were said even about this choice: "These couples will definitely have deformed children," and worse.

The rumors were so hurtful that when my husband's company proposed a transfer to Osaka, we easily agreed. However, perhaps because of his exposure, my husband tired easily. After we moved to Osaka, I would get phone calls from the train station. "Your husband is resting here at the station because he doesn't feel well. Please come and take him home." He underwent examinations that found nothing.

I often got colds, but would recover if I drank cold medicine. Because we were not in Hiroshima, we were not abreast of what was being discovered about "A-bomb disease." We didn't worry much about it, which, in a way, was a good thing.

Later, my husband founded a company that created trademarks for electrical products in Osaka. We kept going by encouraging each other. I led a satisfying life, obtaining a teacher's license, studying clothing design and helping design fashion shows. We moved from Osaka to Tokyo and did not return to Hiroshima until our mid-50s.

That was when we learned that people were continuing to die of A-bomb disease. While my keloids had decreased in size, my fears of A-bomb disease actually grew.

Nonetheless, through referrals by friends, I began to tell my story to students who came to Hiroshima on school visits. More than 20 years have passed since I began this. At first, 10 minutes into the story I would start crying and have to stop. But the somber eyes of the students fixed on me strengthened me to go on. Some would later send me letters. They do so even now. Reading their frank words of appreciation makes me glad I have been able to live this long.

In 2010, as a representative of the Japan Confederation of A-bomb and H-bomb Sufferers Organizations, I went to UN Headquarters in New York to attend the Nuclear Non-Proliferation Treaty Review Conference. It's rude to say so, but I had no interest in that conference. I have no faith in leaders who continue to claim we need nuclear weapons. But if we speak to the next generation, they may grow up and join with each other to get rid of these weapons. Children are the wellspring of peace. In the UK, too, local supporters gave me a chance to talk to schoolchildren.

In August 2015, I underwent surgery for liver cancer. I don't know how long my health will allow me to continue this work, but for as long as I can, I will talk to the world, especially to the children.

Emiko Yamanaka
Scarred in body and spirit, I want to spare others

Born in March 1934, Emiko Yamanaka was 11 years old when she was exposed to the atomic bomb on her way to an eye doctor at Sumiyoshi Shrine, about 1.3 kilometers from the Hiroshima hypocenter. She was in the sixth grade at Eba Elementary School. She has been afflicted with various A-bomb diseases, including thrombocytopenia, cataracts, thyroid cancer and brain tumors. In March 2011, as a Ministry of Foreign Affairs special communicator for a world without nuclear weapons on Peace Boat's Global Voyage for a Nuclear-Free World, she visited 13 countries and told her story at 14 universities and academic institutions.

Cancer in all three daughters

In 1976, my oldest daughter, who had just started college, suddenly developed a dark mole-like stain under her left eye. Soon, a similar one appeared under her nose. My mother-in-law said, "Poor thing, and such a pretty face too. Let's go to the hospital and have these removed." She took her to an orthopedic hospital in the area.

The growth was removed. It appeared to be a tiny mole about two millimeters in diameter, but as they cut, they found it had extended a root a centimeter deep into her flesh. It was skin cancer.

My father had become bedridden and died of multiple cancers. I struggled with several A-bomb illnesses: thrombocytopenia (failure of the blood to clot), cataracts and ischemic cardiac disease. All three of my daughters, though frail, were able to go to college. But fear had always stalked me: "What will happen to my girls?"

The first time my fear proved justified was with my oldest daughter's cancer. Later, the effects of my exposure appeared in the two younger ones as well. My middle daughter complained, "Whenever I go out in the sun, I get sick." We took her to the Red Cross Hospital, where the diagnosis was aplastic anemia. Our youngest, then 19 and in her second year at university, complained of stomach pain. She was examined at the Atomic Bomb Hospital and diagnosed with ovarian cancer. Two years later, she developed thyroid cancer.

Each time my children fell ill, I was terribly distressed. In my heart I begged, "Forgive me!" and pressed my palms together in prayer. I felt a kind of resignation when disease attacked me, but when my children took sick, I wanted only to change places with them.

That was impossible, but for a mother, nothing could be more miserable. "May my daughters conquer illness and find happiness." That was all I wanted.

In 1962, when I was first diagnosed with A-bomb disease, I was a busy mother of three young girls. I was troubled by cuts that did not stop bleeding. If my finger got cut, to stop the bleeding, I would have to wind a rubber band below the cut so tightly that the finger would turn purple. The diagnosis that time was thrombocytopenia. In 1970, I underwent surgery for A-bomb cataracts. Despite my fragile health, my husband and I worked together as best we could to raise our daughters.

In 1974, when our oldest was in high school, I was diagnosed with ischemic cardiac disease. I tired easily and often had to lie down. When I walked, my legs would shake. When I stood by a river, or when a car passed nearby, I felt I was almost being pulled into the flow.

Two years later, our oldest daughter fell ill. Then the middle one, then the youngest. Fortunately, all the surgeries were successful, and they all overcame their illnesses. But before we could breathe a sigh of relief, I was found to have thyroid cancer in 2005. The thyroid is a butterfly-shaped gland below the Adam's apple. The entire right side of mine was removed, and most of the left. The tissue and bronchial tubes in the front of my neck were also cut out.

That surgery cost me my voice. Throughout the 40-day hospitalization, I had to write down whatever I wished to say.

Each time I overcame a condition caused by the bombing, a new one loomed before me. My heart weakened so much I thought it would give out. Even so, I exhorted myself: "Lie down and let this defeat me? I will not!" I learned to shout in order to force sound out, and gradually my voice returned.

The ferocious flash and blast knocked me unconscious

On August 4, 1945, I was an 11-year-old sixth grader in Eba Elementary School. My fourth-grade brother and I left our evacuation site on Kurahashi Island to return to our house in Eba in Hiroshima. We were to stay for two nights and three days.

For some days, I had been waking up with so much mucus in my eyes that it took a while to open my eyelids. My parents decided I should be seen at the Miyake Ophthalmology Clinic near the prefectural office. We arrived at our house in the early evening of the fourth. The plan was for me to be treated on the fifth and sixth and return that evening to Kurahashi Island.

Early on the sixth, I boarded a bus at the Eba Bus Stop for the 20-minute ride to the Miyake Ophthalmology Clinic. When the bus passed the Ikkenjaya, a yellow alert sounded. It was later upgraded to an air-raid warning, and the passengers were told to get off the bus.

When the warning was canceled, I began walking to the clinic.

After I crossed Sumiyoshi Bridge and arrived at Sumiyoshi Shrine, the strap broke on one of my *geta* clogs. I sat down in the shade of a factory nearby and prepared to repair my strap. A man came out of the building and said, "It's hot out here. Come inside and do it." He handed me a length of hemp to replace the broken strap.

I crouched down to replace the strap—and was bathed in a flash as bright as if the sun had fallen onto the Earth. Smashed against the ground with a force that stole my breath, I lost consciousness.

I was about 1.3 kilometers from the hypocenter. Shielded by the wall of the building, I was miraculously spared serious burns. When I came to, I was buried under a pile of rubble. "Help! Help!" I screamed. Through cracks in the debris, I saw army boots with tattered gaiters wrapped around them, then the apron worn by a man who was shouting, "Where are you? Where are you?" He removed debris until he could extend an arm to me.

When I grabbed the man's hand, the skin slipped right off. He immediately turned his palm to face mine so that we could pull against each other's cupped fingers. He pulled me out.

I could see flames rising from the rubble here and there, but fortunately, not yet next to me. I got out as quickly as I could. The scene that met my eyes was not of this world. The morning light was replaced by a murky dusk through which people were fleeing right and left in complete confusion—hair frizzed wildly on heads; half-naked bodies under clothing burnt into tatters.

"I have to get home." As I tried to figure out which direction would take me to Eba, ferocious flames bore down on me. They traveled with such speed I feared they would swallow me. Weeping and brushing off the burning embers, I careened headlong down to the riverbank. I ran for my life. When I made it to the wall around the Yoshijima Prison, I finally felt safe. Once again, a thick wall stood between me and the flames.

Suddenly, a shout: "Hey, anyone trying to get back to Eba?" I looked out to the river and recognized the man who was shouting from a rescue boat that had come down from Eba. I boarded the boat, crying with relief at a familiar face.

The other people in the boat were old men and women, their faces burnt black, their hair standing on end. But when I looked more closely, I realized, "These people are young." I realized at that moment that I, too, might appear to be an old woman.

When I finally got to our house in Eba, I found it had collapsed. No one was around. As I searched the area, I ran into a woman from the neighborhood. "Your mother might have gone to the air-raid shelter at Kaihoji Temple," she suggested. I hurried there, but found no one. I continued to walk around until I found my mother and four younger brothers in a nearby air-raid shelter.

My youngest brother was a nursing infant only three months old. Although my mother was burnt from her back up to her neck, she was frantically protecting her children.

That night, soldiers came to the shelter and said, "You're in danger here—go to the hill over there." Our family was too exhausted to move. The other three or four families huddling there were in the same condition. In the silence I could read deep despair and resignation. "Let's just die together right here."

Fires burning through the night turned it as light as day. Till dawn, we heard the clatter of carts and hand-carts, cries and groans of the injured, desperate wails of children calling their parents and parents calling their children.

The morning of the seventh, soldiers came in trucks to pass out rice balls. We ate them and drank water from broken pipes that spilled out ceaselessly. Where is our father, our relatives, everyone who matters to us? However desperate we were, we could do nothing but wait.

So when our uncle hired a boat and came looking for us, it was like a sudden ray in the darkness. "When we heard that a new type of bomb had been dropped on Hiroshima, we started out right away, but the roads were closed so we couldn't make it to Eba. We rented this boat." So saying, our uncle helped us into the boat. As we traveled from the Honkawa River to the open sea, we thumped continually against floating corpses; the collisions slowed our progress, rocked us and upset me.

When we arrived at my uncle's house, my father appeared. He worked at the Ordnance Supply Depot and had been exposed inside a streetcar going to the Akatsuki Corps headquarters. Worried about us, he had started back to Eba, but when he crossed Sumiyoshi Bridge, he stopped to help soldiers pulling corpses from the river with hooked poles.

Later, my father lost his eyesight as cancer spread through his body. I still remember the diapers my mother made for my father out of old cotton kimonos. They were stained by massive amounts of bloody pus, as though his intestines had melted. In the laundry room of the hospital where my father lay, families of patients in the same condition as my father washed diapers stained bright red and hung them up. As they scrubbed, they all sighed with the same question on their minds: "What will happen now?"

Every day, many patients died, one after another. Barely 10 years later, my father died. He was 53.

After the bombing, I fell ill, first with severe diarrhea. Then my hair fell out, until I became completely bald. My brothers all lost their hair as well, so I didn't stand out so much. When people asked what happened to my hair, I answered, "The *pika-don* (flash-boom) ate it," to make them laugh.

Some who survived without obvious injury and were quite healthy the day the bomb fell came down the next morning with purple spots like small *adzuki* beans all over their bodies—and died. Some suddenly bled from the ears, nose, gums—and died. We saw this happening to people over and over again.

I, too, was suffering maladies peculiar to A-bomb exposure: diarrhea, fever, bleeding from the gums, nosebleeds. Moreover, when the explosion blew apart the nearby factory, I had been pierced by countless pieces of glass. The larger ones were extracted at Eba Army Hospital, but after the war, red lumps would sometimes appear and suppurate painfully on my back and arms.

When my family cut into these with a razor blade, chocolate-colored pieces of glass pushed through the skin. This went on until about 1977.

My post-bombing ills led to many hospitalizations at the Mizuno Hospital at Togiyacho, but treatments gradually restored my health. At 18, I got a job at Fukuya Department Store. Around that time, an older girl from my high school introduced me to a student at Hiroshima University. He was two years older than I.

It was just eight years after the war. A fresh breeze wafting in the air foretold the dawn of a new age. He fascinated me as he talked about his dreams for a tourism-oriented Japan. But then I was diagnosed with tuberculosis and entered the hospital again.

He loved to read. He would visit my bedside toting books that inspired him by Nietzsche, Tatsuzo Ishikawa and other writers. We talked for hours in my hospital room.

In time, he proposed to me like this: "If I pass the exam, I'll work for the Foreign Ministry. Let's live together in Tokyo." Then, this: "I want you to attend my graduation ceremony wearing a kimono."

At the ceremony, I met his mother, who had come from Fukuoka. Then I visited their Fukuoka home a number of times. These were the best times I had ever had. But one day, his mother took me aside and said, "Promise not to tell my son what I am about to say to you. I simply cannot accept you, a survivor of Hiroshima, as a bride in our family."

I was dumbfounded. Shock turned everything black for me, but

I did my best to retain my composure. I politely turned down the money she offered me as compensation and promised to relinquish the relationship without giving her away.

If I throw myself into the Bungo Channel, my body will float out to sea and never be found... Riding the boat back to Hiroshima, I could think of nothing but dying, right then. When shall I jump off? When shall I jump? I was still struggling frantically with myself when the boat landed in Hiroshima.

I called him on the telephone. "I have TB. I don't know what will become of me, so I can't marry you." Over and over he pressed me, "Why did you suddenly change your mind?" But I could not cause him to resent his mother. I remained silent.

After that, his father wrote me a long letter apologizing for breaking off the relationship. When I told my mother why his family had broken off the discussions of marriage, she was furious. "Anyone who would say such things! Why, we reject them!"

After that, we changed the official location of my exposure to the bomb from Sumiyoshi Shrine (about 1.3 kilometers from the hypocenter) to our home in Eba (about 3 kilometers away).

Because my father ran a contract company for Mitsubishi Shipbuilding, my mother asked him to look for a suitable candidate among the employees. One day, she called me at work to announce that my father was critically ill. Shocked, I hurried home. I arrived breathless at the front door, announced, "I'm home!" and opened the door to see a young man, a stranger. I quickly grasped that Mother had invited him there as a prospective suitor.

I protested, "I'm already seeing someone! And I'm not well from TB yet!"

He replied, "I can wait until you change your mind."

Still longing for the boy I had been forced to let go, I kept trying to chase him away, going so far as to bring out an X-ray of my lungs.

But, as the young man later told me, he had already decided

to marry me the moment he heard me call out, "I'm home!" His subsequent single-minded pursuit finally touched my heart. At the age of 23, I married him and became a wife.

But first, I burned in the oven all the love letters from my university boyfriend. When we returned from our honeymoon, I heard he had tried to commit suicide. That was too sad an ending.

It was very hard for *hibakusha* to marry people of normal health. Although my husband had quickly been attracted to me, much later he told me what he and his mother went through. When he told her I was a *hibakusha*, she had responded, "Her poor health will plague you your whole life." He countered, "Weak people can become stronger after marriage, and strong people can get weaker. These things happen—marriage is a gamble." She gave in. "All right then! But don't you tell anyone she's a *hibakusha*."

Two years after I became a member of the Yamanaka family, I became pregnant with our first daughter. Because I still had a hole in my lungs from tuberculosis, the doctor said, "Your body will give out completely if you have this baby." My husband agreed. "Your health is more important than any baby. Let's let it go." I appreciated his concern, but I felt I had been given this chance for a reason. I dearly wanted this baby.

I had already shown symptoms of thrombocytopenia, so the doctor warned, "This means you can't have a Caesarian section." When my labor started, I was so weak I quickly tired and fell asleep. Undergoing childbirth while unconscious is very dangerous. The fetus can get stuck in the birth canal and die.

It took three days and three nights, but I gave birth to a baby girl weighing 2,000 grams (4.4 pounds). When she emerged, she looked like Hotei (a Buddhist deity with a long, thin head). She looked so adorable, I was head over heels in love.

However, I had to pay the price for having the baby despite my poor health. After she was born, I felt so ill I was bedridden much of the time. My husband and his mother took great care of me and our baby.

In time, I became the mother of three daughters. Seventy years have passed since the atomic bombing. All three of my daughters regained their health, married and had children. I am now grandmother to seven.

I will never forget commemorating the end of World War II at the Nippon Budokan Hall on August 15, 1995. That year, representing the bereaved families of the Hiroshima *hibakusha*, I was given the opportunity to offer flowers at the ceremony. After the ceremony, I was deeply touched when Empress Michiko honored me with kind words.

In 2011, I visited 13 countries and told my story at 14 venues in universities and academic institutions. I was a Ministry of Foreign Affairs special communicator for a world without nuclear weapons on Peace Boat's Global Voyage for a Nuclear-Free World. On March 13 that year, I gave my testimony at UN Headquarters in Geneva, Switzerland.

"We can never repeat this horrific history. For the sake of peace, I will tell my story, however much it pains me to recall it." Clinging fast to this conviction helped me share my story. However, just after speaking at UN Headquarters, I collapsed. In fact, I had been worried for some time about my legs giving way. When I returned home, I went to the Kure National Medical Center and was found to have a brain tumor. I underwent frontal lobe brain surgery. Fortunately, I recovered, but it is clear that no part of my body escaped damage by the A-bomb. I can't bear the thought of others going through this.

A dozen or so years ago, my granddaughter's composition won the grand prize in a prefectural competition. The title was "The Atomic Bombing of Hiroshima." She wrote, "I'm grateful to my grandmother, who did everything she could to survive." I am so thankful that even my granddaughter's generation is inheriting the A-bomb stories we strive to leave behind.

It pains us to talk about experiences we wish not to remember. But my mission is to pass my story on to the future, so I continue to talk to students who come to Hiroshima. For 30 years, I have served as president of the Kure Hibakusha Association.

Ritsuko Seidai
Grateful for my life, I live to be of use to others

Born in November 1927, Ritsuko Seidai was 17 when she was exposed to the atomic bombing at Hiroshima Women's Higher School of Education, 1.6 kilometers from the hypocenter. Seriously burnt, she received treatment in her hometown, Onomichi. She went to a dressmaking school and then married. Her second child died 17 days after birth. She divorced when she was 31, and raised her daughter while running a coffee shop. She received a commendation from Fukuyama City for her long contribution as a volunteer in a nursing home.

My dream of becoming a PE teacher was blown away by the bomb

"I should never have gone to Hiroshima!"

I was tormented by regret for a long time. Dreaming of becoming a teacher, I went from Onomichi, a city in the eastern part of Hiroshima Prefecture, to the Women's Higher School of Education in Hiroshima City. I returned home two months later in tatters.

I was the middle of three siblings. I had an older sister and a brother five years younger. I was so physically active, my family called me a tomboy. My dream since childhood was to be a physical education teacher.

The Women's Higher School of Education in Hiroshima was established to train female teachers, and it opened the year I graduated from Onomichi Girls High School. This school was necessary because all the men were off at war, so they ran out of schoolteachers. I was desperate to get into that Women's Higher School of Education.

I would have to live in a dormitory, so I needed extra money beyond the school expenses. It was not easy economically. However, my father offered to pay all the expenses because he wanted me to follow my dream. My father ran an extensive business trading straw ropes and mats, so my family was relatively well off. Also, my brother-in-law was a teacher and suggested that I become one too. These men supported my effort to go to that school. I was the only one from Onomichi attending it.

I had never been to Hiroshima City, so my father accompanied me to the entrance ceremony and handled all the procedures, including getting me into a dormitory. My life in the dormitory began.

The school was so new that some of the buildings were not yet completed. Our school temporarily rented rooms. Because of building problems, school started in June instead of April. I remember lessons in the classroom explaining "the proper attitude of a female student preparing to be a teacher." Just as I was taking this first step toward my dream, a single atomic bomb cruelly shattered that dream.

Hiroshima had vanished

That morning, cicadas started singing very early, telling us the day would be hot. I was preparing to go to school when the dreaded siren issued a yellow alert. I quickly put on my air-raid hood, grabbed my emergency bag containing medicine, daily necessities, a flashlight and a few other things, put it over my shoulder and headed for the air-raid shelter in the playground.

In the shelter, my classmates pulled air-raid hoods tight over their heads, bent their knees and crouched in the approved posture. Everyone was silent.

When the alert was cleared, smiles came back to faces, and we all streamed back to school. I went up to my classroom on the second floor where I waited for the teacher.

Shortly before the start of our first class, at 8:15, a brief, powerful light like a camera flash filled the room. With no time to think what happened, I lost consciousness. Our school was 1.6 kilometers from the hypocenter. When I came to, I was trapped under the fallen school building, and it was hot. The area was dark. I couldn't see much. A big beam leaned heavily on my back. I called the name of the classmate who had been sitting next to me, but got no answer. My entire body was in pain, maybe because of burns. The right side of my body was hot and spongy.

I gathered all my strength and tried to move, thinking, "I have to get out of here!" I managed to get free and sensed a dim light over my head. I climbed upwards.

The Hiroshima I saw from the roof was an empty field. All the tall buildings were gone. Hiroshima had vanished, leaving hardly a trace. The window beside my desk had been open, so I was not pierced with broken glass, like some, but my right side, or window side, was burnt.

One of my teachers stood firmly in the rubble like a demon. With a fierce look he shouted, "Get away quick! Run east!" Smoke was already rising from the collapsed building. I ran to the east with several classmates who had also crawled out from under the debris. They had burns and other injuries, some severe. Glass fragments pierced their faces, arms and legs. Blood oozed out here and there, but we had no time to treat such injuries. We pressed both hands on large wounds, then desperately ran away from the school.

The situation on the street was more tragic. A person whose face was bloody all over was gasping for breath. A half-naked mother was hysterically screaming her child's name. A child covered with serious burns wandered around crying for his mother. A person with skin completely peeled off was groaning, "I'm hot! Hot!"

Dead bodies lay scattered like logs. Their hair singed and bristled, their faces and bodies covered in ash and black soot; they were indistinguishable even as male or female.

We found a first-aid station set up by the Army and entered. It was already full of seriously injured victims. Then, I saw thousands of corpses loaded on a big truck. I wondered where they had come from.

In the scorching summer heat, I waited for my turn to receive treatment, enduring the terrible stench that made me nauseous, as well as the intense pain. I felt as if the flesh had been ripped away from the upper right part of my body. Finally, my turn came. They applied a thick layer of oil on my arms, neck and face, then hung my right arm in a triangular sling.

We received some dry bread and sugar candy as we left. I put the sweet sugar candy in my mouth and gained some strength. I headed straight for Kaitaichi Station with my classmates. Several places on my body that had been hit by falling debris in the school started to hurt. Every time I breathed I felt pain in my ribs. My neck was swollen, and I had a hard time holding my head up.

But I was afraid of being left behind by my friends. I did my best to keep up. My friends were all full of fear, so nobody said anything. We kept walking, speechless in the heat. It was morning when we left school and went to the first-aid station. By the time we arrived at Kaitaichi Station, it was twilight.

The station was crowded with people waiting for a train that was not sure to come. People were asking, "What kind of air raid was that?" The number of survivors taking refuge in the station increased. Finally, when it was completely dark, a train came into the station. The train had its lights off to avoid being seen by an enemy plane. That completely dark train filled up immediately. With a desperate effort, we got on the train and left Hiroshima at last. But the train stopped at Hongo, three stations before Onomichi. We went to an inn in front of Hongo Station and explained that we were injured because a bomb had been dropped on Hiroshima, and they let us stay the night.

I used the inn's telephone to tell my parents I was alive. My mother answered the phone. I didn't know the word "atomic bomb," so I said, "I got injured by a bomb, but I can walk, so I'll come home by the first train tomorrow morning."

The friends I was with said, "Finally, we can stretch our arms and legs!" They lay down, but I couldn't. Lying caused too much pain. I leaned against a chair and waited for daybreak.

The next morning, feeling impatient, I got on the first train. The train filled up at Hongo Station with people going to work or school. Daily life was still happening there, and the tragic sights I had seen in Hiroshima seemed unreal. With my hair disheveled, my face burnt and my arm hanging in a sling, I felt ashamed. I hid myself in a corner of the car.

Finally, the train arrived at Onomichi Station. As soon as I saw my father, who had come to the station to meet me, I started to run. I shouted "Daddy!" I clung to him and sobbed.

My father said, "You made it! You made it!" He was stunned to see me with such thick oil on my burns. All he could say was, "Mother is waiting. Let's hurry home!"

I had barely managed to get home to Onomichi a little after 9:00 in the morning on August 7. The first thing I did was drink water. I still remember that delicious cold water.

Seeing my terrible burns, my mother and younger brother were upset. "How horrible! It looks so painful!" Unlike conventional burns, the burns from the A-bomb heat ray were both deep and wide, with foul-smelling pus oozing out. The smell attracted flies, so

I was always under a mosquito net my mother hung up for me.

The next day, I went to a clinic in Onomichi, but the doctor had no idea how to treat burns caused by an atomic bomb. I just got a standard burn ointment. My mother heard from a neighbor that cucumber was good for removing heat. Every day she grated cucumber and applied it to my burns. At the time of the bombing, I was wearing a gym shirt and *mompe* work pants. Mysteriously, my clothes didn't burn at all, and all my burns were on my right side. My arms, face, neck and shoulder were burnt where they had not been covered by my gym shirt. I got keloid scars that remained a long time on my shoulder and arms.

One of the reasons I had gone to Hiroshima Women's Higher School of Education was a suggestion from my brother-in-law. My father never expressed regret openly, but I'm sure he thought, "I should never have let Ritsuko go to Hiroshima." Deciding I never wanted to go to Hiroshima again, I stayed in Onomichi.

At first, my father thought it would be impossible for me to marry. When I was able to go out by myself, he said, "You'd better learn some skill." He had me go to a dressmaking school in Onomichi.

After a year and a half, when the scar on my face faded away, my father started looking for a chance to introduce me to a prospective husband. I was only 19, but it's natural that he wanted me to get married if possible.

My marriage was arranged for exactly one month before my 20th birthday. My husband was the younger brother of my brother-in-law and six years older than me. His eyesight was quite poor, so he hadn't been drafted. He had gone to Southeast Asia as a civilian employee of the army and returned to Onomichi.

Rumors were going around that "A-bomb survivors will die young" or "Survivors will have deformed babies." I believe my father was a bit desperate. He just wanted someone to marry his daughter.

Because it was a time of severe shortages, we didn't have an extravagant wedding, but we did take wedding pictures at a nearby photo studio wearing formal kimonos.

I attended the Coming-of-Age Ceremony about three months after my wedding. The ceremony was held in the auditorium of Tsuchido Elementary School in Onomichi. The scar on my face was hardly noticeable, but I still had a bright red scar on my neck, so I went to the ceremony wearing a high collar blouse. I met classmates from high school for the first time in a long time. I was afraid they would find out about my exposure in Hiroshima, so I left as soon as I could. Later, I went through the whole summer with long-sleeved dresses.

My father prepared a house for us. I tried to pretend that what happened in Hiroshima was just a bad dream. I concentrated on housework, on being a wife, and lived with no serious trouble. But when I got pregnant two years later, I felt terrible anxiety.

I had nobody to talk to about this fear, so I encouraged myself saying, "If I give birth to a deformed baby, so be it!" I was ready to accept my fate. I gave birth not in a big hospital but at home with a midwife. I felt relaxed and comfortable. I gave birth to a healthy baby girl. I was so relieved, thinking, "I was exposed, but it seems I wasn't affected."

Then, I got pregnant again and gave birth to a second girl. Again, we had a midwife come to our home, but soon after the midwife left, the baby's condition changed suddenly. She had a convulsion and died on her 17th day. I have no words to describe my shock and sorrow. I was wracked with fear. "I wonder if this is because of my exposure?"

My husband had never said anything about my exposure. He probably knew I was a survivor, but I thought maybe he didn't see it as a problem because he had his own impairments as well.

My father often spoke to me about my husband, probably wanting to comfort me after we got married. "He could possibly be a big success." But sometimes, later, he followed that in a lowered voice with, "Or, he will be a complete loser, one or the other."

As my father guessed, my husband failed at everything he tried, and each time we had to ask for my father's help. My husband became addicted to alcohol, and my married life became nothing but trouble. We divorced by agreement when I was 31, and I took our eight-year-old daughter with me.

A few years later, my urine suddenly turned dark brown. This continued for weeks, so I went to the hospital for a checkup. I was told, "It might be a thyroid disorder." Whatever it was, that atomic bomb messed up my life.

Later, my father gave me the funds to open a coffee shop called Roman. It was right in front of Onomichi Station, and I ran it for 20 years. I caused my father all kinds of hardship all my life. I feel sorry for him, but I am more than grateful to him.

I was invited to join a volunteer group when I was 57. "If I had been dead, I couldn't have done anything. Because I'm alive and in good shape, I want to be useful to others." With this attitude, I accepted the invitation. I visited a nursing home for the elderly twice a month as a member of the volunteer group. I helped them with meals, cleaning their rooms and changing their sheets.

In 2004, when the group had been working for more than 20 years, we received a commendation from the neighboring city of Fukuyama. I kept up my volunteer work as long as I could, but around the time I turned 80, it became too difficult. I just didn't have the physical strength, so I retired.

Now, I tell my A-bomb experience as a member of the Fukuyama City Atomic Bomb Survivors' Association. That way, I express my sincere desire to build a peaceful world free from nuclear weapons. We must stop all war, because wars inflict too much suffering on too many. I hope I can pass on my experience and this conviction to young people.

Emiko Okada
I tell my story so my sister's death was not in vain

Born in January 1937, Emiko Okada was exposed to the atomic bombing at her home in Onaga, about 2.8 kilometers from the hypocenter in Hiroshima, when she was eight years old. She consequently suffered from pernicious anemia. Her 12-year-old sister never came home. No trace of her remains or belongings was ever found despite an extensive search. Her sister's death motivated Emiko to participate in peace activities. She has told her story in India and Pakistan as a member of Hiroshima World Peace Mission, which sends "pilgrims" around the world to talk about the bombing.

My parents believed that my sister was alive

My 12-year-old sister Mieko went off that morning calling cheerfully, "See you later!" She was working on demolishing buildings to create a fire break in Dohashi, only 800 meters from the hypocenter. She never came home.

For the next three months, my parents searched the burnt ruins and rescue stations. They often trudged to the ruins of the building demolition site, but never found anything that looked like her belongings, much less her remains.

When they heard that some students from First Hiroshima Prefectural Girls High School had made it to Koi Elementary School, they rushed there, propelled by the faint glimmer of hope. At Koi

Elementary, they heard, "On the way, some girls fell into the Tenma River." That sent them to the Tenma River to scour the area for days.

When they learned that many injured people had been ferried to Ninoshima Island, they took a boat to the island—to no avail.

When there was nowhere left to look, every day they made the rounds to pray at the seven temples and shrines clustered around the foot of Futabayama Hill.

I have no memory of me or my little brothers speaking with our parents during that time. They were so desperately focused on my sister that we were not in their field of vision.

We didn't even have a good photograph of my sister to remember her by. Because Japan was at war, we did not take family photos. Years later, when a relative gave my parents a photo taken of her during a Japanese dance lesson, which she had begun when she was seven years old, they gazed adoringly at her image.

If only they could have found something of my sister's in the burnt ruins of Dohashi—anything at all would have helped give them closure.

Having found nothing of her at the site, they went on year after year feeling, "Mieko might be hospitalized somewhere. One day, she might just appear!" Perpetually hoping that she lived, my parents died without ever reporting her death to the municipality. I grieve for my parents and for Mieko.

A childhood of war

Ever since I could remember, it was war, war, war all the time. Every day, we sent soldiers off to the front, waving flags and cheering, "Banzai! Banzai!"

Every day I went to school wearing a cushioned air-raid hood, baggy *mompe* work pants and a top my mother made out of an old kimono. At school, every time an air-raid warning sounded, we hurried to the shelter. We learned hand-flag signals and did other war exercises in the playground. I can't remember sitting at our desks having a real lesson about anything.

The radio announced the aerial bombardment of Tokyo, Osaka and other major cities. Every time B-29s flew overhead, I was frightened. All the healthy males had been sent to war, so women and girls practiced fighting fires with bucket relays. We also practiced sparring with bamboo spears.

When the war turned against Japan, children between the third and sixth grades were evacuated with their teachers to temples in the countryside. At the same time, older children were forced to help demolish buildings to prevent fires from spreading during air raids.

I was eight, a third grader at Onaga Elementary School.

My father was a teacher at Matsumoto Commercial School. Our house stood three doors from his school. Early that morning, my father was out supervising students demolishing buildings. As both Father and Mieko were at work, eating breakfast at home at Onaga were Mother, me and my little brothers, aged five and three.

Just after 8:00, we heard the drone of airplanes, but because the earlier yellow alert had been cleared, my brothers shouted, "Japanese planes!" and ran outside to wave at them. In a clear blue sky, wings glinted in the sun.

Just then, a huge flash. A tremendous shock wave followed. When I came to, I had been thrown onto the dirt in the yard.

The walls of our house crumbled. Pillars bent. Bleeding from pieces of glass piercing her head, my frantic mother came outside. I was sure that an incendiary bomb had fallen right on our house.

Our house was 2.8 kilometers from the hypocenter. My five-year-old brother had been under the eaves and was uninjured, but the three-year-old was seriously burnt on the back, arms and legs. He was screaming. His undershirt and shorts were burnt to rags. Burns peeled his skin from the neck to the left arm. These burns later turned into keloid scars. Even in summer, he wore long-sleeved shirts with high collars to hide them.

Our neighbors' houses tilted, seeming ready to collapse into heaps of rubble. As it was breakfast time, people had been cooking, and here and there houses began to burn. In time, flames enveloped the entire area. The most piteous sight was a child whose mother was trapped under her fallen house as flames approached. He was screaming, "My mother! Save my mother!" But nothing could be done.

The fires spread over a wide area. I can still hear the heart-wrenching screams of a little girl trapped under a pillar as she burned to death.

As we ran away, we encountered people whose clothes were mostly burnt off, their skin hanging in strips. People who could not move because their eyeballs had popped out. "Please give me water! Water!" moaned people burnt so seriously that we could not tell their gender. Eventually they all stopped moving.

Because the city was in flames, people in our neighborhood fled to the safety of the Eastern Drill Ground. I ran with my blood-soaked mother and my little brothers. I must have breathed in radiation, because I could barely breathe. I vomited repeatedly.

The Eastern Drill Ground was a horrible sight—people near death whose faces were split open like pomegranates and covered in blood; people whose arms were so lacerated their white bones were exposed; corpses whose intestines were spilling out. Wandering among the corpses and injured people were countless children, crying and looking for their parents. I saw the charred corpse of a child around four years old. Only the eyeballs were clearly distinguishable from the blackened body, as they had popped out from their sockets.

Soldiers were burning countless bodies. Hundreds of corpses lay in every direction. Those who carried the bodies and those who poured heavy oil on them worked in silence. The whole scene was unreal. Among the bodies were some who still breathed. Now and then, too exhausted to shut my ears, I listened, stupefied, to their final screams.

Because we were in too much pain to move, we lay down on the fields of the Eastern Drill Ground and spent the night among corpses.

For three days and three nights, we listened to the city of Hiroshima burn. The shocking scenes enveloped in the bright red of fires permanently ruined the sight of sunsets for me.

By the following morning, all the wooden bridges that had spanned the seven rivers of Hiroshima had burnt and fallen into the water.

After leaving the Eastern Drill Ground and returning to our broken house, we found strangers taking shelter in it. The second day, my grandmother came to us; it was decided that we would take refuge at her house in Nishi-Takaya.

But Mother said, "Mieko might come home, so I'll stay here!" Leaving her there, my brothers, my grandmother and I boarded a freight train bound for Nishi-Takaya. The freight train was full of corpses. We had no idea where they were going.

Around that time, I started to feel ill. My gums started bleeding, filling my mouth with blood. The smell of corpses made me nauseous and weak. I could no longer stand up. I lay on the floor groaning, "I can't move, I can't move." I was later diagnosed with radiation-induced aplastic anemia.

When the train neared Mukainada Station, a blaring yellow alert siren brought it to a screeching halt. I had no strength to get off and run for cover. The ride to Nishi-Takaya took an hour.

At Grandmother's house, we learned that my father's youngest sister and his oldest sister's family of three were dead. Thereafter, until her death, Grandmother would place her hands together in front of the Buddhist family altar and cry, "It's cruel. So cruel. If only there had been no *pika-don* (flash-boom)."

About three months later, my parents finally moved from our house in Onaga to Nishi-Takaya. This ended their miserable search for my sister. One day, I saw my mother's kimono in the metal washtub, so I thought I would wash it. I poured water vigorously into the tub, and watched it turn bright red. That was when I learned that my mother had been pregnant and had a miscarriage.

In those days, "human bone powder" was considered a good treatment for burns. In the absence of proper medicine, people crushed the bones of corpses and sold this as medicine. We sprinkled this on my little brother's burns.

The site where my father and his students had been working on building demolition was on the east side of Hijiyama Hill. Because they were working in the hill's shadow, they escaped the flash. My father was helping the injured in the Dambara commercial area. It took him three days to make it back to our house.

After the war, children who had returned from their evacuation site in Miyoshi walked around the burnt ruins, crying, "Mother! Mother!" "A-bomb orphans" like these are said to have numbered more than 6,500 in Hiroshima. For at least five years, orphans who survived the bombing fought a different kind of war.

Though they wandered the city to find something to put in their empty stomachs, there was virtually nothing there for them. *Yakuza* (gangsters) fed them, but as payment, they might put pistols in their hands and order them to steal or kill on their behalf. Even 12- and 13-year-old orphan girls sold their bodies to survive.

Typhoon Makurazaki struck Hiroshima a month after the bombing flooded the rivers and swept away many orphans who were sleeping under bridges. One cold winter's night, dozens of orphans were found clustered under a bridge on the Enko River. They had frozen to death, clinging to each other.

In April, a new school year began. I went to see what had happened to my school, Onaga Elementary. It had burnt down. Not knowing where else to go, I headed for the familiar Tenmangu Shrine. On New Year's Day in previous years, I had gone there to view celebratory calligraphy works. This shrine was also where we students would go to pray for good grades on our tests. As I sat down on the stone steps of the shrine, my classmates began to appear, one by one.

"You're alive!" we exclaimed joyfully to each other. Eventually we numbered about 10.

Even three years after the war, when we waded into a river, we'd step on human bones. The cleanup crews had not been able to thoroughly clean the river bottoms. Bones remained there for years.

Because so many children had disappeared without a sign, whenever someone picked up a belt buckle or metal button from a school uniform, people would crowd around asking, "Is that my child's?" "Is that my grandchild's?"

My mother died in 1950. After she was cremated, we picked out some of her bones from the ashes using chopsticks, as is the custom. But the radiation had left my mother's bones so fragile that my chopsticks would break them, not grasp them. I noticed glittering spots on her skull. When I looked closer, they were pieces of glass still embedded in the bone.

After the war, my father was overcome with remorse for having subjected his students to militaristic education. "I'm so sorry for what I did." When he encountered somebody he had known as a teacher, he would offer an apology. And after my mother died, he turned into an empty shell.

What launched my peace activities was something I found after my mother died. Sorting through her things, I came across a three-page letter from my sister Mieko.

She had written it to our cousin Makoto, who was then at the naval pilot training school. "It's starting to feel like late fall at home... When you come home as a hero, you'll feel like a stranger. So many houses have been taken down, and sweet potatoes are growing on the Eastern Drill Ground. It isn't the old Hiroshima anymore."

Mieko, the 12-year-old first-year student at First Prefectural Girls School, was a gentle soul. She and I used to perform traditional Japanese dance for patients at the Army Hospital, accompanied by a record playing on a phonograph. Our family had an organ, which was unusual before the war. Mieko would play for my brothers and me when we sang nursery rhymes and other songs.

Because we never found any trace of her, that letter became my keepsake. The first time I read it, rage against the atomic bomb welled up from the bottom of my heart. I decided to tell people about the horror of that bomb so her death would not be in vain.

I'm a Peace Volunteer, guiding people through the Hiroshima Peace Memorial Museum and telling them about the A-bomb disaster. I joined the Hiroshima World Peace Mission, a project to send "pilgrims" out to speak to the world about the bombing. As a member of the team, in February 2005, I traveled to Pakistan and India to tell my story.

At the end of one event in India, I left the building and was shocked to see a ragged girl of 12 or 13 standing with a baby in her arms—surely, her child. Near a fancy military facility, I saw barefoot orphan girls scrounging through trash for food. When I saw similar scenes in Pakistan, I thought they looked like the orphans I remembered from Hiroshima.

I never want to see children suffering like that again. Children are the treasure of the Earth.

I spoke at schools in India as well and urged, "Be friends with children in Pakistan, your neighbor." I heard retorts like "No!" or "They're our enemies!" The two countries have a complex history, but I was astonished to learn that instead of being encouraged to make friends, children are taught to see them as enemies.

In that moment, I understood that we must have thorough, global peace education if our children are to have a bright future.

Miyoko Matsubara
I join with the youth to appeal for abolition

Born in August 1932, Miyoko Matsubara was exposed to the atomic bombing at Tsurumicho, 1.5 kilometers from the hypocenter in Hiroshima, at the age of 12. She suffered deep burns on her face, arms and feet, leaving her unable to close her eyes or bend her elbows. At 20, she received reconstructive surgery in Osaka. She traveled with the American peace activist Barbara Leonard Reynolds on a world peace pilgrimage, protesting against nuclear testing in 14 countries.

Shocked to see my face in the mirror

When I secretly opened the dresser to see my face for the first time, I was shocked speechless. Even in the dusk, what I saw resembled a red demon's face, swollen, red and covered with stiffly twisted skin, rather than my own face. The skin around my eyes was disfigured like an overripe tomato, and my eyebrows were gone.

"Is that. . . me?" Despair overwhelmed me. Tears flowed without end.

Though my whole body had suffered deep burns, others had rescued and somehow gotten me home that day. As I recovered, I worried increasingly about my face and begged my mother to bring me a mirror. She refused, and the deep burns prevented me from walking. But one day, I crawled to the dresser.

"If you'd given me better treatment, I wouldn't have ended up like this!" With no other place to vent my rage and grief, I would lash out at my mother.

"If only it had happened to me, not you!" she grieved.

Whenever I cried over my misfortune, she wept by my side. "You'd have been better off dying."

Only later did I learn that while I hovered at death's doorstep, my mother took her kimonos to the countryside to sell in order to pay for my treatment. When I learned that she had sold her precious kimonos, I vowed, "I'll never cry in front of Mother again!"

When my seven months of treatment at home ended, I returned to school. Of roughly 250 classmates, fewer than 50 had come back.

Eyes welling with tears, my friend told me to flee

That day, we first-year students at Hiroshima Girls Commercial School had gone to clean up debris from building demolition at Tsurumicho, 1.5 kilometers from the hypocenter. About 500 first- and second-year students and 11 teachers had gathered at our meeting place at the foot of Hijiyama Bridge. It was a refreshing morning under a clear, cloudless sky.

When we arrived at our task site in Tsurumicho, I slid the backpack that held my lunch box and first-aid kit off my shoulders and left them in the work shed. One after another, the groups ordered to join the demolition force at Tsurumicho arrived on the scene—mobilized students in the lower grades of junior high schools and girls' schools from various districts, along with volunteer corps from companies.

Our school divided into teams of four to pick up broken roof tiles, fragments of wood, nails, etc., and drop these into wire containers or baskets. We called out, "Yo-sha! Yo-sha! (Heave-ho!)" as we worked.

Just then, my friend Miss Funaoka shouted, "I hear B-29s!"

The earlier yellow alert had been canceled, so I thought she must be wrong, but I looked up anyway. In front of a white contrail I could barely make out the wings of a B-29. I was looking carefully at the plane when, seemingly from the tail appeared an enormous orange and bluish-white flash. I dove to the ground as a huge roar sounded all around me. I thought I had been targeted.

I don't know how much time passed, but when I came to and looked around, the world was darkened by clouds of dirt and dust. I could see nothing. Where were Miss Funaoka, who had been near me, and other members of my team? Had they been thrown elsewhere?

From the ground up, the air gradually cleared. I looked at my body and was astonished. Having been told that white clothing would stand out to the enemy pilots, we had dyed my white top and *mompe* work pants dusky purple. The heat ray had virtually burnt this dark cloth away. Only rags of fabric over my chest and bottom remained. My white canvas shoes remained on my feet, but burns had swollen my insteps—they were about to burst out. The unbearable pain forced me to take off my shoes. From then on, I was shoeless.

Checking my body more closely, I saw that both hands, my arms, legs and face were terribly burnt. The swollen red skin peeled off, glossy like cellophane, leaving blood-red flesh beneath. The skin of my fingers and arms hung like rags and was turning yellow as blood seeped through it.

Maybe because I had sheltered my face from the flash with my right hand, it was especially burnt. Terrified, I began to run away in the dark, stubbing my feet on rubble, falling down. The way in front cleared enough that I made it to the bridge.

A crowd of the injured huddled at the foot of the bridge. Most were nearly naked because the heat ray had burned off their clothes. Blood flowed from charred black skin. Some corpses were burnt completely black, with only white teeth distinguishable from the rest.

In the river, which was smothered in something like black smoke or mist, a great many people raised their voices together, like an incantation. This resounded in my ears like the roar of the sea.

The raging heat of my body drove me into the river, just like the others I saw. "Aren't you Miss Matsubara?" I looked at the person who had called out, but severe burns had swollen her jaw and neck into each other, so disfiguring my classmate Mit-chan that only her voice told me who she was. The river was full of people like Mit-chan and me, people burnt beyond recognition.

At this point, reason returned. I understood that the bomb had not just targeted me, but everyone. About that time, flames were leaping from the way we had just come, chasing us. Mit-chan and I got out of the river on the opposite side, crawled up the bank and found a road.

People staggered around like sleepwalkers. Torn streetcar cables had tumbled onto the road along with collapsed electric poles. People's heads were plunged into fire cisterns, where they must have died seeking water to drink. People immobilized by injury were slumped over everywhere.

When we got to Kojin Bridge, Mit-chan gazed at me, her eyes flooding with tears. "This is it for me. Go on by yourself!" She collapsed on the ground.

I wanted to carry her on my back to a rescue station, but I was so exhausted, I was on the verge of falling down myself. I left in remorseful silence. Three days later, her parents found her and took her home, but she died soon after. Even now, when I think about Mit-chan, I feel my heart will break.

I made it through the Dambara shopping area, picking my way over the road strewn with shards of glass from shattered shop doors and windows. I passed my school, Hiroshima Girls Commercial

School. When I got to Oko Elementary School, painful burns and the heat finally made me lie down nearby. I collapsed under the eaves of a house by the side of the road. My aunt from Hamamura found me there, carried me home and then to a rescue station on the hill nearby.

For four days, I ran a fever of nearly 40 degrees, suffered diarrhea and bled from the gums. I lost half my hair. Often I lost consciousness and hovered near death.

Daily, my family carried me by stretcher to the rescue station at Oko Elementary School for treatment. Burns covered my face, arms, hands, legs, even my feet.

The doctors warned that staying in bed with my legs straight would cause my burnt and scarred knees to heal without the ability to bend. They forcibly bent my knee joints, which tore off the scabs and sent blood spurting out. The pain was so terrible, I wanted to scream, "Just kill me!"

After the war, food was scarce in Hiroshima. I tried to help my family make ends meet by doing piecework sewing buttons onto clothing. I wanted to be helpful and would sit on the floor performing tasks with my deformed hands such as removing the vines from sweet potatoes.

"You're too weak." "Your face is covered with keloids." These initial reasons for denying me a job were soon followed by: "Radiation exposure might make you sick." Other rumors withered all talk of marriage: "She'll give birth to handicapped children."

Targeted by such prejudice, I was living without hope when I was invited to Osaka for cosmetic surgery. Reverend Kiyoshi Tanimoto of Hiroshima Nagarekawa Church had launched a movement to provide reconstructive surgery for more than 80 young female bomb victims. I was 20.

I was chosen to receive surgery in Osaka. Because my injuries were relatively light, I was in the last group to go to Osaka. Over seven months, I underwent 12 operations. When incisions around my eyes allowed the lids to close properly, I felt a joy I can't describe. Until then, my eyes would constantly collect dust and dirt that formed painful lumps as they rolled around my eyeballs.

Flesh from my thighs transplanted to my bent elbows and fingers finally freed them to move normally. I was overwhelmed with gratitude. I remembered my mother's advice: "Always be good to others. It will come back to you."

I gave up on marrying and vowed to "live for others."

Around that time, my benefactor Reverend Tanimoto opened an orphanage for children who had lost their sight in the bombing. I was invited to work there. The orphanage opened with three children but this quickly grew to 30. I felt very sorry for the children whose sight had been stolen by the bombing. They couldn't even button their shirts. To go to the bathroom, they had to hold onto our shoulders or our hands. One child told me he had lost his sight because he looked at the bomb: "The heat ray ran straight into my eyes. I never saw anything again."

Helping the children gave me a reason to live. I worked hard as a nurse for children who could not see.

And my thinking about the bombing deepened. I understood that it is people who create wars and atomic bombs, and that unless people abhor war and call for the abolition of nuclear weapons, we will make the same mistakes again. I decided to spend my life working to free the world of these weapons.

After eight years working at the orphanage for blind A-bomb victims, I got a temporary job at City Hall issuing Atomic Bomb Survivor Health Books to survivors.

I had originally enrolled in Girls Commercial School because I wanted to work at a bank, but the bombing took that possibility away. Now, because I didn't want to be thought ignorant, I began to study. With the permission of City Hall staff, I began sitting in on classes at Hiroshima University. Especially interested in English, I bought textbooks and studied on my own.

I later got a job at the Hiroshima Peace Culture Foundation, in the section that sends protest letters to governments when they conduct a nuclear test. I was assigned to translate those letters into English, so my English studies served me well.

I worked at the Peace Culture Foundation for 27 years and retired in 1993. Afterwards, I traveled overseas almost every year to share my A-bomb experience in countries like India, the UK, Norway and Greenland.

Because I wanted people to learn about the atomic bombings and nuclear issues and spread the message for nuclear abolition and lasting peace to the world, in 1996 I established the Association to Communicate the Heart of Hiroshima. Most members are young university students and teachers.

We have invited educators from American public schools to visit classes in public high schools in Hiroshima. We have provided opportunities for Japanese and American teachers to exchange views on peace and how to teach history. We eventually created a website and used the Internet to have conversations with people in other countries.

In September 1988, when I was working at the Peace Culture Foundation, I underwent surgery for breast cancer. During my five months of sick leave, my doctor told me that three polyps found in my stomach would need continuous monitoring. In truth, I live with the constant fear of developing another cancer.

Even so, I continue to tell my story, to appeal for nuclear abolition and to try to convince people of the folly of war. I will go on fighting to overcome my fears and keep making this appeal.

Chisako Takeoka
My mother's screams still ring in my ears

Born in February 1928, 17-year-old Chisako Takeoka was a recent graduate of a girls' high school and was exposed to the atomic bomb at home in Koiuemachi, three kilometers from the Hiroshima hypocenter. Her mother, a head nurse at the Army Hospital, was injured so badly her eyeball popped out. Chisako gave testimony in 1982 at the UN Special Session on Disarmament in New York, and in 2001 at a Russian university.

"I don't want to talk about it!"

I saw my mother's false right eye placed at her bedside from time to time. At first glance, it looked like a piece of candy.

The war had recently ended, and there was no such thing as a case for a false eye. She would line a small paper box with cotton, take out her false eye and put it in the box before going to bed. When she couldn't find the right kind of box, she would put it on a small plate and leave it at her bedside.

The false eye would sometimes get dirty with eye mucus, and Mother would wash it carefully with water. As time went by, if there was no water at hand, she would quickly turn her head to the side, put the false eye in her mouth, clean it with her tongue and put it back in as if nothing had happened.

When she first started wearing a false eye, whenever she was about to put it in, I would look the other way, get up from my seat, or find some other way to avoid seeing it. I kind of felt sorry for her.

At first, Mother was also worried about her false eye. When we were taking a family picture, she would casually turn her head to the side that would hide the false eye. When we went to see friends, or when she went to the doctor, she would always take her granddaughter Mariko with her. Mariko's job was to be a lookout on the right, Mother's blind side.

The false eye was not exactly round. It was a bit sunken in the back. It is very hard to make a false eye exactly the same shape as an eye. She had it remade many times.

In the socket, the scalpel had cut away her optic nerve. Red scar tissue clumped up in the hole, like the gum where you put in a false tooth.

Once I tried to get her to tell me about "that time." She pressed her lips together and stayed quiet a long time. Finally she said, "I don't want to talk about it!"

She left this world when she was 62. In the end, I was never able to hear the truth about "Mother's right eye."

Searching everywhere for my mother

In August 1945, I lived with my mother (then 42), who was head of nursing at the Army Hospital in Koiuemachi. I had just graduated from Yamanaka Girls High School. In those days, if you graduated from a girls' school, you were obligated to serve in the Army or Navy. I joined the Women's Volunteer Corps and was assigned to make parts for *kamikaze* submarines (*kaiten*) at the Toyo Canning Plant in Tenmacho, which had become a military factory. I used a big file to smooth out the bumpy surfaces of the parts.

Kaiten were single-seated torpedoes. Young soldiers of 14 or 15 who had just graduated from junior high school would get intensive training for three months, then were expected to steer the torpedoes into an enemy ship. In other words, they were *kamikaze* in the sea.

On August 5, I was on the night shift. Just before dawn we were told, "Women's Corps members only, go home and get some rest." I left the factory. The summer night sky made the whole war seem like a false rumor. It was completely blue, and we could still see stars shining.

We hadn't had a day off in two or three months, so my fellow volunteers Mihoko Kagawa and Kazuko Otsuka and I agreed to rest a little, then go to the beach at Tsutsumigaura.

The beach at Tsutsumigaura had been strafed once, so swimming was prohibited, but we had been swimmers for our school. I was a distance swimmer and could swim for hours on end. This was my specialty, so I was longing to swim again.

We had said we would get together at Koi Station at 8:15 a.m. After hurrying through the wash and other housework, I was in our front porch getting ready to leave. I stopped and took out a pocket mirror to once again check my braids, of which I was proud.

It was that instant. A flash of lightning, and then a tremendous roar. I lost consciousness. My home in Koiuemachi was three kilometers from the hypocenter. When I came to, I was lying in a sweet potato field 30 meters from my house.

"What am I doing here?"

Looking at my house, I saw the roof tiles and windows all blown away, the structure tilting. All the houses in the neighborhood were in the same condition. I wanted to get home, but I was trembling all over and couldn't stand. I touched my head lightly and felt sticky blood.

In the sky, a completely black cloud of smoke or something was roiling up and spreading out. It was strange and unnerving. Injured people covered in blood were everywhere. A man's back was full of glass shards. Old nails on a wooden chip protruded from a woman's split abdomen.

Looking out to the road, I saw crowds of people with burns and covered with soot and ash coming up the slope, their hair singed and standing on end. Their skin was peeling and red, hanging like strips of kelp from their shoulders, down their arms and from their fingertips. They were shouting, "Help! It's so hot! My throat hurts! Water, please!"

People came out of their houses. Shocked by the gruesome sight, they spoke to strangers: "Hold on! Don't die! Where have you come from?" Some people tried to get under the eaves of houses to get out of the sun. They collapsed and fell over dead one after another. Many were burnt so deep into their throats that they couldn't make a sound.

After a little while, it darkened like the end of day just before a completely black rain came pouring down. When those drops hit arms and legs, they made a round stain as if a black bean had been stuck there.

Suddenly, out of the crowd, a woman rose unsteadily to her feet and began shouting, "Chee-chan!"

"Hey, you're calling my name. Who are you?" I asked. She was burnt black all over. Her hair stood on end. Her cheek was gashed, and blood was oozing out. Blood was also coming from holes here and there on her body. It turned out that it was Mihoko Kagawa, one of the girls I was to swim with on the beach at Tsutsumigaura.

At the appointed time, she had gotten onto a streetcar heading for Koi Station. Just before she arrived, the bomb exploded as she stood in the car holding onto the strap. When she came to, she was in the river. She had crawled out and fled toward my house. Kazuko Otsuka, the other friend who was to meet us for swimming, escaped with light injuries—Mihoko, though, was later to go missing.

I went back to my house, fearful for my mother who was working at the Army Hospital.

The next morning, the city was still burning, so I wet my air-raid hood, put it on my head, and went searching for her, carrying a water bottle. My mother had not been home for a week. She was staying over at the hospital, working night and day for soldiers sent back from overseas.

When I got to Aioi Bridge near the Army Hospital, I looked at the river. It was still full of corpses the rising tide had brought in. They were piled right down to the bottom of the river, so many I could hardly see the water. Bodies that had been in the water overnight were terribly bloated, their faces swollen round like rubber balls. There was nothing human about their transformed appearance.

My mother could be one of these bodies. At that thought, I turned down to the river and called, "Mother, Mother!" over and over. On the other side of the river, I saw three men stripped down to loincloths pulling floating bodies out of the water onto the bank. All three were medics from the hospital. They were saying, "We're the only three who survived, we're sorry."

I went over to the three men and said, "I'm looking for my mother."

One of them said, "Almost no one from the hospital is still alive. A few hundred lived until this morning, but most spouted blood from their mouths, noses and ears, and then died. The few dozen who are still alive can't see or hear. They are just waiting for death."

I didn't want to believe that my mother was dead, but since I had come all this way to find her, I started looking at the bodies on the bank to see if she was one of them. I knew I would recognize her three gold teeth. I used two sticks to pry open the mouths of the corpses, but the lips swollen up to five centimeters made it surprisingly hard to open their mouths. Their faces were no longer human. Still, feeling neither fear nor repulsion, I desperately looked into the mouths of 40 to 50 dead people.

But I didn't find my mother.

I remembered that my aunt and my cousin in the fourth grade lived near Takajomachi, so I decided to go and look there. Because it was near the hypocenter, all the houses had burnt to the ground leaving hardly a trace. I found my aunt's name written in charcoal on a water cistern, so I started digging in that area with my shoes. The roof tiles and stones I dug up were still hot.

Turning things over here and there, I found a part of some clothing I had given my cousin. Then, I found the skeletons of an adult and a child facing each other. The bones were burnt clean. They must have burnt quickly.

Strong emotions assailed me, but when I calmed down, I took a few bones from each of them, wrapped them in my handkerchief and took them home.

The next day I went out again to look for my mother. This time, I went to the Red Cross Hospital. On the way, I saw two or three huge rats gnawing at corpses down near the river.

When I got to the open area in front of the hospital, a big crowd was gathered. There were already three large piles of bodies prepared for cremation. I searched through them for my mother. By this time, I felt so much pain I couldn't stand it, so I went home.

On the evening of the fifth day, I started feeling very bad. I was dizzy. When I put my hand to my head, big bunches of my hair would come out. I noticed purple spots the size of eggs on both arms, three or four of them. "Is this how I'm going to die?" I was suddenly wracked by fear.

In the morning of the sixth day, Mr. Takabayashi, a neighbor, said he would help me search. Though I was weak and unsteady, I went with him to Funairi area.

Someone standing in the ruins of Funairi Hospital said, "The injured were taken to Eba Elementary School." We went to look there. There were so many corpses in the halls we could hardly walk. The classrooms were full of burn victims and bodies that stank so much, I could hardly breathe. In the heat, the burned parts and the bodies were all rotting. White maggots were all over them. People were piled on top of each other, their faces destroyed, their bones visible.

Calling my mother's name, I went around looking into the faces of the dead, turning their faces this way and that to make sure she was not among them.

I went to all the classrooms, but my mother was nowhere. As I entered the last classroom, on some desks pulled together, some people were lying in a fetal position, their faces and bodies wrapped in bandages. They looked like dead bodies hardened with bandages.

Next to Mr. Takabayashi, I faced those desks and called my mother's name.

"Chee-chan. . ."

One of those rounded, bandaged bodies in front of me seemed to have called my name.

Mr. Takabayashi said, "If she called your name, she must be your mother. Let's look for her gold teeth." He unwound the bandage to get a look at her mouth.

And there they were, her gold teeth.

"It's Mother! For sure!"

To make sure, I pulled out the bent leg of the rounded body in front of me. Then, I saw what remained of her white nurse's uniform. When I pulled on the skirt of that uniform, hundreds of maggots fell out. They had entered her wounds and were eating her down to the bone. I began to cry.

Mr. Takabayashi took a tomato out of his pocket and tried to have Mother eat it. She had eaten nothing for six days. When the tomato went into her mouth, she moved it slowly. I spent that night next to Mother plucking out flies, one by one. They were huge: they bit down into her flesh and resisted my pull. When I put my strength into my fingers to pull, they would come off with their mouths full of my mother's skin.

The next morning, Mr. Takabayashi got a cart and came to get us.

We took Mother home in that cart. Her right side was burnt black, her left full of glass fragments. The women of the neighborhood were waiting outside. They lifted her out of the cart, brought her into the house and laid her in her room. Then they took off her bandages.

As they did, I heard them shout out in shock.

Surprised, I looked at her face and saw that her right eye had popped out of its socket. Glass shards stuck into her face all over. Her nose was broken so I could see the bone.

It was all she could do to keep breathing.

I heard that the Army Hospital pharmacy, with its doctors and medicines, was now working out of Hesaka Elementary School. We put Mother on a cart attached to a bicycle, and I took her to Hesaka. It took three hours. However, when we got there, a soldier told us, "Just a few moments ago, the doctor and the nurse vomited blood and died." Since I had come a long way, he then said, "The veterinarian who took care of military horses is still alive."

All I wanted was to help my mother, so I decided to have him look at her. Finally, he put her down on a straw mat in the classroom and said, "I'm going to operate on her."

At that, three soldiers came and sat astride her to keep her from struggling. The vet took a scalpel and stood by my mother's head. When my mother saw that, she said, "I don't need this surgery. Stop this now!"

My mother, who was a head nurse, looked at the vet and understood what kind of operation it would be. The vet said, "Deep in your socket, the nerves of the eyes are connected to each other. If we don't do anything, the rot will spread to your other eye and blind you. We have to take your right eye out now and disinfect the wound."

There was no anesthetic or any sort of painkiller.

I desperately explained to Mother, "If he doesn't cut off your right eye, you won't be able to see at all!" The operation began.

I was unable to watch. I left. Through the closed door, I heard my mother's screams, wails and sounds of struggle.

Her right eye was cut off without anesthetic. The horrible shrieks continued for more than an hour. I couldn't bear it. I crouched in the hall, shivering, praying continually. "Save her. Please save Mother!" If he had been a general internist, he probably wouldn't have attempted the operation. I think he was able to do it because he was a veterinarian.

My mother never, ever spoke about her eye. Whenever I remember her, I am keenly aware that the atomic bomb not only scars bodies but leaves wounds that no one can heal deep in the heart.

A year after the war ended, I was working in the Repatriation Assistance Bureau in Otake City, and it was there I met my husband. Our first child we named Hironori. He was a cute little baby with pure white skin. People in our neighborhood came to see him and share our joy. He was our greatest source of hope.

But 18 days after his birth, this baby that had been nursing happily and healthily just two hours earlier suddenly began writhing in pain and died. From his chest down onto his abdomen, the baby was covered with the purpura (spots of death) that I had earlier seen on my own arms. His diagnosis—A-bomb disease. Though the war was over, the atomic bomb was still causing us to suffer terribly.

I still tell my story in the Peace Memorial Museum and elsewhere. My daughter Mariko has become an A-bomb Legacy Successor. Such tragedy must never be repeated. Nuclear weapons must never, ever be used. As long as I have life, I will continue to speak out.

Hiroe Sato
We must be grateful we survived

Born in July 1938, Hiroe Sato was seven years old when the atomic bomb was dropped on Hiroshima. Two days later, she and her mother were exposed to secondary radiation on entering the city. Her older brother was killed. Hiroe began working in the sixth grade, helping to support the family. She joined a peace movement at the age of 48. She was asked by the Hiroshima Peace Culture Foundation in 1991 to organize the Hiroshima Citizens' Peace Gathering, which she has continued to this day. She founded a nonprofit, HPS International Volunteers, in 2005.

"If you put your words on paper, they remain."

In September 2008, I joined the First Global Voyage for a Nuclear-Free World: Peace Boat Hibakusha Project. This remarkable project organized by Peace Boat took *hibakusha* from Hiroshima and Nagasaki by ship around the world, telling their stories and calling for the abolition of nuclear weapons at each port of call. During the nearly four-month voyage, I met people from many countries, exchanged views, discussed how horrifying war is, and learned a great deal.

My greatest encounter was with Junko Morimoto. I can say that meeting changed my life. Junko Morimoto is an artist and illustrator. She was exposed to the atomic bombing in Hiroshima when she was 13. She later moved to Australia and published a picture book entitled *My Hiroshima*, which depicted her A-bomb experience. Maybe because she is the same age as my older brother, who had been mobilized to work outside on building demolition and was killed by the bomb, I felt an instant closeness the moment we met.

We talked about many things, and she said, "The words you speak vanish with the conversation, but if you put your words on paper, they remain. You should put down your thoughts, whatever comes to your mind."

I had been involved in various peace activities, but I had never even completed elementary school. I missed my chance to study proper reading and writing. My feeling about my writing ability went far beyond mere inferiority complex. It was trauma. The characters I wrote looked like the tracks of an earthworm. I could barely read or write Chinese characters properly.

I said, "All I can do is talk." She replied, "Even if you don't know Chinese characters, even if you can't write legibly, we have computers now. Learn the computer." So I began to learn it.

As I started to write, I realized, "It's okay for people to hear my story, but if I publish a book, I can give the reader a chance to encounter many different views from different people, and all without organizing a conference."

I compiled views from a variety of people, from children to experts, in a book. That first book, published in 2013, was called *Pika-don—A Treasure I Found under the Mushroom Cloud*. Atomic bomb survivors called the atomic bomb *pika-don*, which means flash-boom.

I distributed the book to 206 elementary and junior high schools in Hiroshima City. The paper used for that book was recycled from cranes that had been sent from all over the world to Hiroshima Peace Memorial Park. In 2015, I published another book made of paper recycled from cranes, *70 Years since the Bombing of Hiroshima— Messages from Here to Forever*.

In 1991, four years after I became involved in peace activities, I agreed to be the lead organizer for the Hiroshima Citizens' Peace Gathering. Later I formed a Peace Park Volunteer Cleaning Unit to clean and rake up fallen leaves from the many trees on the roads and grounds of the Peace Memorial Park. I continue it today.

I also started a campaign called "Flowers for a Thousand People." We set up a flower stand in the Peace Memorial Park on New Year's Day to enable visitors to offer flowers at the cenotaph.

Our peace movement is a battle against fading interest. To keep it from dying altogether, I continually look for new ways to pass on the philosophy of the Hiroshima's Pioneers of Peace movement. Through this work, I emphasize innovative program planning and enduring commitment. In 2016, I organized a Hibakusha Fashion Show and a Children's Peace Gathering.

Lonely evacuation to unknown relative's house

My father ran a *ryokan* (Japanese inn) called Nagakiya in Mikawacho, 800 meters from the hypocenter. His brother-in-law was a high-ranking officer in the Army, so my father's *ryokan* was designated for use by senior officers. It was also a guesthouse for officers being sent to the front from Ujina Port. Besides family members, we had employees, including women who cooked high-quality Japanese food, waitresses who carried meals to customers on small tables, and a head clerk who was always busy working on something.

I was the second of four siblings. My older brother (six years older than me) was a first-year student at a technical junior high school mainly for shipbuilding. I was in the first grade, and I had a five-year-old brother and three-year-old sister.

One of my fond memories was the *shichi-go-san* (seven-five-three) ceremony that had taken place the previous year when I turned seven. Children of those ages would put on their best kimonos to visit the local shrine and pray for sound growth. This festival takes place in November. My five-year-old brother, three-year-old sister and I were all celebrated together that year. I put a pretty ribbon in my bobbed hair and wore a colorful long-sleeved kimono. Mother took the three of us to visit Tsuruhane Shrine, which was near our house. I tried to look prim and proper, while my brother and sister were just jumping with excitement.

I entered Takeya Elementary School in April 1945, but only went to school for the required pre-school physical exam. Suddenly, I had to leave Hiroshima. Because so many cities were being bombed, we kids in the third to sixth grades were evacuated to temples in the countryside with our teachers and classmates. First and second graders were considered too young to live in a group, so evacuation in class units was not deemed feasible and they could only seek safety through friends or relatives in the countryside.

My father's parents lived in Asahara, 28 kilometers west of the hypocenter. My parents decided I was old enough to evacuate and sent me there. That was in June. My little brother and sister were considered too young to be without their parents. In my family, I had always been indulged by everyone around me and grew up doing nearly everything I wanted to do. I was quite frightened by the prospect of moving to my grandparents' house all by myself.

My mother had to pull me by the hand to Grandfather's place. She let me go when we got there, but I grabbed her kimono sleeve and refused to let go at the front gate. I was afraid to be left alone in this strange place. My mother said, "I know this is hard for you. It's hard for me, too. We have to do it to make sure you survive." I let go when I saw the tears in her eyes.

In Asahara, I was given a two-tatami-mat room beside the entrance, separate from the rest of the family. I had nothing but a writing desk in my room. That night I was alone for the first time in my life. I had to sleep by myself in that scary room. I was terrified by what sounded like millions of frogs croaking just outside my window. I wept all night. My mother stayed in Asahara for a few days to help me adjust, and took me to Asahara Elementary School, where I would be going.

My mother looked at me with great intensity in front of the school gate and said, "When you pass through this gate and enter into this school, you're an elementary school student. Your teachers are your parents here. So you just can't listen to them with one ear. You will listen with both ears and also the third ear in your mind. You'll never forget things you hear with your third ear." After that, I was in Asahara alone. Two months passed.

August 5 was a Sunday, but I had to go to school for a work detail. When I came back, I was surprised and delighted to see my parents, my little brother and my sister in my room. My older brother had just entered the technical junior high school and didn't want to miss school, so he had remained behind, saying, "I'll watch the house. Please go see Hiroe." My father was able to take a few days off for the first time in a long while, so he had brought everyone except my big brother to visit the family grave and see how I was doing.

I wrestled with my little brother. I got down on all fours and let my sister get on my back, while I crawled around like a horse. I had a wonderful few hours with my family for the first time in two months. I was so happy, I felt as if I was home in Mikawacho.

I woke up the next morning, the sixth, to find my father had already left, but Mother said she and my brother and sister would stay one more day. I went to school feeling completely happy.

I stood with the other students in a row in the school ground waiting for morning assembly. I saw a flash in the clear blue sky. A teacher yelled, "Get down!" We had all been carefully trained, so we immediately fell to the ground, putting our thumbs in our ears and covering our eyes with the other four fingers. Then came an order: "Take cover in the air-raid shelter!"

Later, back in the classroom, we were told to arrange ourselves by neighborhood, and then we walked home in groups led by older students. When I got home, my mother looked restless and worried. She had gotten a notice from the town office saying, "Hiroshima was destroyed by a new kind of bomb!" She could do nothing but walk around fretting because she couldn't reach her husband, who had left for Hiroshima early that morning. She couldn't reach her son either, nor any employees of the *ryokan*. That evening, Father came back to Asahara. That morning he had seen an enormous flash and heard an earth-splitting boom on his way to Hiroshima. Then, the sky went pitch black.

He told us that by the time he arrived, Hiroshima was a sea of fire. Burnt, injured people were running this way and that. Their clothes burnt away, most of them were nearly naked. As he came to Koi, the west end of Hiroshima City, he was stopped by soldiers who told him he couldn't go further into the city. He came back to Asahara.

The next day, we made rice balls, wrapped them in the skin of bamboo shoots we got from the bamboo grove behind the house, and boarded a truck bound for Hiroshima. The back of the truck was full of people.

We were going to look for my brother and the workers at our *ryokan*. However, only my father was allowed to go to central Hiroshima. The rest of us had to wait in Kusatsu, a neighborhood near Koi Station.

The next day, the eighth, I finally was able to get to downtown Hiroshima. I could not believe the scene that met my eyes. Hiroshima was a burnt plain, as far as I could see. A military truck was gathering corpses, one after another. The image of a gaiter-covered leg rolling along the ground is burnt into my memory.

As I walked forward drenched in sweat, an ember blown by the wind hit me in the chest. It stuck onto my skin, where it sizzled and burned. It was stuck on my skin and wouldn't let go, no matter how hard I tried to knock it away. I screamed and cried. My mother took a mouthful of water from a water bottle and sprayed it on my chest. She took a towel from her hair, tore it, soaked it in water and applied it to my burn.

After that simple first aid, we started walking again to find my brother. Much more than my burn, my mother was thinking about my brother. She screamed crazily, "He must be alive! He just can't speak because he's injured! He has to hear me calling him! Hideyuki! Hideyuki!"

The burn on my chest got more painful. Finally, I couldn't bear it anymore and started to cry. My mother took off the towel she had used as a bandage and found the wound open so deep she could see down to my rib bone.

For the first time, she realized how bad my burn was. She began to weep. "I'm sorry. I'm so sorry!"

Later, my mother ground up some *dokudami* (saururaceae) leaves and put the paste on my chest every day. Still, it took several months to close, and it formed a keloid scar.

We kept looking for my brother. We went to Zaimokucho (now part of the Peace Memorial Park). My father had heard that students from my brother's shipbuilding school had been working there demolishing buildings for a fire break. We arrived and found human bones scattered all around. We stood in a place where 195 students were all killed instantly. There were some big adult bones surrounded by many smaller bones, probably students with their teachers.

Seeing those bones, my mother said, "Hideyuki is dead." She held me tight. She took the hair towel, opened it, picked up some bones from the ground, put them in the towel and wrapped them carefully. We all put our hands together in prayer.

She spoke to me, but as if she were talking to herself, "Hiroe, we survived. We must be grateful for this. We should do our best and live all we can for Hideyuki, who couldn't live for himself. Let's let our sorrow, grief and tears flow down this Ota River. If we don't let them go, they'll cause continual misery." After that, she never complained or talked about being unhappy or blamed anyone or anything.

We took refuge in my grandfather's house in Asahara. This time, we got to live in a small, separate house on their property. We began working as farmers. The next year my mother gave birth to a baby girl. As an older child, I was soon busy taking care of my new sister, washing her diapers, etc.

 In 1950, when I was a fifth grader, a huge typhoon named Kezia hit western Japan. Our henhouse, outhouse and other farm structures were washed away. Our house was left standing, but was only a skeleton of pillars and roof. The paddy field our cousins had helped plant was filled with mud, with the rice buried under that mud. We lost the entire harvest.

To get money, my mother and I carried heavy charcoal and firewood down the mountain on our backs. We had to pick our way carefully, step by step, then walk to the village to sell them. I was so desperate that I did everything I could. I learned that the municipal government was buying sand and crushed stone to restore typhoon damage, so I collected and sold sand and rocks by the bucket.

Meanwhile, my father had gone to Hokkaido, where my mother's parents lived. He was doing everything he could to find food for the family, such as Hokkaido's famous potatoes and corn. But he was not with us.

At the time of the explosion, we were in Asahara, far from the hypocenter, so we were not directly irradiated. However, we had entered the city two days after the explosion to look for my older brother, so we were exposed to residual radiation. My younger brother passed away at 65 due to cancer. Mother's health was so seriously harmed by radiation that she gradually spent more and more time in bed.

This left me with all the work, from farming to housework. I didn't go to school. During the day, I carried mud in a cart from paddy fields ruined by the typhoon. At night, I wove straw sandals. Then, the next year, we were hit by Typhoon Ruth.

I realized I couldn't keep farming. Though I was only in the sixth grade, I took my family back to Hiroshima City. My mother was soon hospitalized at the City Hospital, which meant we four children were living alone, without parents. As the oldest child, I worked to make a living and support my brother and sisters. I went to a shallow river to dig buckets of freshwater clams. I brought them to a construction worker's camp and sold them. There, I heard about a construction job rebuilding a fire station. I lied about my age and got work as a laborer.

I climbed the unstable log scaffolding where, clinging to a log, I stuffed cement into cracks from a bucket I hung from my waist, smoothing it by hand wearing a rubber glove. Up on the scaffolding, if I looked down, my legs seemed to weaken. When I looked up and saw clouds running through the sky, I felt I was swaying and got dizzy. It was so frightening. I kept my eyes on the wall. This work was so dangerous that my daily wage was an exceptional 250 yen. We could buy 10 cups of rice for 80 yen, and that could feed my family for a few days. I worked desperately at two construction sites.

When I should have been going to junior high, I still had no time for school. If I were not earning money, my siblings would starve. I did every kind of work I could find. I worked as an assistant nurse, a bus conductor and many other jobs, but I never did graduate even from junior high school. That made it impossible to get and keep a decent job.

Ultimately, I made a living carrying salted mackerel on a bicycle and selling it on the streets. Finally, when I was 19, my father came home. Together we found employment emptying old-style non-flush toilets. I have worked like crazy. My leisurely life as the daughter of a prosperous *ryokan* owner in Hiroshima was completely destroyed by that atomic bomb.

When I was 48, something my mother told me before she died drove me to peace activism. She said, "There are things more precious than money in this world. I hope you'll take root in Hiroshima, abandon greed, love your hometown and care for your people."

Through these long years, I have fallen down and been hurt many times, but I have survived thanks to support from many people.

I'm grateful to all those people and am resolved to continue working for peace.

Yukie Tsuchimoto
I speak from experience: War is hideous

Born in September 1935 as the youngest of eight siblings, Yukie Tsuchimoto was exposed to the atomic bomb in a temple on Ushitayama, a small hill 3 kilometers from the Hiroshima hypocenter, when she was nine years old. She helped care for the injured who took refuge in the temple. She married at 19 and had a son and a daughter. She suffered from pulmonary fibrosis and chronic hepatitis. She received a commendation from the City of Hiroshima for cleaning parks for many years.

Why would we repeat that suffering?

"I don't want to remember it!" "I don't want to talk about it!" I made myself believe it had nothing to do with me. I pushed it to the bottom of my heart. All I wanted was to forget.

Then one day, I felt a voice asking, "Is this right? You're going to take it to your grave without telling anybody?"

In my late 50s, around the time my fourth grandchild was born, I began to feel guilty about not telling my A-bomb experience, and this sense of guilt gradually grew stronger. I had never told even my son and daughter about "that day," but suddenly, because of my grandchildren, I wanted to share my story and pass on my memories for the future.

However, the first time I made myself talk, those hateful memories sprang up with full force in my mind. These were not experiences I read in a book or heard somewhere. They were things I had touched, smelled or seen in person. I was overwhelmed by strong emotions and ended up unable to speak. "What am I doing digging up those horrible memories? Plenty of other survivors are telling their stories. Let that be enough."

In the midst of my struggle, some young reporters for a children's newspaper begged me to give them my atomic bomb testimony. I hesitated. What should I do? Just then, I happened to see a TV news item about war.

"Such foolishness is still going on. I can't take it!"

My heart was filled with anger and frustration. It was at that instant that I made up my mind to talk about my A-bomb experience.

I told my story for the first time 68 years after the atomic bombing for a children's newspaper. That was the start of my peace activities.

Caring for the injured

I was born in a temple in Zakobamachi, 1.2 kilometers from the hypocenter, in 1935, the last of eight siblings. My mother passed away when I was six, but I had a happy childhood with the loving care of my father and siblings.

When the war intensified, my second oldest brother joined a regiment in Hiroshima. The next oldest went to Manchuria, and the fourth oldest, who was only a junior high school student, was mobilized to work at a foundry in Ujina.

By June 1945, the war was going badly for Japan. The Army issued an order to temples and certain private homes in the neighborhood. We had to move out to let the Army build a battery of antiaircraft guns in the center of downtown Hiroshima. It was a forced evacuation. They said it was to shoot down US B-29s.

Like it or not, without any compensation, we had to abandon our homes and move to other locations. Fortunately, my family had another temple in Ushita, so we moved there. I was a third grader at that time.

On August 5, I visited my older sister, who rented a room in Hiranomachi. That evening I returned to the temple, which was about halfway up Ushitayama, a small hill north of the city. The following morning, August 6, an air-raid warning sounded, so I took refuge in a shelter near the corner of a field.

Soon, the warning was cleared. I left the shelter, but I could still hear the sound of a plane. I wondered if the plane had left and come back.

I looked up and saw something drop from the tail of the bomber. I instantly covered my eyes and ears as I had been trained to do, and threw myself into the potato beds.

A bright flash was quickly followed by an intense blast and roar.

My father was in a foxhole shelter at the end of a field, three kilometers from the hypocenter. He was blown right out of the shelter by the shockwave. He died of a gastric ulcer two years later. I was down on all fours and had no injury.

I looked west toward Hiroshima but could see nothing but black smoke. Hiroshima burned for three days. The whole city was reduced to ashes.

I don't know exactly how long it was after the bomb exploded, but crowds of victims began arriving to take refuge in the temple behind the hill. They climbed over Ushitayama through Hesaka, the next town. Many who could not be treated swarmed ceaselessly into our temple. Some suffered such serious burns that their skin peeled off to show the bright red flesh below. Others whose faces were blistered became blind as their eyes swelled shut. Some were simply covered in blood.

Our temple's main hall had been protected from the blast by a pine grove, but our residence standing near it was tilted by the blast. Tatami mats were turned over and strewn randomly. Although the temple grounds were damaged, we opened the main hall and residence to accept the fleeing victims. I worked with the adults to help take care of them. We had no medicine, so all I could do was to apply cucumber juice or sesame oil to the burns with cotton.

We were told we should never give water to people with bad burns because they would die if we did. But all of them desperately wanted water, so I soaked cotton in water and wiped their dry, rough lips. No matter how I tried to do my best for them, those with purple spots on their bodies died by the next morning.

I can never forget a young soldier who was carried in on the back of the leader of his troop. There was an opening about 10 centimeters wide on the right side of his head. Something must have hit him during the blast. It was unbelievable that he was still alive. On top of Ushitayama was an antiaircraft battery. He had been stationed there.

The temple was already filled with badly injured people. We had no space to lay the soldier down. We arranged potato leaves out in the potato field and laid him there.

"Captain, Captain..." he called.

Maggots bred quickly all over his body as he called deliriously for his leader. I picked them off one by one with chopsticks, but he died that evening.

I lost all emotion. I didn't feel frightened. I couldn't feel sorry for him. The situation was so extreme, I became numb.

I simply acted out of necessity, trying to help the person in front of me.

However, most of the injured victims died one after another.

My second oldest brother, who was expected to inherit the temple, was drafted by the Army. He was stationed near the hypocenter on August 6, and has been missing ever since. My older sister went to the ruins of the house where he lived with his family, also near the hypocenter: it was burnt to the ground, and three skeletons were piled on top of each other near the bath. They were his mother-in-law, his wife and their daughter, Kayoko, who was 80 days old. Kayoko was my first niece. I had held her several times. Recalling her sweet face in my arms, I felt so sorry for her.

A cousin who was a year older than me was out on the grounds for morning assembly in Misasa Elementary School, about 2 kilometers from the hypocenter. All the students suffered serious burns, and my cousin was badly burnt on her face. She was invited to the US for treatment after the war. She received many painful surgeries to get rid of her keloid scars. Hearing about her treatment, I thought, "They treat those girls like guinea pigs."

Later, though, she got married and had two children. The burns on her heels ulcerated and never healed. The burns on other parts formed keloid scars over closed wounds, but the burns on her heels have refused to close for 70 years. She still can't wear shoes, so she wears slippers, even in winter.

Radiation has the terrifying power to keep injured tissue from regenerating or healing. Even now, the skin on her heels is cracked open, exposing red flesh. She complains that they are constantly painful.

Another of my brothers was a second-year student in junior high school but he was mobilized to work in a factory in Ujina. He came home taking a long route to avoid the hypocenter area. He told us he saw a dead baby on its young mother's back. He saw people jumping into the river seeking water and drowning. He said the rivers and streets were full of corpses.

My older sister was working for the Bank of Japan's Hiroshima Branch near the hypocenter. She was in her room in Hiranomachi getting ready to go to work at the time. She was trapped under the roof when it collapsed in the blast, but she had no major injuries. Her room was 1.8 kilometers from the hypocenter, which is considered close, so she was taken to the relief station on Ninoshima Island, but she came back on her own because she had no injuries.

Our housekeeper at the temple went out shopping early in the morning. She was exposed to the bomb on a bridge near Hiroshima Station and had severe burns all over her body. The worst were on her back, hands and arms. Her hands were fused into permanent fists. If she let her hands stay that way, she wouldn't be able to use them, so every day, she had to open her hands by pulling and stretching her fingers one by one away from her palms. I helped her sometimes and saw the way the scabs were torn apart. Her palms were covered with bloody pus, and she endured a lot of pain.

A few months before I turned 19 years old, in 1954, this same housekeeper whose hands had been burnt by the atomic bomb came to the temple on Ushitayama with a man. He was a craftsman who built the bamboo framing for earthen walls, and she brought him to see if he and I might get along as partners.

I immediately felt he was decent and a gentleman. He was eight years older than me. My older brothers and sisters were all opposed, saying, "It's too early for you!" But my parents were already gone, and I had no job, so I chose to marry him.

My oldest brother and sister were already married. My second oldest sister was single and still working at the Bank of Japan.

My husband was not an A-bomb survivor. He had been discharged from an Air Force unit in Shiga Prefecture, returning 20 days after the atomic bombing. My exposure was not an issue for him.

After we had been married for some time, a US soldier accompanied by an interpreter suddenly visited our house. I got a ride in a jeep to the Atomic Bomb Casualty Commission (ABCC) on Hijiyama Hill.

I was told that all women of 20 or younger were subject to examination. When I told them I was pregnant, I was allowed to leave after a simple pelvic exam.

Throughout my pregnancy, I was continually anxious. If my

mother were alive, I could have shared my concern with her, but I couldn't tell my husband. He had said he didn't worry about me being a *hibakusha*, so I couldn't make him worry at this point.

Around that time, ominous rumors were everywhere. "A-bomb survivors give birth to deformed babies." "Her baby was born black and dead." I felt like my mind was being crushed. "What if I have a baby like that?"

The time came. I gave birth to my baby in a hospital in Hiroshima. What I wanted to know first was not if it was a boy or girl, but whether it was normal or not. I was still barely conscious, but I asked the doctor.

"You have a perfectly normal, healthy baby boy!"

Those words brought me back to myself. I sobbed out loud with joy and relief.

I was fortunate to be given a son, then a daughter, but after each childbirth I suffered poor health during my periods. I would suffer such severe pain, I was writhing on the floor. The lower half of my body went numb, and I couldn't stand up. I never had the symptoms of atomic bomb disease, such as hair loss or bleeding from the gums, but I was certified an A-bomb survivor because I contracted pulmonary fibrosis, a disease in which fibers proliferate in the lungs. I couldn't stop coughing. I was constantly gasping for breath.

Another A-bomb disease was chronic hepatitis. I felt extreme fatigue, as if I had been drawn into the bowels of the Earth, and could barely do the necessary housework.

Later, the pulmonary fibrosis cleared up, but the chronic hepatitis progressed to hepatic cirrhosis. I had surgery for gastric cancer eight years ago, and the incision took a very long time to heal. The opening was stitched together, but it never really closed. It is still festering. I can't soak in the bath or use rough towels. I know in my own body the horrifying effects of radiation.

Still, I am glad to have lived this long. I wanted to serve my community, so I started cleaning the parks in my neighborhood. I've been doing it now for more than 15 years, and I have received awards twice from the City of Hiroshima.

On May 27, 2016, US President Barack Obama visited Hiroshima, marking a new stage in our history. I was moved by this brave decision. The next day, I visited the Peace Memorial Park with my son and grandchild. It was the first time three generations of our family visited there together.

"Let us now find the courage, together, to spread peace, and pursue a world without nuclear weapons." President Obama left this message in the A-bomb Museum, and I hope everyone on this planet will heed his words and strive to create a world free from nuclear weapons.

Kazuko Kamidoi
Mother refused to admit we were *hibakusha*

Born in June 1939, Kazuko Kamidoi was six years old at the time of the atomic bombing. She had previously been evacuated to Kabe, more than 15 kilometers from the hypocenter in Hiroshima. Having nursed A-bomb survivors with her mother, she received secondary exposure. She and her mother suffered liver disorders, cancer and other health problems. Her father walked around the hypocenter looking for his brothers and died from radiation exposure.

Poor health might be due to radiation

"I'll never let anyone know my three daughters are *hibakusha*!" My mother firmly rejected the idea of applying for an Atomic Bomb Survivor Health Book. There was extensive publicity for the new Health Books, emphasizing that survivors could get medical treatment for free. But my mother never listened. We heard too many stories like, "Her husband's family found out the wife had been exposed and kicked her out," or "The engagement was broken off because she was a *hibakusha*."

Eventually my sister and I came to think, "We have nothing to do with the atomic bombing." I assumed all the symptoms that afflicted me afterward had nothing to do with radiation. When I got pregnant and gave birth to a child, I was not worried about radiation effects. I lived with this attitude for more than 70 years. But when I think back, I have experienced many things that might have been caused by secondary exposure.

The first one came four years after the atomic bombing. I was a fourth grader. I had a liver disorder which left yellow stains on my bed sheets for several days. Serious jaundice turned not only my skin and the whites of my eyes yellow, but it also caused yellow perspiration. After I began menstruating, I suffered terrible cramps that kept me from going to school or work.

After I started working, I would frequently develop a sudden high fever close to 40 degrees and feel too weak to stand. But I would recover in a few hours as if nothing had happened if I laid down. I believed I had some sort of abnormal constitution. When I was in my 70s, I developed uterine and ovary hypertrophy and had my womb and ovaries removed. At 72, the age my mother passed away, I developed bladder cancer and underwent another operation.

My younger sister was eight months old at the time of the bombing. A few days later, she seemed to have caught a cold. Her condition worsened rapidly, and she was taken to the hospital in a coma. Her legs were swollen three times their usual size, and the doctor had to incise them to squeeze out the bloody pus. My mother said that the pus filled a bucket. She was hospitalized for more than a month. She escaped death, but remained frail. When she entered elementary school, my mother even went to speak to her teacher, saying, "I want nothing more than for my daughter to be alive. Please don't give her any homework."

I believe her condition has to do with having been carried on our mother's back for several days while she nursed A-bomb survivors.

My mother contracted both stomach cancer and bile duct cancer. She was hospitalized for more than two years before dying at 72. Treating her bile duct cancer was extremely expensive. If only she had had an Atomic Bomb Survivor Health Book, her treatment would have been free of charge. But she adamantly refused to apply.

When her bile duct was blocked, I would draw bile from her with a needle and boil it down to make bile pills, wrapping them in mashed sweet potato to make them easier to take. If bile is not supplied to the digestive organs it can be life threatening, so it had to be returned to her body. Bile smelled terrible when you boiled it down.

Fear is the greatest cruelty

My father worked with paulownia wood, processing it for *geta* (clogs) and chests of drawers. At one point, he employed more than 60 craftsmen. His workshop was in Honkawacho, and our residence was in Sendamachi, but my mother, my sister and I had evacuated to Kamiichi, which was in Kabe, north of Hiroshima.

We planned to go back to the house in Sendamachi on August 5 to get some things we needed. We went to the station to find the train completely full, even the aisles and entrances. We gave up, thinking we couldn't board a train like that with an eight-month-old baby. If we had ridden that train, we would have been killed by the bomb without a doubt.

My mother always took care of others. She was a leader of the neighborhood association until right before she gave birth to my sister. Despite her large belly, she went around the neighborhood calling, "Yellow alert!" We had fire pounders at our house. They were like mops to be soaked in water for use in extinguishing fires ignited by incendiary bombs. My mother kept the fire pounders for the whole neighborhood association and maintained them ready to use.

Kamiichi was more than 15 kilometers from the hypocenter. My mother told me I often used to play with mirrors. That day, when she saw a bright, instantaneous flash, she thought I was playing with mirrors again. She scolded me, "Don't play with mirrors, Kazuko!"

Kamiichi suffered hardly any damage from the bombing. Our houses did not even tilt. Our windows were not broken. Basically, no one noticed.

Therefore, my family expected not to be affected. We had moved to Kabe on March 29 on the last shipping wagon. However, as I mentioned, my mother took good care of others. Many neighbors from Sendamachi visited us after we moved, saying, "How's life out here?" Because she had maintained these relationships, residents of Sendamachi who were exposed to the bombing came to us for help.

They came one after the next, relying on my mother. Because we nursed those people, my mother, my little sister and I (another sister was born after the war) appear to have had secondary exposure. I was six then.

The first visitor after the atomic bombing was the younger of two brothers, sons of a teacher at a dressmaking school. He came that afternoon on a "refuge wagon" bound for Kabe. He entered our house quite cheerfully, calling, "I'm home!"

He was full of energy. He went right away to the river behind our house to catch fish. But that night he came down with a high fever. He started groaning, "I'm tired! It hurts!" He groaned throughout the next day and was dead the following morning. Purple spots had appeared on his face, arms and all over. He had looked so healthy. He had no burns or serious injuries, but he died in three days. It was quite shocking.

By that time, a dozen neighbors exposed in Sendamachi were taking refuge in our house. All were women or children, no men. My mother was extremely busy caring for them—distributing wet towels or helping take off their burnt clothes. And throughout, she was carrying my sister on her back. I was near the survivors, too, helping my mother.

Around the time the younger brother with purple spots died, his older brother showed up. He had serious burns all over his body.

Even his face was wrapped in bandages, leaving holes for his eyes, nose and mouth. I was frightened at first, but he survived.

Soon after the bandaged brother came, his older sister arrived. She had walked through first-aid stations all over the city looking for her two brothers. She told my mother, "You shouldn't be here. I heard it's not good to breathe the air where the injured are housed." She had heard about "contaminated air" at the relief stations.

Immediately, my mother rented three empty houses in the neighborhood and moved some families there. My sister and I moved into a room in a big house we rented from the farmer next door. We slept there.

The girl who told us about the contaminated air developed purple spots and died the following day. Another person we helped was a middle-aged lady who died, leaving her children behind.

We ran into the bandaged brother again later. I didn't recognize him, but he talked to my mother. The bandage was off, so we could see his face. His earlobes had melted. They were just two holes on the sides of his head. One side of his nose was also melted, leaving just a hole. His face was red with keloid scars. I felt sick just looking at his face.

He told us he survived because maggots bred in his wounds. They ate radioactive substances along with the bloody pus.

In Kamiichi, survivors were also accepted at the Obayashi Hospital and a temple. One victim drove a three-wheeled truck into town, stopped in front of a greengrocer's store in Kamiichi and shouted, "Give us things to wear, anything, even rags!" In that truck were people whose clothes were so burnt they were practically naked.

In addition to survivors, we saw many dead people. Bodies filling a large cart were carried to a sandbar in the river. Because the river was too deep, the cart couldn't reach the sandbar, so the men carrying them grabbed the corpses with fire hooks and threw them up onto the sandbar like fish. I guess they were able to do that because the corpses were children and fairly small women.

I heard from others that a few of the "corpses" were still breathing. They groaned or writhed when hooked. Even now when I see a sandbar or fire hook, that sight comes back to my mind and I feel a sense of horror. The corpses on the sandbar were lined up, covered in heavy oil and cremated. When wind blew the smell toward us, I couldn't eat. Of those who took refuge in our house, five died, some were taken to hospitals and the rest had light injuries. Those who could went to stay with relatives. All were gone in less than a week.

On August 21, my father was discharged from the regiment he had served with in Kyushu. He immediately went to see what had happened to his workshop in Honkawacho. His craftsmen had all been killed. They were still lying there on top of one another. Two weeks had passed, so they were decomposing badly.

He walked around near the hypocenter for several days searching for his brothers and their families. He was the eldest of five brothers. He was exposed to a high level of radiation and died at 56.

In July 1948, my family moved from Kamiichi to a new house in Noboricho, a neighborhood in Hiroshima City. I entered Noborimachi Elementary School, and started in the second semester of third grade. After moving there, my mother never went back to Kabe. Nor did she ever mention the atomic bomb. Our neighbors in Noboricho knew only that we had evacuated and come back, so we didn't talk about the bomb.

Even when someone raised a topic related to the bomb, my mother never took part in the conversation. Only once when a neighbor with an Atomic Bomb Survivor Health Book said, "It's helpful. I can get free medical treatment," she muttered with a sigh, "But I have daughters." She was probably aware that she had secondary exposure from nursing radioactive survivors in Kabe.

She lived the rest of her life pretending we had nothing to do with

Kabe or the atomic bomb. Her approach was so uncompromising that we never mentioned Kabe in front of her. Mother weighed only 35 kilograms. She had to have blood transfusions quite often, but even then she insisted that it had nothing to do with the atomic bombing. Thanks to her attitude, I felt no anxiety when I got married at 30, nor when I conceived our daughter eight years later.

Maybe my mother knew that fear is the greatest cruelty.

Keiko Ogura
I tell my story in English

Born in August 1937, Keiko Ogura was exposed to the atomic bomb when she was eight years old near her home in Ushitamachi, 2.4 kilometers from the Hiroshima hypocenter. Inheriting the mission of her husband, the late Kaoru Ogura (former director of the Hiroshima Peace Memorial Museum), who endeavored to connect Hiroshima with the world, she strives to pass on A-bomb experiences. In 1984, she founded Hiroshima Interpreters for Peace. She has received numerous awards: The Hiroshima Mayor's Prize in 2005; the Hiroshima UNESCO Activism Prize in 2009; and the Hiroshima Peace Center's Kiyoshi Tanimoto Peace Prize in 2013.

Hunger impelled me to learn English

For more than 30 years, I have told the stories of *hibakusha* in English—in speech and in writing. I will continue as long as I am able. I believe that I can contribute to world peace by telling people what kind of horror using nuclear weapons will bring.

But when I started learning English, it was not for such a noble reason.

During the shortages following World War II, the United States sent food and clothing under the name "LARA Relief Materials." When my father came home one day carrying a large can of food, we hungry children thought its contents would surely fill us up. Salivating, we stared at our father's hands working on the lid with an old-style can opener. But when he got the lid off, it was brimming with red cherries floating in syrup. My father could not read the word "Cherries" printed on the label.

Trying to repress my hunger, trembling with frustration and powerful determination, I decided to learn English. This is how I developed an interest in English as a child. I used to hum the alphabet song. I even bragged to others, "My English is very good."

Our house stank of pus and filth

One year before the atomic bombing, my father moved us from our home near the hypocenter to Ushitamachi, 2.4 kilometers to the north. I was one of six children. My older sister attended the Girls High School. My oldest brother was in middle school and the next oldest was a fifth grader in elementary school. Then came me at eight years old, followed by a four-year-old brother and two-year-old sister.

That day, my oldest brother was mobilized to work in the sweet potato fields planted on the Eastern Drill Ground north of Hiroshima Station. The next oldest had been evacuated with his class to a temple at the border between Hiroshima and Shimane Prefectures. In the morning, my father said, "I have a bad feeling about today. Stay home from school!" My father was the fastidious type who would never go out without his gaiters neatly wound around his calves. That day only, try as he might, he could not wind them properly, which gave him a sense of foreboding. It also meant he was late leaving the house.

My older sister was in the *futon* closet. I had gotten bored and gone out of the house to play by myself in the road on the north side. I was enveloped in a blinding flash. The next instant, the blast slammed me against the ground and knocked me out. When I came to, all was dark and completely silent.

Because I had been unconscious, I wondered if hours had passed and it was nighttime. But that turned out not to be so. Straining to hear in the darkness, I just picked up the cries of my little brother; that told me which way our house was. The darkness lifted enough to let me get there.

I saw a straw-roofed house in the neighborhood swiftly going up in flames. Our house was my father's pride—a stately structure with many sliding glass doors forming its walls. Because it was summer, all the glass doors were open. Had they been closed, the family would have been wounded, maybe killed, by flying glass. Even stacked to the sides as they were, every glass door splintered beyond recognition, losing its shape as it blew in, glass piercing every wall, ceiling and piece of furniture.

Glass even pierced hard wooden pillars and concrete. What kind of blast was capable of that? Though he was in the house, being on the veranda, my father was sheltered by a large pine tree between him and the explosion, so he suffered little injury. The side of the tree facing the hypocenter was charred black.

My sister in the closet was buried in *futons* and also escaped injury. My mother was in an inner room, safe from flying glass. My brother, however, was hit in the head by flying roof tiles. My little sister's arm was pierced by glass shards and bled profusely.

We could do nothing but sit in a daze. In a while, I went outside to see what had happened to the neighbors and was hit by black, slightly viscous rain. About that time, my brother who had been working in the sweet potato fields at the drill ground came over the hill to get home. His face and arms were burnt.

I cried, "They bombed our neighborhood." Having seen much more than we, he replied, "Not just us. Hiroshima's a sea of flames!" He described the big cloud he had seen from the hill. It was like layers and layers of ice cream, with a top layer of pink.

Our damaged home quickly filled up with injured relatives,

neighbors and friends. My sister wept as she pulled out of our uncle's back one piece of glass after another. Our house filled with the smells of bloody pus, burnt hair and excrement.

Having heard that our neighborhood was not the only place bombed, I decided to climb the hill beyond Waseda Shrine and see for myself.

Both the east and west slopes had stone steps leading to the shrine and beyond to the shrine office, now a rescue station. When I reached the steps and looked down, fumbling its way up both the west and east steps was a squirming, writhing black mass of burnt people seeking shelter. Hair was singed. Sooty, dirty faces were swollen large. Eyelids drooped, lips turned up. Burnt skin was peeling off, hanging from fingertips.

Most people in this ghostly, speechless procession were soldiers and students in singed uniforms. The crowd grew larger and larger. In time, the shrine path was as packed as if it were a festival. I even saw someone pulling a horse by its reins, as if for an injured officer.

Once people reached the top of the hill, lacking the strength to climb the stone steps to the shrine, they squatted or fell down on the steps. Soon a huge number of people covered every inch of space.

Strangely, no one spoke. There was something very eerie about an enormous crowd of people falling over in silence. I saw no one who looked like a doctor. There was a soldier on the steps carrying a bucket of zinc oxide oil and a brush to apply it to the badly burnt.

One thing I can never forget. As I was climbing the hill, my ankle was suddenly grabbed. I looked down at a charred person covered in blood. The person begged, in weak desperation, "Water, please give me water." The silent ones around started to murmur, one after another, as if chanting, "Water, water, water..."

I ran down the hill and brought back a kettle full of water. Their arms strained for the kettle. They drank, some gulping with happy screams. One, however, upon swallowing a mouthful, threw up the contents of his stomach and screamed a last scream. The head dropped; the person was dead.

Frightened, I tossed down the kettle and ran back to the house. I was sorry for what I had done. At the same time, I vowed never to tell anyone.

When my father came back that night he told us, "You all know not to give water to people who are heavily burnt. You haven't done anything like that, have you?"

"No!" I blurted, my body trembling. I was too young to know about such a rule. I couldn't tell anyone in the family what I had done until after my father died. For years I had nightmares about it.

At some point, a burn victim rushed into our house, calling to my older sister, "Let me use your bathroom," as she ran into it. Her hair was loose, disheveled, drenched in dripping blood; her eyes were swollen. She appeared ghoulish. My sister almost fainted. For some time afterwards, she avoided our toilet.

My father's conscription exam had graded him Class C, which meant he could not be sent to war. His job was to organize our neighborhood. Therefore, we owned a bicycle and a telephone, both unusual at the time. When the town office telephoned to order him to notify the neighborhood of a firefighting drill, he would hop on his bicycle and ride around telling everyone. After the bombing, as our neighborhood Citizens' Defense Reserve representative, my father helped cremate bodies in Ushita Park.

He told us, "Don't you children come near the park!" He resisted talking about the cremations, but I pressed him anyway. "How do you burn them?"

Speaking with difficulty, he told me that they dug deep holes in the park. It took two people to carry a corpse to a hole. As most young men were off at war, my father, still on the young side of the men available, had to carry the heavier top half of the corpse; someone older would carry the bottom half. Holding the head, he could not avoid seeing the corpse's face. Those with open eyes made him very uncomfortable; he tried not to look at their eyes.

After 10 corpses had been laid in a hole, they poured heavy oil over them and lit it. Later, they arranged the bones so that the remains could be distinguished one from another. To the people cremating them, these were corpses—but to the bereaved, they were family. People who had lost family members came to watch the cremations. A person who witnessed cremations told us that once, just before the fire was lit, amazingly enough a woman recognized a patch of clothing on a corpse and cried, "That's my daughter!" Another woman who was watching said, "What a loyal daughter you have. How lucky you are!" That woman's child was missing; she envied anyone who knew what had become of their child.

Not having their child's remains was unbearable to parents. Of those who never received their child's remains, those who at least knew where their child died were on the lucky side. Knowing where the child had died settled their hearts a bit.

When a child's status was "missing," parents would cling to the belief that the child was alive somewhere. They let decades go by without filing a death report. Finally, they would give up, but still lacked a sense of closure.

In photos taken after the bombing, the city appears to be motionless ruins filled with rubble. However, when I looked down from the Waseda Shrine hill the next day, smoke from cremation fires rose from all around. It was an unearthly scene. Especially from riverbanks and beaches, smoke rose like beacons. Because bodies decomposed and drew flies quickly in the summer heat, the lines of rising smoke almost seemed to race one another. My father said that the temporary cremation site in the park cremated about 700 corpses.

Because the entire city was now piles of rubble and a great amount of wood, it might seem that finding wood for cremation would be easy; in fact, the number of corpses overwhelmed the quantity of waste wood available. In order to cremate his mother, one man climbed a nearby hill in search of dead trees and fallen branches; but others had been there first. He wept, telling us over and over that he had to abandon his mother's partially burnt body on the pyre as he climbed the hill again to scrounge more wood.

Taking the mantle from my husband

Last year, on the 70th anniversary of the atomic bombing, for the first time, my siblings and I gathered at a hotel in Osaka and talked the night through about what happened "that day." Until then, whenever we had gathered for family memorial services and the like, we had never spoken of it. On the contrary, if someone brought it up, others would change the subject or get up and walk away. This was also because we were married to people whose families had suffered tragedies from the bombing, so we wanted to respect their feelings.

Hibakusha stay silent not only because "remembering is painful." Various other factors press us into silence.

Last year, because our parents were dead, we seven children (a fourth brother was born after the war) made up our minds to talk about it. My younger brothers and sister had only vague memories, but my older sister and older brothers spoke with much emotion, as if a dam had broken to release what had been locked in for 70 years.

They even vied to speak. "This is how it was." "No, it was like this!" Though I had been playing outside and only 2.4 kilometers from the hypocenter, I was lucky to be protected behind a large storehouse. I did not suffer from A-bomb disease.

It was the sudden death of my husband, Kaoru Ogura, former director of the Hiroshima Peace Memorial Museum, in 1979, that forced me to directly confront the atomic bombing. I was 42. Our friend Robert Jungk, a writer and Holocaust survivor, is known for having told the world about Sadako Sasaki, a Hiroshima victim who folded paper cranes.

When I was sunk in despondency after my husband's death, Jungk contacted me: "I'm coming to Japan to get material for a story on nuclear issues. I want you to interpret for me." Although I had majored in English literature at college, I had never studied overseas, and I certainly didn't know the specialized terminology of nuclear issues. I turned him down.

"Keiko, you're just right for this! You've experienced the death of loved ones, and you know the horror of the atomic bombing." Half forced into it, I became an interpreter for Robert Jungk. I studied frantically, striving to do a good job for him. I determined to take on my husband's mission of engaging with the atomic bombing and nuclear issues.

I began working as an interpreter and coordinator for peace activists, media personnel, writers, artists and scholars who came to Hiroshima.

At a mock antinuclear trial in Nuremberg, Germany, I related my A-bomb experience in English. I attended the First Global Radiation Victims Conference in New York and met nuclear victims from around the United States. At a summit for former world leaders, I again told my story in English. I have been fortunate to participate in many deeply meaningful events.

In 1985, I published the *Hiroshima Handbook*, which gives information on the bombing in Japanese and English.

To help foreigners who visit Hiroshima, in 1984, I established Hiroshima Interpreters for Peace (HIP). HIP trains volunteer guides to take visitors around the Peace Memorial Museum and Peace Memorial Park in English. Along with the other members, I guide and interpret for guests. I often tell my own story.

However, I have found that people hold widely varying views and feelings about the atomic bombings. Some have a hard time understanding the truth of what happened. For this reason, I have long tried to adapt the content of my explanations to each individual I speak to.

I'm constantly struggling to find a way for my message to reach people's hearts. I have vowed never to stop trying to convey the truth about the horror of nuclear weapons and the sanctity of life.

Nobuko Suzuki
Glass shards emerging after 33 years

Born in February 1925, Nobuko Suzuki was exposed to the atomic bombing when she was 20 years old at her home in Sendamachi, 1.7 kilometers from the Hiroshima hypocenter. Glass shards remained inside her body for decades; she often had to have her skin cut open to have them removed. After the war, she suffered severe anemia while helping her mother-in-law run a restaurant. After getting divorced, she worked to hold down a hard-won job, still struggling with anemia. She remarried in 1956.

I think it actually made me stronger

I wonder how glass shards buried in the body come to the surface. They seem to move around inside the body and suddenly pop out from some unexpected place. They get on your nerves and make the area prickle, and when you touch it you can feel a strange, hard lump under the skin.

It does not bother you much at first, but the prickly sensation gets stronger and you go to the hospital. When the doctor cuts into the skin, a glass shard about five millimeters across shows up. I don't remember exactly how many times, but I think I underwent this process at least four or five times.

I had the last piece taken out in 1978 at the Hiroshima City Hospital, from the outside of my left knee.

"Keeping it in your leg for 33 years, it should have turned into a diamond, but it seems to still be glass. It won't do you any good," the doctor laughed.

For me, those 33 years had felt like both the distant past and yesterday.

I also suffered from anemia. Soon after the war ended, I worked in a restaurant run by my mother-in-law. When I had my period, my anemia would become almost unbearable. I would climb up the stairs to get something from upstairs, get so dizzy and almost stumble. If I did manage to make it upstairs, I would stagger and almost fall down the stairs.

Later, I divorced my husband and had to find another job. I had a hard time. After a long search, I landed one at the central wholesale market with the help of a friend. The medical examination van from the Public Health Office would come once a year for all market employees to get health examinations. Every time, I was diagnosed with anemia and sent to the hospital for a closer examination.

At the market, when we received an order, we had to work together to quickly put together products into packages by the deadline. My colleagues knew I was frail, so they would offer to cover my part, saying, "Don't push yourself." However, my father was a carpenter, and I grew up watching him work on each of his projects in a tightly united team. I couldn't rest and just watch others work.

I continued working hard even when I was so weak I desperately wanted to lie down. Looking back, I think that actually made me stronger.

Glass shards all over my body

In 1945, I had an arranged marriage at the age of 20. My husband was the same age as me, and was drafted only a week after the wedding to join his regiment in Iwakuni, Yamaguchi Prefecture.

That kind of thing was nothing unusual in those days.

My father-in-law worked for a fire station and was busy demolishing buildings to make way for a fire lane. He had a bedridden son (my husband's older brother) who was mentally unstable. Someone threw a snake at his chest when he was in junior high school; the timid boy began crying uncontrollably and had never really recovered since.

My task was to attend to my brother-in-law's personal needs and carry him on my back to the shelter when an air-raid warning sounded. But as the war got more intense, he and my mother-in-law evacuated to Itsukaichi one month before it ended.

On August 6, I was at home behind the Red Cross Hospital in Sendamachi. Early that morning, my father-in-law had gone out to Kakomachi for building demolition. I finished breakfast and was putting on *mompe* work pants to go out into the field.

I didn't see the flash. I didn't hear any roar. I just experienced a huge blast. When I came to, I found myself in nothing but my underwear. While I was changing, I had been thrown into the backyard. I was barefoot.

Glass shards were piercing my whole body, and my white slip was covered in blood. With no idea what had happened, I thought, "I have to get out of here." I climbed up the embankment on bare feet with blood gushing from my right leg.

As I crossed Minami Ohashi Bridge (1.75 kilometers from the hypocenter), the bleeding was so bad I was losing consciousness. I recovered my senses just before I would have fallen off the bridge. I made it across only because someone helped me.

"I have to get down below the bank! I'll be targeted and shot by an enemy plane!" I fought my way down to the river and hid behind a boat moored in the river. An old woman crouched by the boat holding her dead grandchild tightly. Her shoulders shivered as she cried, "How can I apologize to my son?" I saw a boy of 14 or 15 crying. I approached him and saw his mother dead by his side. Her face was completely uninjured and she was still beautiful.

I have only hazy memories of that time. I don't remember if I talked to anyone or not. I think I might have talked to a worker from the factory nearby. I think he told me that a truck that was to go to their plant in Itsukaichi was waiting in Koi, and that he could give me a ride to Itsukaichi. I must have told him my mother-in-law was there.

We walked toward Koi. I got light-headed on the way, then sick. I clearly remember shouting, "Leave me here!" I have no memory of how I got to Koi or what kind of vehicle I rode in. Somehow I managed to get a ride in that truck. I stayed that night in the plant in Itsukaichi.

The next morning, I headed for my mother-in-law's designated evacuation site. I was walking on the riverbank filled with anxiety thinking, "Is she okay? Will I find her all right?" Unexpectedly, I ran right into her. I clung to her without thinking and sobbed out loud.

One month later, my mother-in-law put me on a cart and took me to a hospital in Hatsukaichi to get the glass fragments removed. The hospital was packed with survivors. I don't remember exactly who was there with me, but I do remember a man in his mid-30s with a fist-sized hole in his chest. He looked like he was dying.

A glass fragment two centimeters across was buried in the back of my right knee. Because the blast came from that side, the glass was buried mostly in my right side. More than a month had passed, so the glass was covered by flesh.

The pain I felt when those pieces were taken out was so bad I can't help shivering even now as I recall it. The doctor cut my leg and removed the glass without anesthesia.

On the day I arrived in Itsukaichi, my mother-in-law started going to Hiroshima to look for her husband, as he had been doing building demolition. She even went out to Ninoshima Island, and there she learned the bad news that he had been taken there and had died on the island. Because she was busy with the search, then dealing with her grief, the treatment for the glass in my leg didn't start until one month later. During that time, I had been busy limping around taking care of my brother-in-law.

My father-in-law's mother lived in Hiroshima with his sister. She died shielding her grandchild. She was found holding the child tight to her chest. She was completely charred. It seems they were burned alive.

The war ended, and my husband came back from the front a month later.

Near the end of spring 1947, my mother-in-law started selling food in front of a streetcar stop in Ujina. She had managed a restaurant in Sendamachi, but when the war turned against Japan, she had nothing to sell, so she suspended her business. We couldn't eat unless we did something, so she sold fruit, laying it out on a wooden door. She couldn't get any rice, but sometimes she could make and sell side dishes. Some time later, she started her restaurant again.

Since I had lived with my husband for only one week after our marriage, we knew nothing about each other. One thing I learned after living with him for a while was that he didn't like work. Jobs were very hard to find, even for military veterans, but he didn't even try. He spent his days doing nothing but playing around. No matter how busy we were in the restaurant, he never showed the slightest will to help. He seems to have taken it for granted since childhood that he didn't have to help.

When we started selling snow cones from a night stall during a neighborhood event, he thought that was fun, so he helped on one or two occasions. But after that he stopped, saying, "I'm tired!" Those were the only times I saw him working.

Our first daughter was born the next year, then a second daughter three years later. Both deliveries were relatively easy. I had no concern about the atomic bombing. The restaurant was always busy, and I had to take care of a bedridden invalid. I had no time to worry about anything else. My brother-in-law passed away in October 1948.

My husband had an affair and was often away from home. One day he asked me to change our second daughter's dress. After I did so, he took her to the other woman's house. I endured it all thinking, "I will bear all this for the sake of our daughters. Maybe he'll change someday." But after seven years of a bad marriage, I divorced him.

My two daughters were adopted by my in-laws, and I returned to my parents' house in 1952.

My own father was a carpenter. He usually went to work in Mitaki every day. But on August 6, he had a stomachache and stayed home, 1.5 kilometers from the hypocenter. He was killed by the bomb there.

My mother was working at the Mitsubishi Plant in Eba, more than four kilometers from the hypocenter. She was safe.

She immediately started walking around the city looking for my father, my sister and me. She walked all over, became exhausted, entered a school building that was still standing and fell asleep. This was Honkawa Elementary School, not far from the hypocenter. The next day when she woke up, she was astonished. The school was full of huge piles of dead bodies.

Every time I talk about the events of August 6, I feel pain in my heart, as if another piece of glass hidden in my body is coming to the surface.

Sachiko Yamaguchi

I pray there will never be any more *hibakusha*

Born in April 1928, at the time of the bombing Sachiko Yamaguchi was 17 years old and a first-year student at Hiroshima Red Cross Nursing School. She was in the school kitchen, 1.5 kilometers from the hypocenter, but was uninjured. She went back to her parents' house in Mihara, and later married. She showed no signs of A-bomb symptoms and never thought herself an A-bomb survivor. Her friend told her she was eligible for an Atomic Bomb Survivor Health Book, so she applied. She developed gallbladder cancer, then colon cancer after the age of 80.

Escape through a crowd of corpses

I was the third of three sisters born to parents who ran a salt farm in Mihara, a city in the eastern part of Hiroshima Prefecture. I was the tomboy. Every day I would come home from school and climb the big hemp palm standing next to our salt farm because I loved to watch the town from atop that tree.

It seems my father was thinking, "With no sons, we can't send a soldier to the front from my family. At least I could serve the country if I had one of my girls become an army nurse." Because I was so physically active, he chose me to send to the Hiroshima Red Cross Nursing School on the grounds of the Hiroshima Red Cross Hospital. I went right after I graduated from girls' school. (In those days, the Red Cross Nursing School had one course which consisted of two years of education after graduating from girls' school.)

Half the third floor of the Red Cross Hospital was a women's dormitory which accommodated some 30 students, while another dozen or so lived in the two rooms of a one-story house on the side of the hospital called the Annex. As a first-year student, I was assigned to a room in the Annex.

Dormitory residents ate meals in a dining room attached to the Annex. Next to the dining room was a kitchen where female cooks prepared meals assisted by a few students who were assigned cooking duties, taking turns a week at a time. At 6 a.m., we started putting tableware and big kettles of tea on the tables.

The morning of August 6, 1945, I was on kitchen duty. After finishing breakfast, which started at 7 a.m., everyone returned to their rooms. I was washing utensils with Miss Hiraoka, the other student on kitchen duty. Suddenly, we saw a brilliant flash. It seemed to me the light was not that big, but the violent, roaring boom that followed made me think our dorm had been hit by a bomb.

About a week earlier, a B-29 had flown over and scattered a massive quantity of handbills. Some of the bills landed in a heap in front of our dormitory. Head nurse Taniguchi came out with a bucket shouting, "Don't touch them! Don't read them!" She was collecting the bills in her bucket, but they were everywhere, so we could read them without picking one up. On a bill the size of a postcard, an illustration of a plant with a chimney carried Japanese text that said, "We're not fighting citizens. We're going to drop a bomb soon. We demand your immediate evacuation!"

I was washing plates, but the instant I heard the boom I dove into the space between two cauldrons for cooking rice. A beam from the ceiling fell down and my classmate who was working with me was trapped under it and killed.

The lights in the building went out, so it was pitch black inside. In fact, no light was coming in through the window either. It was dark as night outside. Buildings had collapsed, so we couldn't tell what building was what.

I desperately screamed, "Dad, Mom, help me!"

Soon I realized there was no way my parents were there. Thinking, "God must be here," I started screaming, "God! Help me!"

The sky outside was wrapped in black mist, but at times, from gaps in the mist, beams of white light burst through. My mouth was so dry from fear I couldn't say a thing. Then I thought, "I'll be in trouble if I stay in here!" I cried out loud, again and again. Fortunately, someone outside removed some rubble and I was freed. Watching my step carefully, I quickly climbed out of the building.

The black mist obscured everything from about one meter around me. Very slowly, this mist or smoke lifted. As if a black curtain had been rolled up, the area around me grew light again.

I looked around and was shocked. I saw people who had fallen with blood covering their faces. Others were groaning, with arms or legs torn right off. The clothes had completely burnt off one victim, leaving only a belt. A mother held a baby whose skin seemed to be melting off. One person with skin peeled off was so burnt I couldn't tell if I was looking at their face or the back of their head. Such misery spread before my eyes. Dead bodies were scattered everywhere.

Meanwhile, fires ignited and blazed.

Some already burnt victims had no idea which way to go so they ran aimlessly this way and that. Soldiers were shouting, "Go to the Army Air Field!" I didn't know which way the Army Air Field was, but I followed the crowds.

The ground was hot. The rubber soles of my shoes immediately melted and fell off. I found one *geta* (wooden clog) and a military boot on the street so I wore them. I went from place to place looking for safety from the fire, and then waited for daybreak.

The next morning, I went back to the Red Cross Hospital, but the Annex where I lived had vanished.

Fire had also broken out in Yamanaka Girls High School next door. The whole school had been gutted by fire during the night. I went inside the burnt ruins of the gymnasium. One of my friends from Nursing School was sitting on a balance beam with no strength left in her. Glass fragments filled her face, which was covered with lines of dried blood.

The windows in the dormitory were all shattered, and many students had been seriously injured by flying glass. The glass windows in the kitchen were protected by wire netting, so I had been spared glass fragments.

When I saw a charred mother die while nursing her baby in front of the hospital, I was suddenly terrified. I thought I should go home to Mihara.

No matter where I tried to cross the river, the bridges had all burnt down. I kept walking and looking for a bridge. I went forward for a while, then, at a desk placed near the road, I saw a soldier who was issuing Disaster Certificates. I told him, "I want to go home to Mihara."

He hardly looked at me as he wrote a Disaster Certificate and handed me a paper about the size of a credit card. I carried the paper as I walked to Mukainada Station, which took a long time.

I heard that a few days earlier, a unit of the Akatsuki Corps from Osaka had come to Hiroshima. They were lining up in front of Gokoku Shrine on the morning the bomb exploded, and hundreds of them were killed. At Mukainada Station, I wondered how they had prepared such a huge number of plain wood coffins. I saw hundreds of white coffins loaded on a freight train. Each coffin carried a unit code and name.

When I showed my handwritten Disaster Certificate to the station attendant, he said, "If you don't mind riding with coffins. . ." I sat leaning back against a mountain of coffins. Swaying on that freight train, I just wanted to go home.

When I got off at Mihara Station, people were surprised and gathered around me. I had gotten off a freight train, which should not have been carrying any passengers. They threw many questions all at once. "You came from Hiroshima?" "What happened there?" I escaped from them and hurried home.

When I arrived at my home, my mother was amazed. Her eyes grew round and she burst into tears. "I heard Hiroshima was totally destroyed. I'm so happy you made it home!" My father had regretted sending me to the Red Cross Hospital. He sobbed, "I'm sorry, I'm so sorry."

The Hiroshima Red Cross Hospital started treating atomic bomb survivors immediately after the bombing. But many doctors and nurses had been killed, so they were badly understaffed. I received several telegrams asking me to go back to the hospital.

Because I had seen such painful scenes, I had no desire at all to go back. Every time a telegram came to my house, I took my time and tried to postpone making up my mind. I think my father went to the hospital and apologized for me.

"You should go at least once, if only to greet them!" My father finally told me, so I went to the hospital three months later, on November 4. My father went with me. There, for the first time, I learned that many of my classmates had died. I was so shocked and prayed sincerely for their peaceful repose.

I settled down in my parents' house in Mihara and resumed flower arrangement and tea ceremony lessons. One day, an elderly lady there suggested, "I know a good person for you. Would you like to meet him?" He was two years older. He had trained as an elite special submarine navigator and was assigned to be a "human torpedo."

Just before he made his one-way sortie, the war ended. His attack was canceled, and he survived. He came back to Mihara the year after the war ended.

My family owned a saltpan and was relatively wealthy, so the go-between lost confidence and told the young man, "Her family is rich. They might reject you. I know another good one who's the daughter of the owner of a cigarette store. Shall I introduce you to her?" But the boy was highly competitive and was offended by her second suggestion. He simply said, "I don't need a cigarette store girl. I want that saltpan girl." So we got married.

My husband was not a *hibakusha*. I was in the Red Cross Hospital, 1.5 kilometers from the hypocenter, but I was in the well-shielded kitchen, so I was not sure if I could properly call myself "exposed." I generally felt that A-bomb effects were things that happened to others.

Since I felt that way, I shared with my husband the things I had seen in Hiroshima immediately after the bombing. He was appalled, of course, but he, like me, assumed that the experience had nothing to do with us.

I had no A-bomb symptoms like bleeding from the gums or losing hair. Neither did I develop any serious illnesses. I thought, "I'll never be affected by the atomic bomb exposure." So when I got pregnant with my first daughter, I had no fear and delivered her with no problem.

About 30 years after the war, I ran into an old friend from the girls' school. She worked for the prefectural government office and was in charge of organizing documents related to the atomic bombing. She said, "That day, I just passed through Hiroshima Station in a train, but I got an Atomic Bomb Survivor Health Book." She went on to suggest that I was eligible too, as I had been near the hypocenter.

To do that, I needed to have someone testify that I was in Hiroshima at that time. I looked for Head Nurse Taniguchi at the Hiroshima Red Cross Hospital. She was old, but in good health. She confirmed that I was in the hospital, so I got an Atomic Bomb Survivor Health Book.

After receiving the Health Book, I developed colon cancer, followed by gallbladder cancer. I've had a third of my liver and my gallbladder removed. I have no idea if my illnesses were effects of the atomic bombing, but I can't eliminate my fear or my feeling that the bombing caused them.

I pray for genuine peace on Earth and that we never create any more *hibakusha*.

Part 2

Hiroshima August 6, 1945
A Silence Broken

Testimonies of men from Hiroshima

Shigeru Nonoyama
Beginning to tell my story

Born in January 1930, in Nagoya, Aichi Prefecture, Shigeru Nonoyama was the youngest of three siblings. His two sisters were much older, and were already married and living in Hiroshima when Shigeru was a child. During 1945, major cities throughout Japan experienced air raids, but Hiroshima was never attacked. More and more people moved there, Shigeru and his parents among them. They lived with his two sisters and their families. His sister Tsuneko had six children, and his other sister Harue had two. Altogether, the 15 of them lived in two adjacent houses.

Shigeru was 15 years old when he was exposed to the bomb while swimming in the Tenma River at Hirose Kitamachi, 1.1 kilometers from the hypocenter.

Exposure while swimming

Our house stood on the bank of the Tenma River. We would catch gobies, river shrimps and crabs at low tide. At high tide, we would jump into the water from the bridge. I was 15 years old at the time of the bombing. Coming from Nagoya, where we had no rivers nearby, I wasn't used to playing in the water. The local kids made fun of me for not being able to swim, calling me "Nagoya." I was so humiliated that I sneaked out to the river at night and practiced swimming between the piers. The effort paid off, and I acquired some swimming skills.

I graduated from the Communications Staff Training Center and started working at the Hiroshima Telegraph Bureau. We worked in three shifts. On August 6, my shift was from 2 p.m. to 10 p.m., so I was at home that morning. My sister Tsuneko's eldest son Hideaki was with me. He was a sixth grader and until the previous day had been evacuated with his school to Imuro. He had just returned home.

"Let's go swimming!"

Just when we took off our clothes, the yellow alert sounded. The tide was high but was starting to go out. We could only jump from the bridge when the tide was high, so we waited impatiently, and finally the alert was lifted. We rushed out wearing nothing but loincloths and jumped from the handrail of the Kita Hirose Bridge.

We found some driftwood trapped between the bridge girders. Hideaki and I got it loose and pushed it upstream. The river was deep, and Hideaki couldn't stand on the bottom. He clung to the log as I was pushing it upstream.

The roar of B-29s came from nowhere.

"Let's not get shot! Hide under the water!" I shouted, but looked up at the sky. At that instant, I saw a bright flash, like lightning.

At the same time, Hirose Elementary School, which stood by the river, was blown away in pieces. People also flew through the air. I saw countless hot water balls of different sizes like baseballs or ping-pong balls running across the surface of the river, as if a blacksmith had put the blade of a sword red-hot from a forge into cold water. The surface of the river grew hot.

I felt danger and quickly ducked into the water. The pressure from above was so great I couldn't swim or even move. Several times I swallowed water full of sand coming up from the river bottom.

I used all my strength to get to the surface and get my face into the air. The sun that had been blazing above us just moments before had vanished.

It was pitch dark. "What was that flash? Why is it so dark?"

Not being able to comprehend what had happened, I stood in the middle of the river.

After a while it gradually grew light.

I heard Hideaki's voice.

"Shigeru, what happened to you?"

I looked at him and saw that his hair was burnt and shriveled. The skin on his face and chest above the water had peeled off and was dangling like seaweed from his chest. The skin from his hand was dangling from his fingernails like rubber gloves. He and I stared at each other. Both of us had been utterly transformed. Hideaki and I looked just the same, but neither was aware that it had also happened to us.

We scrambled up the bank and stood stunned. There were no houses left standing normally. Hijiyama Hill to the distant east was usually hidden from view by houses, but it was right there in front of our eyes. Our houses had been crushed. They were built on a riverbank, so the sloped area was like a basement, which we used as a kitchen. My mother was there and unharmed.

I found Tsuneko with blood spurting out of an open chest wound. I tied my loincloth around her wound like a bandage.

My other sister Harue's face was bleeding from shattered glass. Her two daughters were miraculously unhurt: they had both been shielded behind a cow pulling a wagon that had come to clean out waste from the toilets.

People crawling out from the destroyed houses started to flee. We decided to escape to a safe place on a hill. We saw people with melted ears stuck to their cheeks, chins glued to shoulders, heads pointing in unnatural directions, arms stuck to bodies, fingers joined together and unable to grab anything. Not merely one or two hundred, the whole town was in chaos.

I saw that the lady from the shoe shop had her leg caught under a fallen pole, and fire was approaching. She was screaming, "Help me! Help me!" There were no soldiers and no firefighters around. I later heard that her husband had to cut her leg off with a hatchet to save her.

Each and every scene was hell itself. I couldn't tell the difference between the men and the women. Everybody had scorched hair, burnt clothes and terrible burns. I thought I saw a doll floating in a fire cistern, but it was a dead baby.

A woman trapped under her fallen house was crying, "Please help me, help me, my dear!" But her husband had no choice but to leave her, weeping as he went.

My family fled with my mother leading the way. Kita Hirose Bridge where we had been playing had been knocked down by the blast. Half the bridge was under water. It was low tide now, so we were able to slide down the bridge and cross the river. After walking about a kilometer, and just before we reached Aki Higher Girls School in Yamatecho, I could walk no further. I lay down between two ridges in a potato field. The sky grew darker and darker, and then suddenly big black drops of rain started to fall. The rain grew so strong that my body was soon submerged in water with my face just barely above the surface.

Shigeru's father was on his way to work in Misasa when the bomb was dropped. The heat ray came from behind, leaving his neck badly burnt, but he was determined to look for his family. The black rain turned his white shirt black. His two daughters were so transfigured he couldn't recognize them. He was in no better condition. His face was so swollen that he couldn't see. Fortunately, he recognized his wife, Shigeru's mother, who was unscathed, and the family was reunited.

Tsuneko, known for being kind and caring, was loved by many. One who cared for her was a farmer named Tamura in Furuichi, Asa County, 8 kilometers away from the hypocenter. The Tamura family offered to take us in. They were not even our relatives. It was mostly because of Tsuneko that our large family was able to take refuge with the Tamuras.

We thought that we might be attacked by enemy planes during the day, so we waited to move by night. Our mother borrowed a cart from a farm in Yamatecho. In it we carried Tsuneko on the verge of death with an open chest wound, Harue with her face covered with blood and broken splinters of glass, Hideaki with severe burns on his torso and Tsuneko's two-year-old, Hiromi. We pushed the cart all night and reached the farm around daybreak.

Hideaki, who had always hung around me like a little brother, passed away that day.

Later, a neighbor came to tell us that Tsuneko, who had moved to stay at her parents-in-law's house in Imuro, died on August 15 after a great deal of suffering. My mother was probably in shock. She just groaned and shed no tears.

Tsuneko's third daughter, Masako, a student at Shintoku Girls School, remained missing. She was supposed to be on her way to school at 8:15 when the bomb exploded over Hiroshima. Harue's husband, Hirotaka, worked at the Army Munition Depot in Nagoya. He had taken a few days off work to see his family in Hiroshima, as it had been a while since he saw them last. He arrived in Hiroshima on August 6 and was exposed to the bomb. He passed away at the end of August. Tsuneko, Hideaki, Hiromi, Hirotaka and Masako: my mother's children and grandchildren departed one after another.

Maybe she couldn't afford to lament each time. I, myself, was on the brink of death and have little memory of that time. Glass shards filled Harue's face. Little purple spots like *adzuki* beans appeared on her face and body after about a week. When these spots appeared from face to chest, a person's hair would fall out one clump after another within a week. Although we didn't talk about this, we all thought that she would die soon.

She started throwing up jelly-like clumps of blood, enough to fill a bowl quickly. While my mother dumped one bowl of this congealed blood, she filled another one. My mother dug a hole in the garden and buried the blood day after day.

Harue miraculously recovered. She later said it was perhaps because she threw up all the bad blood. She lived to the age of 96 and passed away on February 6, 2013.

I hovered between life and death for three months from August to October. When a fly landed on a festering wound, it would bleed white maggots in a few days. My mother shooed the flies away with a fan throughout the night. She must have been desperately determined not to lose any more sons or daughters. My dangling skin dried and turned hard like paper. My mother picked off the dry skin. She made a cream of straw ash mixed with cooking oil and applied it to my burnt head, face, chest and fingertips, turning me black. It stung at first, but soon the hurt went away. When the wounds dried, they were covered by scabs. She soaked the scabs in cucumber juice and removed them. She applied the black cream again, and removed the scabs again, and kept repeating the process.

Even after burns healed, they were often covered by thick scar tissue known as keloids. Decades later, my name was called in a streetcar by someone whose face was unknown to me. It turned out that he was an old friend, but with a keloid scar. That was an everyday occurrence in Hiroshima after the war. For years I saw many people with keloids in the public baths.

However, I developed no keloids and no scars anywhere on my body. All that remains is a faint line between my upper body, which was above water and exposed to the heat ray, and my lower body, which was in the water while I was in the Tenma River. I believe my unscarred skin is a gift from my mother, who so tenaciously did her best to save me.

I recovered and returned to work at the Telegraph Bureau

in November. I received a medical checkup at the Hiroshima Communications Hospital at the same time. The director of the hospital, Dr. Michihiko Hachiya, who performed the checkup, said, "You're probably the only person who survived the bomb in the river. Your skin is clean enough. Take care and don't overdo it." Dr. Hachiya was also a *hibakusha*. He was injured, but he examined and treated survivors in the wreckage of his hospital building.

On the way to work in Fukuromachi, a wooden sign read, "Navy Officers Burial Site." Around the sign lay a thin layer of dirt. Anyone who dug in the ground there would find dead bodies with rotten skin peeling off. Many wooden signs like that could be seen throughout the city.

I simply thought the atomic bomb was "a new type of bomb." None of us knew anything about radiation. Many people came to Hiroshima looking for family members and were exposed to radiation. They had no other injury, but they tired easily and soon became feverish.

Doctors would say, "I wonder if you have pneumonia." After a while, they developed red spots on their bodies. They would think, "What's happening to me?" They lost their hair and vomited blood. Many died without any understanding of what had happened. The dead were cremated on the ridges of rice fields. There were no coffins available. They covered the corpses with firewood and burned them in the fields every day. Corpses quickly decomposed in the summer heat and attracted maggots—turning the bodies white. The stench of the burning bodies filled the town.

Shigeru married when he was 40. His wife, Kimie, was also a survivor. She had been in Funairimachi, two kilometers away from the hypocenter. Before Kimie met him, she was engaged to someone else. However, the wedding was canceled because the fiancé's family did not want their son to marry an A-bomb survivor.

Since we were both survivors of the bomb, some said, "They won't have healthy children." We were fortunate to have three healthy children. I now have five grandchildren. Three of them are about the age Hideaki was when we were swimming in the river. What if my grandchildren suffer an atomic bombing? Just imagining it makes me shudder.

But I fear not only for my grandchildren. No one deserves to be exposed to such a horrific weapon. The human family does not need nuclear weapons. When I drink alcohol, my burnt upper body becomes bright red. Even now, when I think of my mother, who lost so many loved ones at once and took such good care of me despite her grief, tears come to my eyes.

Shigeru has come this far almost never talking about the atomic bomb to anybody. But when his grandchildren went to the Hiroshima Peace Memorial Park and asked him about it, he decided to share his story.

In 2011, I told my A-bomb experience to an audience in Italy. I was in Rome on January 30, then Florence on February 1. I was invited by some peace groups, including the Pugwash Conferences and International Physicians for the Prevention of Nuclear War. I was not used to taking turns speaking with an interpreter, but I spoke with my whole heart. Everyone who listened to my story responded enthusiastically. My sister Harue was still alive at that time, and when I said, "Harue is over 90 years old and is in good health," the whole audience stood up, cheering and clapping their hands. I was deeply moved by the sweet, warm treatment I received from the Italians, who were delighted by the fact that Harue had lived through that tragic experience.

Nobel Peace Prize laureate Betty Williams encouraged me, saying, "Thank you very much for coming all this way." After my speech, people came to meet me. One hugged me and said, "I was touched. Grazie." Another shook my hand and said, "I have read Dr. Hachiya's book." I had to get up some courage to go to Italy, but I was extremely happy I did, and I feel that I did the right thing.

I hope to see the world filled with the smiles of our children and grandchildren.

Human beings do not need atomic bombs.

Katsuyuki Shimoi
The accident in Fukushima prompted me to talk

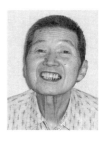

Born in January 1930, Katsuyuki Shimoi was exposed to the atomic bomb when he was 15 years old at the house of the neighborhood association president in Shimo Yanagicho, 1.2 kilometers from the Hiroshima hypocenter.

Katsuyuki had just graduated from higher elementary school and enrolled at Second Shudo Middle School. However, the students were mobilized to work in a war factory as "volunteer labor." Beginning at 7:00 every morning, he worked on engine parts for airplanes at Kurashiki Aviation's Hiroshima plant in Yoshijima. He was in charge of inspecting the completed components. He dipped the finished parts in liquid to make sure there was no crack in them. He then chiseled anchor marks on the parts that passed the inspection. In addition to male students, housewives and female students were mobilized at the factory. They didn't have enough strength to use chisels, so they used drills to cut the anchor mark. Katsuyuki later heard that all the window glass in the factory was blown out by the blast. The inspectors always worked by the windows where there was plenty of light. All the housewives and female students who were at work were pierced by glass shards in their faces and heads. They died in pools of blood.

My brother died with the face of an old man

I lived in a row-house facing a narrow street. The authorities planned to demolish the building to prevent the spread of fires resulting from incendiary bombs. My family had been informed that we had to either move out or demolish the house by the end of September.

Air-raid alerts sounded frequently in those days. People living in densely-built areas were required to evacuate their homes to prevent fires from spreading and provide evacuation routes.

On August 6, I took the day off, submitting a medical certificate from my doctor to the factory. The day our house would be demolished was approaching, but we had not found a new place to live. We had no choice but to ask the president of the neighborhood association to keep our belongings temporarily in his house in Shimo Yanagicho. As soon as I confirmed that the air-raid alert had been lifted, I changed into my work clothes and went out. The president's house was about 50 meters from ours.

He had agreed to keep our belongings on the second floor, so we were bringing his furniture down to the first floor. I used a rope to let the tilted furniture slide down a ladder. The president and some neighbors received it at the bottom.

We had just started this work when suddenly I saw a brilliant light, thousands of times brighter than the flash of a camera. Then I heard a tremendous booming roar. In an instant, the second-floor room I was in rumbled and collapsed. My body fell down, as if being vacuumed into an abyss. At that time, nearly all houses had earthen walls, including the president's house. They were fragile and fell apart immediately.

It was pitch dark. I was trapped between a wall and a pillar. I tried with all my strength to move my body, but I couldn't. My left leg was wedged under a fallen beam. I was in pain. It seemed I had injured my ankle.

"Help! Help!" I shouted.

"I'm stuck as well! Can't move!" An angry shout rang out.

I heard someone nearby saying, "Somebody's caught down here." Hearing that voice, I calmed down a bit. I waited for a while. Some of the rubble shifted, and I was able to move a little. If I crawled under the pillar above my left shoulder, I thought I might be able to get out.

But I couldn't get my head under the pillar. With all my might, I bent my neck as if willing to break it. Finally I was free! I started to crawl, little by little. I fought my way out by crawling toward a ray of light in the roofing. I was assuming that only the president's house was destroyed, until I got to the roof.

I pushed my face up over the roof, then stood up. I was stunned. The blast had toppled every building in town, all in the same direction, like dominos. All I could see were roofs. Debris was everywhere. I could see the Fukuya Department Store and Chugoku Newspaper buildings in the distance. I later heard that the president's wife, his daughter and some others were found on the first floor, burnt to death. I couldn't find the president or the person that yelled back at me. Suddenly I felt the wind and instinctively felt that a fire had started somewhere.

My aunt, who had survived an air raid in Osaka, had told me, "When a fire turns a corner, it creates a wind as strong as a tornado. Be careful!"

I breathed in a lot of dust and dirt from the walls blown up by the wind. I got sick, and before I knew it I was vomiting a lot. Still throwing up, I managed to crawl over the roof and escape. It was summer, so I was wearing shorts and an open-necked shirt. My clothes were torn to pieces while I was trapped under the house. Roof tiles and debris were all over the road, making it difficult for me to walk with my bare feet. (I had taken off my shoes because I was indoors.)

I walked along the road, then on top of roof tiles from roof to roof. I found some sandals in what looked like a shoe closet in a fallen house. I put the sandals on and headed for the Kyobashi River, dragging my left leg in pain.

I passed a community kitchen on the way and saw an old lady trapped under a telephone pole. She couldn't move and was screaming, "Help!" I pulled her out from under the pole. Apparently she thought I would leave her there and clung hard to my waist. Taking her with me, I got as far as a field on the riverbank.

By the bridge was a group of eight to ten women. They were all at a loss. Fire was breaking out here and there. They didn't know where to go. Their hair and clothes were all burnt; they were essentially naked. They crouched down trying to cover their bodies with wood and newspapers. The old lady I was helping saw someone she knew, so she joined that group. Many people had fallen to the ground. Countless bloated and black-scorched bodies were tossed everywhere.

I ran up to the riverbank and looked over the town. All the houses were leaning or crushed. Of all the tall buildings nearby, the Chugoku Newspaper Building and the Fukuya Department Store were the only ones still standing, and smoke was rising up from both of them.

"There must be a first-aid station on Hijiyama Hill!" This thought spread from mouth to mouth. The people on the riverbank stood up and started heading toward Hijiyama Hill. I followed the crowd. When we reached Yanagi Bridge, it ignited and started burning right before our eyes. The fire spread, and in a minute or so the whole bridge was burning. Nobody could put it out. We couldn't do anything but stare at the burning bridge.

Yanagi Bridge had been frequently washed away in the past by floods. At this time, the bridge was under repair, and building materials were piled up around it. It is thought that those materials caught fire and spread to the bridge.

The bridge was burnt out. If we wanted to get to the other side, we would have to wade and swim. We were fairly near the Inland Sea, so we had to wait for the tide to go out. Besides, a strong wind whirled through the air, and the waves were quite high.

In Dotemachi on the opposite side of the river, the fire was raging bright red. I could feel its heat in a hot wind all the way from the other side. The fire was so strong, I felt as if it would spread to our side of the river. We were so hot we went into the river to cool down. We brought tatami mats from a collapsed house and put them in the river. We put the heavily wounded on them. Then we just waited for low tide.

Finally the water was low enough, and we were able to cross. Everything in Dotemachi was burnt out, but the fierce fire had subsided. We crossed the river pushing the tatamis. The severely injured were shivering, though it was midsummer. By strange good fortune, I found my father on the other side. It was a miracle. My father was not a soldier. He was in the National Volunteer Corps in charge of building demolition. He also went to factories to help. He had been on his way to work at the Asahi Weapons factory in Jigozen.

When he saw the mushroom cloud above Hiroshima, he came to look for us by boat from Jigozen. He was thinking, "There are no houses on Hijiyama Hill, so it won't catch fire. My family will take refuge there." On this assumption, he had walked to the hill.

After I was reunited with my father, we decided not to go to Hijiyama Hill. We headed for a house we had rented in Katako. It took probably 30 minutes, crossing Kojin Bridge, which had lost its handrails to the blast. There were dead bodies lying everywhere, charred like coal. We couldn't tell the men from the women.

I saw so many miserable people. I saw one whose clothes had been burnt off his back by the heat ray, and the skin of his back was hanging down to his feet. Another was walking along dragging the skin of his back. Another's face was red, black and terribly swollen, having been hit by the heat ray from the front. All of them walked like ghosts with their arms out in front of them, their skin hanging from their fingertips.

My mother and younger sister Rumiko (then five years old) had previously evacuated to the house in Katako. Although the house was ruined by the blast, they were both safe. However, many people in Katako had severe burns and other injuries. When my mother saw us coming back safe, she was overjoyed and said, "I was so afraid, seeing so many people fleeing!"

Then my younger brother Akio came back. He was 13 and mobilized at the Toyo Canning Plant. He was at Nagarekawa on a streetcar at the time of the bombing. He told us that most of the people around him died instantaneously because of the heat ray and the blast. Because my brother and his friend Nakamura were small, they were shielded by the adults all around them.

The fires had not started yet, so the two of them managed to make their way home. My brother had been wearing a hat at the time of the bombing and it was burnt onto his head, a deep, black burn. He looked as if he were sick.

I could not believe that despite the horrible disaster Hiroshima had suffered, my entire family had survived and reunited. I could not help smiling when I thought about this simple reality. We told each other how fortunate we were.

That day we ate fried rice using the rice rations my mother had put aside for emergencies. The kitchen was destroyed, so we built a stove using an oilcan on the earth floor. My mother put a pan on it and made fried rice. All of us, including Nakamura, surrounded the oilcan and keenly watched my mother cooking. Thinking back, I know it was simple rice fried with cooking oil and a little soy sauce, nothing else, but it was a great feast at that time. I remember that taste even now.

The next day, the fire had died down in most of the city, except Atagomachi. Nakamura spent the night with us, and I walked to Tokaichimachi Station with him. We saw a scorched streetcar that was burnt brown.

"You were on that thing!" I was impressed by the fact that my brother and Nakamura had both survived even in such a completely destroyed streetcar. We noticed the ruins of the Industrial Promotion Hall (the A-bomb Dome) as we crossed Aioi Bridge and headed for Tokaichimachi, following the streetcar track.

After about 20 days, my brother's hair started falling out, and red spots appeared all over his body. "You'll be fine! It's just the poison coming out of your body. Be strong!" My mother encouraged him, but he just lay there looking weak. It seemed like she was trying to convince herself.

His shoulders and arms got thinner and thinner until they were like chopsticks. My mother massaged and encouraged him continually, but he died on August 29. He had been a mischievous, very masculine boy. Our personalities were quite different, but we always played together. I remember I could never beat him at sumo wrestling, marbles in the alley or most other games. After watching a samurai movie, we would wear wooden swords on our waists and fight like the heroes in the movie. My brother was dominant in that kind of fighting as well. For the harvest festival in early winter, he always made himself up as a red or blue demon and chased other children around the neighborhood. Sometimes he went a bit too far, but if I tried to stop him, he would just get wilder and wilder. He loved military drills and always said, "I'll go to the Naval Aviation Preparatory School as soon as I turn 15."

My mother's grief and suffering were so deep, I couldn't stand to see her. Every day she wept silently, holding tight to a can of ointment she had applied on my brother's burns. My brother was only 13, but he looked like an old man when he passed away. His skin was tattered, and his arms and legs were so skinny he looked like a skeleton. I later heard that his friend Nakamura passed away on the same day.

Although I was only 1.2 kilometers away from the hypocenter,

I had no burns, nor did I experience acute A-bomb disease. My doctor thought it was strange. He said, "You were probably well shielded." I think that being indoors was the main reason. Still, I have gotten sick easily the rest of my life. I always feel tired. I used to get vitamin injection shots, and I never had the strength to participate in physical training at school.

Right after the war, I developed a strange cough and went to a clinic. I was diagnosed with tuberculosis and took streptomycin. Rumor spread that moxibustion (a type of heat therapy) would help if radiation had lowered the white blood cell count. After that, moxibustion became a popular form of treatment. When I was not feeling well, I used to go to get a moxa treatment.

I can't say for sure that it's related to the bomb, but my father died of liver cancer in 1963 at the age of 58. In 1990, my mother passed away from colon cancer, aged 80. My sister married, but later lost her sight due to hemorrhages in the eye and other complications.

In 1946, a friend's sister died in an accident. I heard he was planning to dance at her memorial service, so I went to watch him practice. That was how I first encountered Japanese classical dance.

Lessons were held on the eighth floor of the Fukuya Department Store. "You can borrow my fan and sandals, so just order a *yukata* (summer kimono) and I'll teach you," the teacher told me. I thought dance might make me stronger, so I decided to become an apprentice under Master Mitsuyuki Hanayagi of the Hanayagi School. I was 17 years old. When I first started, I didn't have enough strength. I fainted during practice several times. But dancing worked. I gradually became stronger.

I became an accredited master in June 1953. My master allowed me to inherit the Chinese character "Ko," meaning happiness, from him, and so I got my dance name Kojiro Hanayagi. My master later changed his name to Kaji Hanayagi and became one of the best dancers in the Chugoku region. I continued dancing for 60 years.

In 1956, I received an Atomic Bomb Survivor Health Book. I was within three kilometers of the hypocenter. But to apply for the Health Book, I needed someone to certify that I was there. The president of the neighborhood association filled in a certificate to vouch for me. It was the same president who had helped me move our furniture. His face had been burnt by the heat ray and was disfigured by keloid scars. When I went to get the certificate, I said, "You've been through a lot, haven't you?" He replied, "I'm okay. Only my face was burnt. It was just fate that this happened to me. You take care of yourself, Katsuyuki."

The Atomic Bomb Survivor Health Book is a small book with a yellow cover. Nobody applied for them in the beginning. At the time people were going around saying, "A-bomb disease is contagious."

A radio drama called "The Yellow Book" was broadcast to promote the book. By showing the Atomic Bomb Survivor Health Book and your health insurance card, you can get free medical treatment. As people learned more about this system, they started getting the book. Those who could not find someone to certify their presence would advertise on the radio, saying, "Anyone who knows Mr. X, who used to live in XX, please contact me."

I got married when I was 31. One of the senior dancers used to warn me, saying, "If you don't get married by 30, it will get harder to find a partner. You'll be single all your life. If you find someone you like, get married right away!"

My wife was from Tokushima Prefecture and did not experience the atomic bombing. There was a rumor that *hibakusha* would have handicapped babies, so when my wife was pregnant, I was so worried I could not think of anything else. Fortunately, my two daughters are both healthy.

At the time, there was talk about issuing Atomic Bomb Survivor Health Books for second-generation *hibakusha*. I was asked if I wanted to apply for my daughters, but I declined. Living with my own A-bomb experience was enough for me. I did not want my children to carry this burden.

I live near the Peace Memorial Park and the Cenotaph for the A-bomb Victims. I wake up at 5:00 every morning and go there and pray. I have almost never before spoken in detail about my experience of the atomic bombing.

Katsuyuki changed his mind about talking about his experiences after the nuclear power accident in Fukushima caused by the Great East Japan Earthquake of March 11, 2011. According to the International Nuclear Event Scale, the Fukushima accident is rated at the highest level, 7, which is the same as the Chernobyl accident that occurred in 1986. Renowned antinuclear activist Ichiro Moritaki said, "Human beings cannot coexist with nuclear power." If an accident occurs again, it will be too late. Now, whenever Katsuyuki has the chance, he talks about his experience. He says, "Although the power of a single person is small, if we all put our voices together, we can cause a change."

I saw a worker at the Fukushima nuclear power plant on TV. I think I saw a rash on the worker's arm—the same kind of rash I saw on my brother's body. It made me shudder. The situation inside the reactors has not even been confirmed yet, but the government quickly declared the accident to be under control. Radiation is not that simple. The government should not be so vague. We *hibakusha* know the horrors of radiation from the tragic experience inflicted by the atomic bomb. I believe it is time for us to raise our voices.

Senji Kawai

"Who else is going to pass on the story of the atomic bombing?"

Born in February 1930, Senji Kawai was 15 years old when he was exposed to the atomic bomb at his home in Kami Tenmacho, 1.2 kilometers from the hypocenter in Hiroshima. He receives treatment on a daily basis for various aftereffects such as keloid scars on his back, prostate cancer and heart disease. He worked in construction until he was in his 70s.

"My mother used to be a geisha, so she was flamboyant and generous," says Senji. His father was serious and totally devoted to his work. He explored ways to improve workmen's heavy-duty shoes, and eventually commercialized his product. Senji was their second son.

I still suffer from the aftereffects

Two young employees worked with sewing machines in a workshop on our premises. We also had two housekeepers. My mother was always ordering them to do this or that. My father's business was successful, and we were quite prosperous. Our house was in Kami Tenmacho. It was a big two-story house about 9 meters wide by 30 meters in depth. I was pampered as a little boy. Every New Year's Day, we would serve all our guests *sake* and *zoni* (soup with rice cakes) and vegetables. People we didn't even know would hear about this and stop by. "Come in!" My mother didn't care who they were. She just invited them into the room where we served food and drinks.

She often took me to the *ochaya* (where patrons are entertained by geisha), and I saw her generously handing tips to the geisha.

Once I started school at First Commercial Middle School, a lot of friends came to my house. It was a boys' school, so they were all boys. I got a taste for *sake* at a young age. There was a liquor store next door where I would take home as much *sake* as I could put on my parents' tab. When my friends came to my house, we always drank *sake*.

In 1945, I was in my third year of school with one year to go before graduation. Middle schools under the old system covered five years, but during the war this was shortened to four years.

One of my classmates was accepted to the Naval Aviation Preparatory School, so five of us took him out to celebrate. We partied by drinking and singing at a string of restaurants. The next day, I was exhausted and took the day off from school, as we were to work hard clearing fire breaks. Four of my friends who had partied the day before also decided to cut classes while on their way to school, and came to my house. "If you're not going to school, we can't be bothered to go either," they said. We talked about nothing in particular and hung out on the second floor.

An air-raid warning cleared, and we could no longer hear the antiaircraft guns. "I bet they ran out of ammunition!" we joked.

That instant we saw a blinding flash followed by a tremendously loud roar, and my house collapsed. I felt like my body was being squashed into a mold. I used all my strength to crawl out onto the roof.

All of the surrounding houses were down. I could see the ruins of the Industrial Promotion Hall (the A-bomb Dome), a building I normally could not see at all from my house. In the Tenma River, I saw people screaming as they were washed away along with window frames, furniture and horses. It was still morning, but it was dark as night. It felt like I had crossed the River Styx, because the sights I was seeing were not of this world.

I heard my father call, "Senji! Your mother is trapped. Come and help!"

Our house was a wreck, so I had no idea where anything was. I ducked back down under the roof and tried to find the first floor. My mother was lying on her back with her left arm trapped under a doorframe. Her arm was badly broken, and white bone was protruding.

My mother was so pale—she looked as if she was dead. She didn't utter a sound. "She won't make it!" I felt intuitively. My father and I dragged her out from under the frame and carried her to the bank of the Tenma River behind our house.

"I'm going back to look for our employees! Take your friends and get out of here," he told me, then ran back to the house.

I realized that my younger brother was lying on the ground right beside me. He looked up at me and struggled to stand up.

"Senji," he said. The hands he stretched out to me had skin hanging from them.

Senji's younger brother was on the school swimming team. He was planning to help clear buildings to make fire lanes, but changed his mind and went to swim in the river. He was on the steps by the river and was directly hit by the heat ray. He was 13 years old.

With my brother and four of my friends, we fled to Mitaki. My brother's body was hot, and he shouted for water, heading for the river.

"Don't let him drink the water! He'll die!" shouted a firefighter from a distance. I couldn't let him have any water.

At the bottom of a nearby hill, relief corps members were giving treatment to the wounded. I left my brother there and walked up the hill with my friends. Our bodies were covered in blood from shards of glass and pieces of bamboo from the earthen walls that had stuck into them.

Meanwhile, it started raining a thick black rain which got heavier and heavier until it was pouring down. That's when I realized blood was running down my back. Countless small pieces of glass had punctured my back. Washed by rain, the blood was running. I grew cold.

The village had a Shinto shrine. We entered the shrine, tore down a banner, wrapped it around ourselves and rested.

The rain stopped. I suddenly wanted to go to the toilet. It was unbearable. "Go ahead," I told my friends. I stayed back and defecated near a garden. It was amazing. I excreted an enormous amount of black feces. "Is all of this coming from my stomach?" It was an unbelievable amount.

A doctor later told me, "It's good that you relieved yourself. You probably let a lot of the poison out of your body."

After resting a bit, we started toward the house of a friend who lived nearby. But then one of my friends said he was going home to Mitaki. The rest of us decided to head for Gioncho. We had heard rumors that they were offering treatment there. However, when we got there, we found piles of dead bodies and not enough people to treat the wounded.

We walked to Furuichi. Omei Elementary School was being used as a first-aid station. There we saw a soldier who was near death in a crouched position with his head down leaning it against the wall. His back was severely burnt and completely covered with maggots.

"I wonder if he's dead," I said. The soldier turned around and glared at me. "Humans don't die easily," I thought. He had burns all over his back but was still alive. What I didn't know was that my back looked just like his, severely burnt and covered with maggots.

One of the classrooms was being used as an examination room. People with burns were waiting in line. Mercurochrome was put on our burns with cotton, and the next person would be called. This was the only type of "treatment" available. I picked some of the glass out of my back; the remaining glass was buried under my skin, leaving tiny bumps.

Chairs had been put out in the corridor, and victims were lying on them. Many were almost dead; some had already died. Pieces of dry bread were put beside their pillows. Thinking, "It's a waste to leave that there," I stole some of them and shared them with my friends. It was the first time I had ever stolen from someone.

All the infirmaries were overcrowded. The military were refusing to treat civilians.

I heard someone shout, "Get the badly wounded onto this truck! We're going to Kabe where there are doctors!" I saw a truck loaded with severely injured victims. It was not a military truck; it was a private citizen's truck that someone had got to take injured people to Kabe.

We got onto the truck with many people who were near death. There were over 20 people on the truck. Most of them were burnt black. We couldn't even tell if they were male or female. The injured were lying like fish on the floor of the truck, begging in whispers for water. They were too weak to move. The firefighters and the four of us were the only ones sitting, our legs carefully positioned between the injured.

Before we got to Kabe, two young women died. Their skin had peeled off, revealing black and red flesh. Their faces were burnt and unrecognizable. They were so pitiful. They had been lightly dressed because it was summer, so they were almost naked as their clothes were burnt by the heat and blown to tatters by the blast.

"These two are dead! Let's get them off!"

The truck stopped, and the firefighters lifted them down.

We covered their private parts with leaves and prayed for them to console their souls. We had no tools, nor the time to bury the bodies. After we had removed the dead, another injured person got in. There was no point in carrying the dead.

After a while someone on the truck suddenly had a spasm. It was my friend Chuji Sugita: his calm and mature personality earned him the nickname Oji, or old man. His eyes rolled back, and he began to moan in pain. It looked like he was about to die. I got on top of him and shouted, "Oji! Don't die! We're going to your house!" I slapped him, and he came to.

The police station in Kabe was crowded with survivors. The injured got Mercurochrome on their wounds and bandages wrapped around them. Firefighters came to a vacant lot behind the police station. They used hand hooks on the dead bodies, dragging them to an area where corpses were piled on the ground. Nobody could afford to treat us here either. Mothers with babies and small children were ignored. They sat on the ground, not knowing what to do.

We decided to travel to a friend's house in Oasa. We got on another truck filled with injured near death. When we arrived at the friend's house, his mother was surprised to see us.

"I only have women's clothing," she said and put the three of us in *yukata*, a summer kimono. She prepared a truck that had old tatami mats in the bed. We got in and decided to head for Sugita's house in Mibu. We found his mother in a hat store nearby, and she went to borrow a large cart from a neighbor.

The three of us got a ride on the cart and were finally seen by a doctor. The doctor put Mercurochrome on us and picked out the glass fragments and bamboo splinters in our backs. The backs of the women's *yukata* we were given in Oasa were bright red with blood and pus. Sugita's mother gave us new shirts to wear. We stayed there for a week, going to the clinic every day on the cart. The wounds treated with Mercurochrome dried and became scabs.

There was a big hospital called Kasabo Hospital near Senji's house at Kami Tenmacho, owned by the Kasabo family. They would always tell Senji's family, "Our parents live in Kabe, so if the war gets any worse you're always welcome to stay out there." Senji's parents would reply, *"If something happens, we'll evacuate to your parents' house."* Recalling this conversation, Senji made his way to the Kasabos' house in Kabe.

I entered the premises from the front gate. As I walked past the garden, I saw a small person sitting on the porch. "That's my mom!" My mother always sat up straight and was smart-looking. She sat in the way she always did. "It can't be true! I must be dreaming." But the person in front of me was, indeed, my mother. Without thinking I ran up to her and hugged her. "Mom!"

I didn't know what to say. I cried out loud. The fear, loneliness, hardship, pain—all the feelings I had endured burst out all at once, and I kept sobbing. My mother started crying, too. "You're alive! I'm so glad you made it, Senji." She held onto me tightly and didn't let go.

This was 10 days after the bombing. All this time she thought I was dead. She had a bandage around her arm but was alive. A kind young Korean man had saved her. That young man made a simple shelter for her with some burnt galvanized tin under a bridge. He carried her there and told her, "Rest here." However, my father, who had gone off to look for his employees, was missing, as was my brother, who I had left for treatment at Misasa Bridge.

When I last saw him, my father was alive and well, so I couldn't understand why he hadn't come to Kabe. A month passed in great anxiety. In those days, a Ouija board-type of game called "Kokkuri-san" was popular in Japan. I used a five-yen coin and chopsticks to find out if my father and brother were alive. The game told me that they were both dead.

My brother was directly exposed, so he would not have survived. Since he was doomed, I still feel I should have given him the water he was so thirsty for. I think my father may have gotten caught in a fire or breathed too much smoke.

Senji stayed at the Kasabos' house for a year. His elder brother, who was four years older, was discharged and came home from Gifu Prefecture. Senji, his mother and brother began to build a new life together.

I developed leukemia and needed blood transfusions. My older brother donated his blood by intramuscular injection to my thigh a number of times. Meanwhile, he got sick with fever and diarrhea. He was diagnosed with typhoid fever and was put in isolation. That put an end to my blood transfusions. I got more and more tired. Eventually I couldn't even lift a teacup. A big typhoon called Makurazaki hit in September. Water flooded in under the floor, but I couldn't move. I just stayed in bed.

My mother had many expensive custom-made kimonos at home in Hiroshima. During the war, she kept the kimonos at the Kasabos' house in Kabe. My spoilt older brother was home, but he showed no inclination to work. My mother started selling her kimonos to keep us alive. She didn't need to go out to trade her kimonos. People around us willingly helped her. It may have been because of her character. Somehow she had always been well liked.

She never had to carry kimonos around to exchange for potatoes. Farmers got together bringing vegetables to our house. My mother would line up the kimonos and show them like a salesclerk. There was even a farmer that had brought a cow and asked for a set of kimonos. My mother never lost her dignity.

After about a month at the Kasabos' house, my hair started to fall out. I would run my fingers through my hair, and it would come out in clumps. Eventually I lost my eyebrows and all other bodily hair. My gums turned purple and started to rot. They bled easily, and pus would ooze out. When I brushed my teeth, pieces of jelly-like flesh would get caught in my toothbrush.

I have no idea why, but after about a year, the blood and pus stopped. My hair started growing back. My whole back was covered with scabs. They itched and drove me crazy. My skin was bumpy like a lizard's. I would scrub my back with a dry towel until the scabs rubbed off. Although it stung a little, it felt good. Then my back would get hot, and pus would appear. After a while the scabs would reappear. Then I would get out a towel and repeat this cycle over and over again.

I had keloids that stretched my skin all over my back. They made it hard to move my body. I was a gung-ho boy, and that made me quite competitive. That's probably why I have lived so long without letting anyone know about my keloids.

The Kawai family lived in Kabe for two years. Senji was concerned about the house and factory, so he went to Hiroshima alone. He was surprised to find that his cousins had restarted the factory. "I can't believe you survived!" They were happy to see him. He still remembers that they treated him to rice porridge with sweet potato. Around that time, he overheard the local doctor tell his mother, "Senji will probably not live past 30."

I was always a tough guy, but after I heard this, I was scared of nothing. I thought that since I had only 10 more years to live, I didn't care if I died. My life grew wild. When I was 19, I spent most of my time in the red-light district. I had googly eyes, so people called me "Googly." There were red-light districts on the east and west sides of the city. I was known as "Googly, the playboy of the west."

There was another reason why I was out of control. I wanted to work, and I passed the written exams, but I would always fail the physical checkups. That was because of the keloids on my back. When I got sick and went to the hospital, doctors would see the keloids on my back and say, "Let me take some pictures." None of them knew how to treat them.

My scars made people uneasy. I avoided going to the public

baths and bathed at home even in the winter. I never went on trips either. I was ashamed of myself. But I was never able to become a real gangster. At one point, I heard there was a job carrying flour at Ujina Port. I applied, but I didn't have the strength to lift flour, so I was told to go home.

Later on, Senji was apprenticed to a plasterer, a position introduced by a friend. After a while, he was able to work as a plasterer. He got married in 1974 when he was 44 years old. His wife was from Kure, a city to the southeast of Hiroshima, so she was not affected by the bomb. He still suffers aftereffects from the radiation.

It's almost 70 years since I was exposed to the atomic bombing. When it rains, the scars on my back start to itch and purple spots appear on my thighs and arms. I've had prostate cancer and heart-related illnesses. Going to see doctors has become a daily routine.

Someone said that countries with nuclear weapons are evil. I absolutely agree. Unless the US experiences an atomic bomb, they can never understand how hard it was for us. It's not just the US, of course. All countries with nuclear weapons—Russia, China, France, the UK—they're all evil. They hold onto their nuclear weapons, while not allowing other countries to have them. I can't understand how they can say, "We have these weapons, but you shouldn't." It's very strange.

I still hate the war for making me like this. I think it's a natural feeling. I can't ignore my feelings because that bomb ruined my life. I have suffered continually from it all my life.

Senji's wife told him, "Every year there are fewer people who went through what you did. If you keep quiet, who will speak out?" Strong encouragement from his wife made him overcome his reluctance and caused him to give us this testimony. Still, he expresses mixed feelings about speaking about the bombing. "No matter what I say, those that haven't experienced an atomic bombing will have no idea what it feels like. Only one who is hungry can understand a hungry man's heart. It's the same with this. This is far deeper than words."

Kazunori Nishimura
For the friends who saved me

Born in November 1932, Kazunori Nishimura was 12 years old when he was exposed to the atomic bomb at the foot of Hijiyama Bridge, 1.5 kilometers from the hypocenter in Hiroshima. He has been president of the local neighborhood association and the crime prevention council for 10 years.

He shares his atomic bomb experience in the community to teach children about the dignity of life and encourage them to think about how to protect it.

Kazunori was 12 years old at the time of the atomic bombing, in his first year at a private school, Matsumoto Industrial School. When asked about his childhood memories, Kazunori sang a number of songs, one of which went like this: "Thanks to the soldiers I can go to school with my brother. Thanks to the soldiers who fought for our country."

His was a generation that never questioned the justice of the war.

My teacher said, "They're both dead."

I was the third child of six. I had two older sisters and was the first son. My oldest sister especially adored me. I relied heavily on her for help.

On that day, I was one of 20 first-year middle school students assigned to clear houses for fire breaks. The train departed from Shiraichi Station, and students got onto the train at seven other stops on the way to Hiroshima Station. When we were near Saijo

Station, the air-raid warning sounded. The train conductor notified us that the warning had been cleared before we reached Hiroshima Station. We were to help out in Tanakamachi.

We reached Hiroshima Station and marched in line heading for Yayoicho. All the students wore khaki school uniforms with field caps and gaiters, but the color and the size of our uniforms didn't match, due to a lack of supplies. Not only uniform colors varied, but the caps were also different.

While we were marching along the Kyobashi River near Yanagi Bridge, we heard the roar of a B-29. Since the B-29 was a large bomber, the sound was full and loud compared to other bombers. There had been almost no air raids in Hiroshima, so we had no experience of diving into air-raid shelters. We kept on marching.

It was like a TV monitor turning off all of a sudden. That was what happened inside me. I don't remember any flash or roar. I suddenly lost my sight and consciousness—for how long I don't know.

When I came to, I was buried under timbers and rubble. Buildings in those days were mostly made of wood, so the debris came from surrounding houses. Through a crevice in the pile above me I could see a crowd of people fleeing. I was able to free my upper body, but my left leg was caught under a big piece of timber.

Fire broke out at a house about 50 meters away and headed toward me. The flames were approaching me quickly. "Big sister! Father! Help! Help!" I shouted out without thinking. "I want to go home again!" Many thoughts came and went. My whole life flashed before my eyes. When a person knows that death is approaching, he recalls the moments of his life one after the next. "Help!" I kept shouting desperately, but no one could afford to care about others. "Help! I don't mind losing my leg!" When the fire was a meter away, I was thinking, "No help. My life is over," and I started wondering what it would be like to die. I still clearly remember that moment as I prepared my mind for death.

Just then, I heard someone say, "I'm coming to get you!" I think it was a military policeman or a soldier from Hijiyama Hill. Clearing away the rubble, he used a piece of wood as a lever to lift the timber. I pulled with all my strength and was able to dislodge my leg.

"You pulled me out! Thank you! I'm saved!" I barely avoided burning to death thanks to this man.

I then noticed that I had severe burns on the right side of my body. I had lost consciousness the very instant I was trapped by the flying debris, but it seemed that the heat ray hit the right half of my body directly. From face to shoulder, arm, waist, down to the gaiters on my foot—my entire right side was burnt.

The debris spread as far as I could see, so I couldn't tell where the streets were. Some joints in my left leg that had been trapped under the timber were broken. I could hardly walk. I collapsed on the ground on my back.

My father would surely find me when he came to search for me! With this faint hope, I faced upwards because I wanted him to see me. The sun was so bright and harsh it made me dizzy. I don't know how much time had passed, but I heard someone calling out my name. I saw a very black face covered in soot. Some skin was peeled off here and there from the burnt raw face. Do I know this person?

"Who are you?"

"I'm Yanagida."

It was my classmate Yanagida, with whom I had been walking in line. He always got on the train at Nishi-Takaya Station, the station after Shiraichi. Since we always sat in the same seats, we would meet every day on the train and go to school together.

"If they come again, we'll be all killed! Hurry! Let's escape!"

"I can't move. My leg is injured."

"Then I'll carry you!" Tender and big, Yanagida was a boy who took care of his friends. He was a kind of boss among us. Carrying me on his back, he started walking toward a school in Onaga. But he was soon out of breath. "Yanagida, let me down. I think I can walk a little!"

So saying, I got down and hopped on my good leg while holding onto what I could for support. Yanagida saw that I could hardly walk and carried me on his back again.

"Yanagida, this won't work. You go on ahead and tell my parents." I yelled this at him over and over. Then, I heard someone else call out my name. It was Nishikubo. He was a boy from a rich family who had a lovely face with white skin.

"Okay, why don't the three of us go together?" I borrowed shoulders from Nishikubo and Yanagida; I was almost hanging on them. We made our way to the school. We thought that once we got to the school, they would have medicine, and we would receive treatment. But our expectations were crushed. The school had burnt to ashes; nothing remained.

"We're close to Funakoshi. Let's go to my house," said Nishikubo. I started walking again, hanging on their shoulders. Eventually we came to Ochigo Pass, known as a difficult place.

What we saw there was hell. Most of the people who had fled to this point had used up all their energy and had fallen to the ground. As they died, people fell on corpses already there. A mountain of bodies piled up in layers. Once a person fell down, it seems they could not get up again. Tremendous numbers of people had died there. All these people had families! Those just arriving would push their way into the crowd and walk on the dead, step by step. Some of the "dead" were still alive. They grabbed the legs stepping on them and screamed out for help.

I have no idea how we got through Ochigo Pass, but once over it, we reached Nukushina, and a creek. I was hot so I put my arms into the creek. As soon as I did so, blisters appeared on my arms and shoulders. Yanagida washed his face, and most of the skin of his face peeled off, dangling around his mouth. One eye he couldn't open at all, the other he could, but just slightly. Nishikubo appeared to have few injuries. We found some tomatoes in a nearby garden. We plucked them and bit into them.

Yanagida cried out loud: "I can't eat this tomato!" The skin on his face was blocking his mouth so he couldn't eat. It was so pitiful.

"He carried me in this condition?" I was filled with regret. Tomatoes still remind me of Yanagida.

My arms were burnt and covered with blisters that hurt in direct sunlight. Whenever I let my arms down, the blood rushed to my fingertips, giving them furious pain. I put my arms above my chest like a ghost and advanced, leaning on the shoulders of my two friends. We finally reached Nishikubo's house in Funakoshi.

As soon as his mother saw her son, she came running out of the house. She cried as she pulled Nishikubo into the house. Yanagida and I were left standing in front of the door.

An old lady next door said, "Come to my place." We stayed the night with her. She served us a meal, but Yanagida could not eat. The old lady said, "You have to eat!" and made porridge for him. She lifted the skin that was blocking his mouth and fed him porridge, spoon by spoon. "Oil is good for burns," she said and put cooking oil on the right side of my body.

The next day, the old lady got on a train with us and took me home to Kodani. When I arrived, my mother's surprise and joy were overwhelming. I must have looked grotesque, because half my body was burnt and my leg was injured.

"Kazunori, I'm so glad you made it home!" Crouching down, she began to cry. "We heard that a bomb was dropped on Hiroshima and terrible things are happening. We were all so worried for you."

My father had been looking for me in Hiroshima and was gone the day I arrived. He came home from Hiroshima that night and was thrilled to see me. I felt nothing but relief that I had survived and made it back home. I didn't feel any pain or itching for some time.

All I did was concentrate on surviving each day. All my feelings were paralyzed, numb.

After a week, I started to feel pain and itching. We didn't have a clinic in our village. If we wanted to go to a clinic, we had to go to Saijo, and it was impossible to go there because of my terrible burns. Nor did the clinics have appropriate medication. There was a shortage of medication in Japan even before the bomb was dropped.

"I cannot leave you as you are. I will do everything necessary to heal you." My mother asked around on how to treat burns and tried various methods. She used steamed *dokudami* (saururaceae plants), turning it into a paste, but this had no effect. Next, she heard that potatoes absorbed heat, so she mixed mashed potatoes with ground root of red spider lilies and cooking oil. Potatoes applied to my burns absorbed the heat and soon dried. She would remove the dried paste and put on a new layer. She kept repeating this, and eventually my burns turned into scabs.

Since I could not take baths, we cooled a towel in well water and put it on the wounds. All we could do was wait until I healed naturally. I couldn't lie down on my back or stomach. Anything that touched my right side was painful, so I had to lean on my left side against folded *futons*.

We had cows on our farm, so there were a lot of flies. They would swarm around my wounds. My sisters used a fan to keep them away, but no matter how they tried, the flies came. They were bothersome. Then, white maggots began crawling around on me. It was my body, but it didn't look human any more. My sisters removed them with chopsticks and toothpicks.

Thanks to the devoted care of his family, Kazunori was able to go back to school in February the following year. He thought it had taken him a long time to heal and that his friends would already be well. He was excited to go back to school to see them.

I did not see Yanagida or Nishikubo in the classroom. I had a bad feeling and asked my teacher, "What about Yanagida and Nishikubo? Why are they absent?"

He said, "They're both dead." It was unbelievable. Everything turned white. I thought he was lying. I pulled myself together and looked around the room and noticed that only half the students were present. I later learned that nearly all the rest were dead.

I survived because of my two friends. If not for them, I would have died. When the bomb exploded, we were marching along the Kyobashi River toward Yayoicho. The hypocenter was to our right. We were right by the river, so nothing shielded us from the flash. All of us were exposed directly to the heat ray.

Yanagida had probably turned his eyes toward the bomb at that instant. That is why his face was charred. I got burns on the right side of my body from my head and right ear to my neck, shoulder, right arm, waist, thigh and ankle. It took the longest time for my waist and thigh to heal.

My father passed away two years after the bombing in 1947. He was bedridden, and his hair fell out. Eventually he started throwing up blood and became weaker. The doctor had no idea what was causing the symptoms, but in the end he was diagnosed with tuberculosis. We heard that diseases of the lung required nutrition, so I would often go all the way to Saijo to buy milk for him. I now believe that my father had acute leukemia. He went into Hiroshima to look for me right after the bomb was dropped, so he was exposed to residual radiation.

Kazunori graduated and went to work at the Satake Manufacturing Company. He learned about machine coating. Because of the disability in his left leg, he worked harder than other employees. After a year, he started his own business. He received many orders for rice milling machine coating. In 1961, he joined Toyo Industries (Mazda today).

There he began a career coating cars, moving to product management, and finally into the personnel department education center. He retired at 60.

After retirement, he studied the repapering of fusuma (sliding doors) and the mounting of scrolls at a training center for the disabled. He received many orders for repapering fusuma at Mazda's company housing. He was always busy but grateful. He found it extremely difficult to carry the heavy fusuma into company housing that had no elevators, but he managed to get them up the stairs, while protecting his disabled left leg.

I married when I was 28. I was in my second year working at Mazda. My wife was from Kure City, so she was not affected by the atomic bomb. A friend from the village introduced me to her. When my wife's father found out I was a *hibakusha*, he said that he wanted time to think about our marriage. My wife and her mother persuaded him, and we were allowed to marry.

I was especially worried when my wife was pregnant with our first baby. A rumor was going around that *hibakusha* couldn't have normal babies. Even now, I still feel uncomfortable when talking about marriage. My daughter and sons married around 30 years ago. It was clear that their partners' parents would be concerned if they found out, so I never told them my A-bomb experience. Now, it's my grandchildren's turn to get married and, again, it seems my wife wants me to avoid talking about it if possible.

In the summer of 1945, when it became clear that Japan was losing the war, the Chugoku and Shikoku regions were constantly being hit by air raids. Okayama was attacked on June 29. Three major cities in Shikoku (Kochi, Takamatsu and Tokushima) were attacked on July 4. Matsuyama in Ehime was hit on July 26. Many cities around the country were being attacked. Until August 5, Hiroshima had still not been hit.

It is said that the US military intentionally prevented an air raid in order to see how much damage would be done by the atomic bomb.

"The US used the people of Hiroshima in an experiment," says Kazunori angrily. Three aircraft participated in the bombing. The Enola Gay dropped the bomb just after an air-raid warning was cleared. In other words, the US created a situation that maximized the effect of the bomb in order to conduct a test.

I have lived into my 80s. The two classmates who saved my life were killed at 14. Had they not helped me, I would have died. For the sake of my two deceased friends who saved me, I believe that I must talk about my experience.

In the fall of 2010, I told my story to children at the Fuchu Elementary School. Later, I participated in an event that premiered a new song, "We Will Never Forget That Summer." The children wrote it after they heard me and other *hibakusha* tell our stories. I had wondered if they really understood the bombing, but they clearly grasped it firmly. I was grateful.

The people in Fukushima are going through hard times now. In our day, we had no concept of the horror of radiation. We built shacks and lived on radioactive soil. We resumed living, focused on getting through the day. Then for some of us, nosebleeds would not stop; hair would fall out; people would die without knowing what was happening to them.

Now we understand the ferociousness of radiation, and large numbers of people of Fukushima are still unable to go home. Not being able to move forward is painful and difficult. But no matter what, they must never lose hope or give up. I want them to stand up and display their strength. I wish this with all my heart. How can they stand up again? How can they challenge reality? I believe there is always hope as long as you take on the challenges presented by adversity.

Kazukuni Yamada
The peaceful use of nuclear power is a lie

Born in March 1930, Kazukuni Yamada was exposed to the atomic bombing at his home in Hakushima Nakamachi, 1.7 kilometers from the hypocenter in Hiroshima. He was 15 years old. He worked as a junior high school teacher, on the Board of Education, and eventually at a university. He is committed to contributing to his community as president of the local neighborhood association and social welfare council.

"I won't forgive you if you die before me!"

I was a student at Hiroshima Higher School of Education at the time. I went there because my father encouraged me to be a teacher. Classes had ceased long before, and the students were mobilized for military service every day.

Our first task was to fold and carry waterproof tents manufactured at a tent factory. After that, we were assigned to loading bombs at the munitions depot run by the Akatsuki Corps (Army Marine Headquarters) in Ujina. I was supposed to go to the Akatsuki Corps that day.

I was at home in Hakushima Nakamachi with my mother. My father was an executive at a military factory in Yoshida. He had to stay the night at the factory and was not home.

The air-raid warning had been lifted, so I was getting ready to leave for work. While I was leaning on the wall to put on my gaiters, I heard the drone of some bombers. An instant later, a bright light turned everything white.

I heard a tremendous roar, but before I could even think, I was blown a few meters away with the doors. The ceiling collapsed, and the floor caved in with all the tatami mats. I was covered in blood. My mother was hurled into a glass door in the kitchen and was cut by glass from shoulder to chest. Blood was gushing out of her wounds. I carried her on my back and got us outside.

What we saw is the most tragic scene I have ever seen. Telephone poles were down, so electric wires were coiled up on the street. Store signs, pieces of wood and galvanized tin sheets lay everywhere for as far as I could see. Most houses were smashed, their roof tiles covering the narrow streets. Countless dead and injured were scattered all around, their bodies burnt black and so unrecognizable it was impossible to identify even the gender.

And yet, the leather shoes and belts worn by soldiers remained unburnt.

I was shocked by the appearance of the people who were fleeing. When you steam potatoes, the light brown skin peels off. The people looked exactly like that. Their skin hung like potato skin from their faces and hands.

My mother and I headed for the nearby Nagayama Clinic, but we found it in ruins, unable to treat patients. I lifted my mother again and headed for the Communications Hospital.

What I saw along the way was gruesome. People who were outside when the bomb exploded had melted faces, arms and legs. Their hair and clothes were burnt, leaving them half naked. Those who had been inside houses were trapped under beams or pillars, unable to move. I could hear them screaming for help under the debris, but there was nothing I could do.

The railroad overpass was destroyed, so we couldn't get to the other side. We walked against the crowd. I was pushed back a number of times as I was carrying my mother on my back. We had to give up on getting to the hospital.

Soldiers kept shouting, "Run north!" So we headed north, picking our way through the crushed houses. We reached the riverbank near Engineer Bridge that connected the areas of Hakushima and Ushita. That was a scene from hell. People would arrive, then collapse in the weeds on the riverbank. Maybe their will was somehow weakened by the smell of weeds and living creatures. Hundreds of them fell down and died right there.

Many bridges had fallen under the blast, but Engineer Bridge, a suspension bridge, miraculously remained intact. This bridge was built to connect an army post with the military training grounds. There was a training ground for the Corps of Engineers beneath the bridge. Normally, guards stood at each end of the bridge, and residents were prohibited from entering. To escape the fires pressing from behind, many survivors crossed the bridge that day. "The bridge of life" saved many lives. Years later, a plan was made to tear the bridge down and replace it, but local residents opposed it. The bridge was strengthened and preserved.

On the other side of the bridge, a group of soldiers sat on the ground. They had all been blinded. Because they couldn't see, they held onto each other's shoulders. They were constantly moving their faces this way and that, trying to find something they could see. Their faces, badly burnt by the heat ray, were swollen red and black.

"What did you see?" a voice asked.

"A fire ball!"

"A huge fire ball was flashing!" came the replies.

Those who looked directly at the flash had burns in their eyes and died one after another. Those with burnt bodies were groaning and calling for water. Some crawled down the steps to the river, went into the water and were swept away by the river. While floating down, they reached out their hands as if asking for help. But if you took hold of a hand, the skin on the entire arm peeled off. You couldn't even lift the fallen survivors. It was absolute hell.

When you got burnt by the heat ray, your clothes would burn off in a matter of seconds. You would be naked with a few rags hanging around your body. But you had no feelings of embarrassment. Those who could flee, did. Those who couldn't, died. Those who fell while fleeing were trampled by those who were determined just to get away. Many must have been killed by the trampling. Everyone was consumed solely with fleeing and had no capacity to care for others.

Time passed, but we had no concept of what had happened. My mother and I were unable to think anymore. We were just pressed on by the crowd and crossed Engineer Bridge.

Asked for help by a woman who was almost naked, I got her some clothes from a crushed house. There were many women like her at the foot of Engineer Bridge.

We crossed the bridge and went further north. We didn't see many with terrible burns or injuries after leaving the riverbank. "Residents of Hakushima Nakamachi should flee to Nagatsukacho if something happens." Each neighborhood had a designated evacuation area in the event of an emergency.

We rested at the riverbank until noon, and I remember it happened just as we were about to leave for Nagatsuka. The sky suddenly became black, though it was midday in summer. I later heard that black rain fell nearby. Luckily, the black rain did not come to where we were.

We reached a grove of trees near the village shrine in Nagatsuka at midnight. I looked by chance toward Hiroshima, and saw that the whole city was burning. Even the hill in Ushita was on fire. The light from the fires was so bright it was possible to read a newspaper. We slept outside among the trees.

"It hurts!!"

"Water, water, please!"

Moaning, crying voices gave me no sleep at all. The next day, a farming family in that area offered us a temporary room. I still remember how grateful I was when I lay on tatami mats. We were finally able to relax and tend to our injuries. We picked the glass fragments from our skin and cleaned our wounds. I felt like a decent human being again for the first time. We were given some tomatoes, and they were so delicious. My mother and I stayed at the farmer's house that night, and the following morning we left for a relative's home.

My father's sister and my three cousins lived in Kabe. My cousins were often mobilized to work at my father's factory, so we knew each other. My mother's wounds from her neck to her shoulders were suppurating.

"It hurts! It hurts!"

She cried out in pain, but I could do nothing for her. School classrooms were being used as an Army Hospital in Kabe, so there was hardly any proper equipment. They couldn't even take the glass shards from a patient's wounds. All they could do was sterilize the wounds with their only medicine, iodine.

Then, before a week had passed, my body went through a strange change. My body was so fatigued I couldn't keep standing. I had no will to do anything. My gums bled and would not stop. Mosquito bites would remain red and swollen and wouldn't heal. I got my blood checked, and it turned out that my white blood cell count was 100,000 when normally it should have been between 7,000 and 8,000. It seems I had acute leukemia.

My mother also had acute leukemia, so her wounds wouldn't heal for a long time. I felt so sorry for her. I now believe that it's a miracle that she survived. I also think it was good we left Hiroshima as soon as we could.

We had no idea what was happening to our bodies at the time. All we knew was that we had been hit with "a new type of bomb." We had no clue that it was the cause of our leukemia. Since information was not available, we didn't even worry about it. Not knowing was our only consolation.

Kazukuni and his mother stayed in Kabe until the fall. In October, he was finally able to go back to school. Later, the school system changed, and his school became part of Hiroshima University. He continued his education there, graduating when he was 21 years old. He became a social studies teacher at Noborimachi Junior High School. However, he was destined to face the effects of the atomic bomb again.

When I started teaching in 1951, I was a seventh-grade homeroom teacher. One of my first students passed away due to the atomic bombing. Her name was Hideko Yumoto. She was a quiet girl with porcelain white skin and bobbed hair. At the end of the year, she fell ill and stopped coming to the school. In April the following year, classes resumed, but she didn't come to school. We let her move up to the next grade and kept her name on the school register.

I went to visit her at the hospital. When I stood in front of her room, I heard her moaning. I couldn't open the door and go in until her voice quietened down. Leukemia often causes sharp pain all over the body. When I entered the room, I was relieved to see her smile delightedly.

She had the brand-new eighth-grade textbooks right by her pillow. I opened the social studies textbook and told her, "We're on this page right now." She nodded her head many times.

Soon after that she passed away. I couldn't go to her funeral because I had to teach. I visited her family later to pay my condolences. All her classmates knew she was in the hospital due to the bombing and was unable to come to school. There were many children like

Hideko, who had been exposed to the bombing when they were very young. Although I knew it would cause those children to feel anxiety, I told them about her death. I can't express how hard it was for me. I didn't teach her directly, but Sadako Sasaki, the model for the Children's Peace Monument, was also enrolled at the same school.

I taught for almost 40 years, and was transferred to other schools five times. At each school, there were always a few students who had been exposed to the bomb as a baby or in their mother's womb. One I will never forget is Kaoru Hikichi. He was in my ninth-grade class and an excellent student. He took a leading role in school volleyball tournaments. He was excellent at both studies and sports. I am sure his parents had great expectations for him. However, immediately after Kaoru was accepted to one of the most prestigious public high schools, I received news of his sudden death. He had leukemia due to radiation exposure as a baby. I was shocked speechless.

"As I experienced these incidents one after the next, I realized that teaching is a cruel job," says Kazukuni. He lost many students to the A-bomb disease. "I was exposed, too, but having to see my students die is more painful."

"Mr. Yamada, so-and-so died from leukemia last year." Whenever I attend class reunions, I hear about the death of someone I taught. A survivor can develop A-bomb disease even after the age of 60. It's unbearable. One of my students who was married and living in Tokyo, now a grandmother, told me one day, "My hair is falling out, and I don't feel so well." She passed away recently.

At every reunion, I always tell my students, "I won't forgive you if you die before me!" I have lost about 25 students, including those who died after graduation, to A-bomb disease. For the sake of those children who were killed so young, I have to make the most of my survival by telling my story, getting the facts out. Even as a teacher and after retiring, I have spoken at every opportunity about my experience. My wife and I sometimes encourage each other, saying, "We have to talk about the atomic bombing as long as we can remember it."

Kazukuni married in 1956. He was within 2 kilometers of the hypocenter, which is designated the "direct exposure area." His wife was 2.3 kilometers away, so they are both survivors.

Of course, I worried about the aftereffects. I decided that we should help each other since we are both *hibakusha*. If my wife were not a *hibakusha*, her family would have opposed our marriage, but no one did. We have three children. I was quite worried when my wife was pregnant with our first baby.

"Don't believe the rumors. It's not true." My wife's brother was a doctor, and he encouraged me. His words were really reassuring.

Kazukuni points out that there are three types of damage from the atomic bomb. One is burns due to the heat ray. Next is injuries caused by the blast. Like his mother, many survivors were struck by glass shards or trapped under fallen houses. The third type of damage is the radiation.

You can't see radiation. Those who entered the city after the bombing or were exposed in the womb develop A-bomb disease without even knowing where they had been exposed. If I had known about the dangers of radiation, I would never have returned to Hakushima Nakamachi. I would have stayed in the countryside, just like the people of Fukushima who have fled from the power plant.

Soon after the war ended, the US opened a research institute on Hijiyama Hill called the Atomic Bomb Casualty Commission (ABCC). Its purpose was not to give treatment, but to conduct medical checkups to collect data on the effects of the atomic bomb. It was a time of severe food shortages in Japan, and if you went for a checkup, they would give you curry rice and chocolate. I went there several times. I remember that they even came to pick us up by car.

Radiation is said to be "the science of death." We knew nothing about it, so we built shacks, cultivated gardens and grew vegetables on the scorched land.

Many people were unable to work due to overpowering fatigue. We used to call it the "idleness disease" or "lazy illness." Over a 10-year period, these people passed away one after another.

In 1957, the government announced for the first time that the cause was radiation. This was the first time that A-bomb disease was officially acknowledged. The 10 years preceding this is called "the lost decade." We have many monuments dedicated to the atomic bomb victims throughout Hiroshima, but those erected in the early stages do not use the term "atomic bomb." They probably had to avoid using it because of the media censorship established under the US Occupation.

Kazukuni worked as a teacher in public schools in Hiroshima almost until retirement. He then worked on the Board of Education, and also taught at Hiroshima Bunkyo Women's College until he was 70. He chaired the local neighborhood association and social welfare council. He also served as a probation officer for more than 20 years. His many contributions were acknowledged when he received an award. His father had also received a similar award, so he was able to follow in his footsteps. His face softened for the first time when he told us this. However, when he resumed talking about the atomic bomb, his expression once again became solemn.

I was 15 when the bomb exploded, and now at the age of 83, I feel like my life has been a continuing series of atomic bomb diseases.

When I was 25, a decade after the bombing, I developed a liver ailment. In my late 40s, I got severe stomachaches from eating anything oily. I was diagnosed with inflammation of the gallbladder and had it removed. Now, I'm taking medication for a thyroid gland malfunction and prostate cancer.

This is why the nuclear power plant accident at Fukushima is not just something happening to someone else. Tokyo Electric Power Co. and the government have not told us the whole truth. I believe that the peaceful use of nuclear power is a lie. Nuclear power and human beings absolutely cannot coexist.

Tadashi Kihara
I will never let people forget

Born in February 1927 to a family that ran a Japanese confectionary store, Tadashi Kihara was exposed to the atomic bomb on a train stopping at Hiroshima Station, 1.9 kilometers from the hypocenter, when he was 18 years old. He worked for the Hiroshima Railway Bureau, and after the atomic bombing, he took over the family business. Later, he started working for a company where he was recognized for his skills in calligraphy.

I will tell my story as long as I live

I was the fourth child of eight and had four brothers and three sisters. I was the third son. My parents ran a small Japanese confectionary store in Tsuyama, Okayama Prefecture. My whole family worked for the store. I was making sweet bean paste with my brothers and sisters by the time I was six or seven. My father was a strict craftsman, so he would scold us if we were not meticulous enough, sometimes even hitting us with a piece of firewood.

I was good at making bean-paste-filled wafers called *monaka*. I placed the wafers upside down on a wet dishcloth. When the edges were moist enough, I would scoop bean paste onto one wafer and place the other on top. The pair would seal together perfectly. I would enjoy sneaking a spoonful while stewing the sweet beans.

In April 1941, Tadashi began working at the signal section of the electric repair workshop at the Facilities Department of the Hiroshima Railway Bureau. He was 14 years old. The National Railway Company had eight such bureaus in Japan. The workshop was highly specialized, mainly in charge of regular inspection and repair of the relays that switched railway signals, as well as clocks and switchboards.

My workplace was more like a factory than a railway company. I worked as an engineer and handled plating, coiling, woodwork, casting and lathe work. When my boss wasn't watching, I would sometimes make belt buckles, rings and climbing axes. At the time, the National Railway transported military supplies and soldiers. Because of labor shortages, we received assistance from the military. I would see soldiers in white military uniforms shoveling coal into the furnace of a freight train. I guess the military gave the National Railway special treatment, because the employees seemed to be conscripted much later than people of other occupations. Still, five of my colleagues received draft notices.

On my days off, I would often go hiking and camping with my colleagues to Mt. Dogo, which stands between Hiroshima, Tottori and Okayama Prefectures. As we worked for the railway, we did not have to pay the train fare. We would ride the Geibi Line and head for a cottage, carrying carbide lamps after about 9 p.m. One of our group was killed by the atomic bomb; another was never found.

Food shortages became increasingly serious in 1945. Tadashi and his colleagues decided to make a salt field in a vacant lot by the railroad tracks near Koyaura Station on the Kure Line. The bottom of the slope by the tracks faced the Inland Sea. The plan was to spread sand on the vacant lot, carry sea water with buckets from the beach and let it dry in the sun to harvest salt.

August 6 was to be the first day of work in the salt field. Sixth graders from Niho Elementary School had been mobilized to help in our workshop, but they were too young to perform difficult tasks. They were assigned simple chores, like carrying tools here and there. That morning, five of us were planning to take 10 students to the salt field. We met on the Kure Line platform at Hiroshima Station.

The train arrived about 10 minutes late that morning. That was a cruel twist of fate. If the train had left Hiroshima on time, it would have arrived in Mukainada or even Kaitaichi Station by the time of the bombing. If they had made it that far, they wouldn't have been exposed to the bombing.

I saw the B-29 bombers in the sky just before I got on the train, but since no air-raid warning sounded, I didn't think anything of it. I had the children get on the train first, and I followed. I stood near the entrance to the coach and chatted with the children.

The train master always told passengers to close the wooden shutters before departure, but we left the windows open because the children were too excited. For them, it was like going on an excursion, and it was hot, too.

Departure time was 8:15.

All of a sudden, I saw a flash, hundreds of times brighter than the magnesium flash of a camera. I felt as if my eyes had been scooped out in an instant. At almost the same time, a tremendous roar shook the train hard. All the slates fell off the station roof. The fallen tiles and dust made the world dark.

There had been no air raids in Hiroshima, but I knew that incendiary bombs were being dropped like rain on other cities. I knew the attack wouldn't end with just one bomb. I thought, "We have to get out of here before the next bomb comes."

Crying out loud, the children covered their eyes and ears with their hands as they had been trained to do and were lying on the floor. All the children were injured by shattered glass from the windows. I helped each child down from the train onto the track.

Each child held onto the belt of the one in front and followed the track. I headed for the Osugacho railroad crossing about 200 meters ahead. I wanted to take them to the Railway Hospital near Sakae Bridge, but a flood of people from the city came rushing down Sakae Bridge toward us. They all had terrible burns on their faces and arms.

We were engulfed in the whirlpool of people and forced to go into the Eastern Drill Ground. I had no choice but to gather the children into a corner of the ground. They were all bleeding from their faces and arms, crying and shouting. I said, "Stay here! I'm going to get some medicine. I'll be right back." I headed for my workplace in Minami Kaniyamachi.

There I found the building broken, with the walls and windows shattered. There was no way to enter. Still, I somehow found a first-aid kit and went back to the drill ground, but the children were nowhere in sight. I wondered if they had been moved somewhere else for some reason. I decided to wait for them there for a while, and it was only then that I realized that I was injured.

I thought I probably got injured when I stumbled over a tie on the railroad track on my way back to the Eastern Drill Ground. My white short-sleeved shirt was red with blood from my shoulders to my waist. My right leg was also bleeding. The wound went all the way down to the bone. I took out some medicine from the first-aid kit and stopped the bleeding.

I waited for them for an hour, but no one came back, so I returned to my workplace. A few days later I found out that the children had decided that staying in the city would be dangerous, so they made their way back to Niho, walking along the paths in the hills near the drill ground.

Since I had been in a train, I was not directly exposed to the heat ray. I only had wounds. My colleagues at the electric repair workshop were busy tending to the injured. I was put in charge of night duty and told to work that night with four assistant stationmasters. We put some boards and straw mats in the front yard and slept under a mosquito net. That night, I connected an electrical cord to a miniature light bulb and made an electric lamp. I used an extra-large battery used to test traffic lights. Using this light, we looked for injured people in the alleys or under the collapsed buildings nearby. My workplace had over 100 employees before the bombing; we were reduced now to around 20.

When I went around on watch, the injured who saw my light would beg for water. In the darkness I saw a woman suffering from burns, naked from the waist up. She held a baby in her arms and said, "Soldier, please give me some water!" She probably thought that anybody coming near her was a soldier. Her voice was feeble but intense. The baby in her arms held a nipple in its lips, but it was already dead. Its body color had changed. It was probably the mother's reflex to keep holding her dead baby. She had particularly severe burns from her face to her shoulders. There was nothing I could do for her. I pressed my palms together and apologized, and walked away. This still causes pain in my heart.

There were many survivors who died soon after drinking water. Therefore, most people did not give water to survivors even when they begged for it. In reality, they would have died anyway.

The Eastern Drill Ground where we were was a huge area of land. Soldiers used it for bayonet practice or marching in file, but after the bombing it was completely full of survivors taking refuge. Some with injuries were lying down. Some families crowded together. There were so many people it was impossible to tell how many were there. But as the days passed, the numbers fell rapidly. Some evacuated to relatives' homes, but many more simply died. Dead bodies were loaded onto a cargo train and carried away. One day I looked into one of the empty cargo cars. The stench that hit my nose made me feel like throwing up.

The roofs of the surrounding wooden houses were bent in waves. The atomic bomb exploding in the sky must have pressed down on them with tremendous force.

During the night, raging flames enveloped Atagomachi, near the Eastern Drill Ground. Firefighters ordered civilians to help put the fires out with manual water pumps. A few days later, I saw heavy oil being poured over lines of army horses that had been killed by the heat ray. They were being cremated. The legs of the horses killed by the bombing were thrust out straight. Their bellies were bloated and they looked like inflated balloons. The stench was horrible.

Ten days after the bomb was dropped, I continued to have diarrhea. Then my hair started falling out. Now I know those were symptoms of A-bomb disease. Long after the bombing, we saw many women in Hiroshima wearing scarves on their heads. I always thought they had lost their hair like me.

Tadashi continued to work at the Hiroshima Railway Bureau until April of the next year. He then started training at a Japanese confectionary store in Kobe to take over the family business. He later returned to Tsuyama to help his father.

My father knew only the old way of making sweets and was delighted to learn the new techniques I brought from Kobe. The new sweets were popular. There were even other shop owners who offered to sell my new sweets. We decided to stop retail sales and concentrate on production. I was 27 or 28. I heard that survivors could obtain an Atomic Bomb Survivor Health Book. With the Health Book, you could get medical care free of charge. I was within 2 kilometers of the hypocenter, so the book was issued immediately. However, I really didn't want to get it because I thought it would affect my chances of getting married. I wanted to be a "normal person" as much as I could.

But my physical condition got worse and worse. As a result, the Health Book was very helpful. I had a bladder operation when I was 32, and an intestinal obstruction when I was 45. When I was 55, I had gallstones removed. After three abdominal operations, my navel disappeared. I was able to survive these serious illnesses because of the Health Book.

Tadashi started working at the Sanyo company, a job he found in the classified section of a newspaper in 1967. Eventually he was recognized for his calligraphy ability and was mainly asked to write certificates and addresses on business envelopes. He worked at that until retirement age, but his clients continued to request his hand-brushed calligraphy. In 1995, he started his own company called Kihara Kikaku, where he still works as a calligrapher.

When I was young, I hid the fact that I was a *hibakusha*. After turning 65, I resolved to tell my story to future generations. First, I told my friends and people I knew. Then I started telling my story in public. What shocked me most was that young people were not interested in the A-bomb. I don't want to let them forget that terrible bomb!

To keep that hellish event from happening again, I believe I have to keep sharing my story now, and I will do so until I die.

Yoshiharu Nakamura
My mission is to do my best for peace

Born in May 1927, Yoshiharu Nakamura worked for the National Railway after graduating from Hiroshima Commercial School. Aged 18, he was studying to be a train conductor in a building within the Hiroshima Station Conductor Section, 1.9 kilometers from the hypocenter, when the atomic bomb exploded. He fled to Ochiai, then evacuated to his mother's hometown in Saga Prefecture.

No reply from my best friend

I was the youngest of four siblings, with two sisters and a brother. We used to play soccer in a vacant lot until sunset with three brothers who lived in the neighborhood. I have fond memories of New Year's Day from the time my father was still healthy. To make *mochi* rice cakes, he would pound steamed rice with a wooden mallet. My mother would turn the rice in the pestle between each whack. Then my sisters would roll the rice dough into little cakes. My father loved sumo wrestling. Whenever he could, he listened to sumo matches, putting his ear close to the radio.

Yoshiharu was in middle school as the war grew increasingly intense. He studied in the classroom up to the first semester of the second year, but was then called out for student mobilization. Day after day, he welded and bent pipes at the Mitsubishi Heavy Industries Hiroshima shipyard.

School lessons took place only once a week. A teacher would come on Saturdays and teach in the shipyard dining room for just three hours.

My father used to hire craftsmen to deliver window frames and other fittings to the Navy, but he fell ill and was bedridden by that time. Fresh fish had long been unavailable to ordinary people, so I often brought home the braised mackerel served at the shipyard cafeteria, which always made him happy. It was a time of severe food shortages, and we could hardly get any food. When you heard dumplings made from rice bran were on sale, you would quickly run out to buy some. If you were lucky, you would be able to get some. If not, you had to go home empty-handed.

There was also a shortage of medicine. My father had bronchitis, so when he started coughing hard my mother would rub his back. Other than that, all he could do was stay in bed. That was his "treatment," the best we could do. My father got weaker and weaker. He passed away in 1944, at the age of 56.

In March the following year, Yoshiharu turned 18 and graduated from Hiroshima Commercial School. He got a job at the National Railway.

There was almost no employment other than in military-related industries. Most of my classmates kept working in the shipyard. Aside from that, the only choice was to work for the National Railway as conductors for freight trains carrying military supplies. In those days, we had no choice of occupation.

My mother wanted to move back to her hometown in Saga Prefecture after my father died. One of the reasons I entered the National Railway was because I thought that I might have a chance to be transferred to Saga. But I later found out that the cargo trains coming to Hiroshima were either from Himeji or Shimonoseki. There was no chance of working in Saga, which was in a different district.

Yoshiharu's main job was switching the cargo train couplings. This sounds easy but is in fact a complicated job. You had to consider the horsepower of the locomotive to determine the number of cars to connect. You also had to plan the order of the cars that would be decoupled at each station, putting the freight for the first stop at the end, that for the second stop in front of it, etc.

We mainly used steam locomotives such as D-51 and C-31 at the time. The D-51 had four sets of driving wheels and was capable of pulling 30 cars. D is the fourth letter of the alphabet, corresponding to four sets of drive wheels. Thus the C-31 had three sets of driving wheels. 51 and 31 were class numbers. You had to pass an examination to become a cargo conductor, so on my days off, I studied for it.

On that morning, I was studying as usual with 12 coworkers. We were on the second floor of the Conductor Section Building, a wooden structure next to Hiroshima Station. I was by the window at 8:15 a.m. At that moment, my body was hurled through the air with a bright flash like sparks from locomotive wheels. I heard nothing. It was a clear sunny day, but it turned pitch dark. I groped for the handrail of the stairs and followed it down to the first floor, and got out of the building.

I saw a gruesome sight. As the darkness lifted from the ground little by little, black dust rose up into the sky. It didn't rain where I was, but I wonder if that became the "black rain."

I realized I was covered in blood from my shoulders to my arms. Countless glass shards had pierced me through my navy blue hard-collar railway uniform. I had just become a conductor, so my collar badge was white. It was red with blood.

The area in front of Hiroshima Station was in chaos, filled with a tremendous crowd. The extension of the station building had totally collapsed.

I shouted to my boss, "May I go home to see if my family is all right?"

"Go ahead!" So I left with permission.

I ran out of the station and headed home as fast as I could. My home was about a 20-minute walk away. The Dambara Elementary School in front of it was burning furiously. My home was smashed to pieces. My mother and sister, who had been blown by the blast and were covered in blood, were just standing there stunned. Having crawled out from the collapsed house, they were badly injured. I could not believe they had managed to get themselves out of the rubble. Their hair was a mess, their faces black with soot.

Behind our house, three medics were starting to put up a first-aid tent. They put oil on burns and wrapped bandages around open wounds. I received first aid there. Then, my other sister, who was working at the Army Ordnance Depot as a member of the Women's Volunteer Labor Corps, came home. She said that the Ordnance Depot was crushed by the blast, but she was unhurt. My brother, who worked for the Telephone Bureau, had been drafted and assigned to the communication corps of the Ozuki Unit in Yamaguchi Prefecture. We assumed he was safe. My whole family was really lucky to be alive.

The Nakamura family headed for Ochiai, the designated evacuation area for their neighborhood. On their way, they saw many people who had been badly burnt from the bombing.

I had no ability to feel horror or pity on seeing those people. I must have been emotionally numbed. Telephone poles had fallen. Electric wires were scattered here and there. Burnt bodies were everywhere. We walked through tremendous numbers of bodies, carefully avoiding stepping on them. Countless bodies were floating in the river. We received some dry bread from two soldiers who were distributing it on the way. We fled across Higashi Ohashi Bridge along with other evacuees.

We arrived at Ochiai in the early evening. It had received no damage from the bombing, and the atmosphere was quite peaceful. I remember that when we got there, my strength left me all of sudden. We had been assigned to stay with a certain family. That night, they put up a mosquito net for us. I remember feeling acutely grateful.

The Nakamura family had no place to return to. This meant that they would have to rely on a distant relative. The next day, they headed to Kabe where their late father's sister-in-law lived.

On August 6, the people in Kabe had seen a giant mushroom cloud in the direction of Hiroshima. I heard them saying, "I have no idea what that was, but it seems something terrible is happening." Four or five days after we arrived there, I developed a high fever of unknown cause. I was so weak I couldn't even stand. All I could do was stay in a crouching position. It was about half a year later that I realized this was one of the symptoms of the A-bomb disease.

On August 15, the Emperor announced the end of the war on the radio. Just a week before, the mere word "Emperor" would have made everyone stand straight at attention. But we just stood in a daze as we listened.

It was the first time that ordinary people ever heard the voice of the Emperor. People were saying, "Is it true? Is the war over?" But many simply said, "I couldn't understand anything he said."

The day the war ended, my family left for my mother's hometown in Saga Prefecture. My health had improved a bit, and my family helped me get onto a train. We had a Disaster Certificate, so we didn't have to pay for the ride. The soldiers were handing them out along with dry bread on the day the bomb was dropped on Hiroshima. People living in the same neighborhood fled together to the same designated evacuation area, so the soldiers probably didn't bother checking the identity of each person. These were just pieces of paper saying "Disaster Certificate" with no name or date of birth on them. We would later exchange them for Atomic Bomb Survivor Health Books.

We left Hiroshima Station and arrived at Otake Station, beyond which the railroad tracks had been severed by air raids. We crossed a railway bridge over the Oze River and made our way to Iwakuni on foot. From there we got on a train to Saga. My mother's parents' home was in Kashima, Saga Prefecture. The *Nishi Nihon Shimbun* (Western Japan newspaper) I read there said that Hiroshima had been devastated by a new type of bomb. My mother's relatives thought we were all dead. When my mother, my two sisters and I showed up, they were astonished.

My brother was discharged on the day the war ended, so he also visited us there. My sister found a job at a noodle factory across the street, but the rest of us had no means to make a living. Eventually, my other sister and brother went back to their former workplace in Hiroshima, the Telephone Bureau. I also got a job there, thanks to their help. Due to the war and the atomic bombing, they were understaffed, so they gladly hired me.

We rented a room from my father's parents in Atagomachi so the three of us could work in Hiroshima. My mother and my oldest sister stayed in Saga. Thus, our family members lived apart for some time.

The following spring, the lymph glands in my neck started swelling, but almost no doctors or hospitals in Hiroshima were able to treat me. I went to Saga to look for a doctor. At the hospital in Saga, I was told to have surgery right away. I took leave from work and had an operation.

Eventually I recovered, but I had to return to Saga once every two months. One of the reasons was food. There were still food shortages in Hiroshima, but in rural Kashima plenty of rice and potatoes were available.

My mother always worried if we were eating enough and would make me take home rice and vegetables. I hid the food in the bottom of my backpack. If the police discovered rice out of the rationing system, they would confiscate it. At Moji Station, passengers had to line up in four rows in the underground passage under the station to have their luggage checked. My rice was safe because I always put the vegetables on top of it.

At some point, I came across a friend from Hiroshima Commercial School. His family had been wealthy and lived in a mansion. But the atomic bomb destroyed everything, so they built a shack over the ruins of his house in Nagarekawa. When I asked him, "Do you mind if I build a shed next to yours?" he happily replied, "You are more than welcome."

I quickly built a 40-square-meter shack next to his. The walls were made of wooden panels, and the roof was made of bark sliced off tree trunks. It had two six-tatami-mat rooms with a kitchen and a toilet. I lived there with my brother and sister for nearly three years.

My oldest sister, who had lived with my mother, got married. Our life settled down, so we were able to invite our mother to live with us. We moved to Rakurakuen in Itsukaichi, where the four of us lived together. Later, I married and left home. I was 34, and my wife was 26. She was from Hiroshima, but she was not there at the time because of school evacuation. Her family did not complain about me being a *hibakusha*.

Yoshiharu's sister got a job at a trading company in the Mitsubishi Group. The employment conditions were so good that he went to work there too. The company delivered goods like furniture and refrigerators to families of the Occupation Forces living in Kure. This task ended when the Occupation Forces left Japan, and the business was closed down. He got a job at a securities firm with the help of his brother. He was later headhunted by Hiroshima Sugar Company, and worked there until retirement.

One aspect of the atomic bombing that I will never forget has to do with my best friend from Hiroshima Commercial School, Goro Mitsuda. He was an excellent gymnast, especially good at swinging up on the horizontal bar. He was the class hero. His family sold baby chicks at their store called Mitsuda Chicks. When I moved to Saga, I needed work, so I wrote him a letter saying that I wanted to raise chicks and have them lay eggs. He never replied. Instead, I received a letter from his brother informing me of his death. It was a short letter, but I was devastated.

On August 6, Goro had left home at 8 a.m. to get a special cadets medical checkup at the Hiroshima Chamber of Commerce and Industry Building, which was only 260 meters from the hypocenter. He was so strong and fit, but he died young. I am skinny and not very strong, but somehow I am still alive. This makes me believe that our lives are ruled by fate or destiny. This is why I have pledged to always do my best in whatever I can do for peace.

Toshio Morimoto (Korean name Kim Soo-gab)
In memory of the Korean victims of the A-bomb

Born in Busan in Korea in 1929, Toshio Morimoto came to Japan when he was four years old with his parents. His father's younger brother, who had arrived earlier, ran a laundry. Many Koreans lived in the neighborhood. In 1939, his family was forced to change their family name from Kim to Morimoto at the order of the Japanese government. At 16, working as an assistant truck driver transporting military supplies, he was exposed to the atomic bombing under a truck in Matsubaracho, 1.7 kilometers from the Hiroshima hypocenter.

I recognized him only by the belt buckle...

That day, we were carrying 60 bales of rice on the truck. I say truck, but it was a charcoal-driven vehicle that gave us nothing but trouble with the engine and electrical system. On that day, as always, the engine was not working properly. When we got near Hiroshima Station, the power dropped to near zero. "I wonder if the oil is leaking. Check it," the driver told me. I went under the truck to see about the oil.

The instant I crawled under the truck, a dazzling flash, so bright that I couldn't open my eyes, filled the air.

Then, "boooom," a tremendous explosion like nothing I had ever heard. Then, a powerful wind. Pieces of wood and all sorts of things flew all around. A huge cloud of smoke rose high into the sky, then things like dust and dirt started falling down like rain.

Fortunately, I was saved because I was under the truck. The driver was also uninjured because he was in the truck. We immediately decided to walk back to the branch office in Ujina. On the way to Ujina, we saw incredibly horrible sights on the streets along the Hijiyama streetcar line. Pieces of wood and roof tiles from collapsed houses were scattered all over the ground. The streetcars were standing still. People were walking around with their hair burnt and frizzled, wearing nothing but rags for clothes. Many were barely able to walk; many couldn't walk at all.

Although the Ujina branch office building was not damaged, we were told to return home immediately to check on our families. We all had no choice but to walk home. After crossing Miyuki Bridge, I passed the Hiroshima Red Cross Hospital and came to Takanobashi shopping arcade. There, crowds of people were running around nearly naked, trying to escape. When I crossed the Meiji and Sumiyoshi bridges, I looked down the rivers and saw hundreds of people floating in the water. No one dared try to rescue those people. Most of them were probably already dead. All I could do was watch and pray for their safety.

After a desperate journey, Toshio finally approached his house in Kawaramachi. His home was completely destroyed. He then headed for a house where his family had decided to go in the event of emergency.

My family had decided to gather at a friend's house in Kouchi in case of emergency. We had already taken a wooden chest and various household necessities to that house. My mother, younger sister and youngest brother were already there. My father, who worked at a cannery for the Army Provisions Depot in Ujina, came and joined us. He had a few cuts on his head from broken glass.

Only my younger brother, who seemed to have been playing outside near our house, was missing. We searched for him everywhere but couldn't find him. I went mainly to look in schools used as shelters. I called his name out loud, but no answer came. I continued to look at the face of each injured person.

Three days after the atomic bombing, I was told that a boy who looked like my brother was at Kusatsu Elementary School. I hurried over there. Hundreds of injured people filled the classrooms. Among them, I found a badly burnt boy lying on the floor. He had hideous burns all over his body, which was almost naked. His head and face were so severely burnt it was hard to tell who he was. I recognized him only by the belt buckle he wore with his trousers. It was one I had made, but had given to my brother because he wanted it so badly.

I then remembered that my brother had a scar on his right ankle. When I checked the boy's right ankle, I found that scar. I shook the boy and called out his name. He nodded slightly. I was finally convinced he was my brother. Thus, all of my family was still alive. However, my brother's life after that was complete misery. When I helped him sit up, I saw that the wounds on his back were infested with maggots. We went so far as to make him take powdered human bones as medicine, as we were told that human bones worked wonders on wounds.

On New Year's Eve that year, my family and two other Korean families talked about returning to Korea. It was decided that my family would return first. At that time, I already had a job in Hiroshima, and I couldn't speak any Korean. I had grown up in Japan since I was four. What worried me most was that I couldn't speak, read or write Korean. The mere thought of this made me hesitate to go back. Some of my relatives and friends decided to stay in Japan. I, too, decided to stay in Hiroshima.

I started to work at an eatery in front of Hiroshima Station. A relative, also a Korean resident in Japan, had started a coffee shop and restaurant right in front of Hiroshima Station. The owner was married to my aunt, which was why I was able to work there. At that time, the Enkobashicho area right by the station was a black-market district that had rapidly recovered after the war. There were intense battles over territory. The conflicts between crooked peddlers and gangsters became nationally known due to a hit movie series called *Battles Without Honor and Humanity*, distributed by Toei Production Company.

That coffee shop and restaurant were later born again as a music cafe called "Musica" and continued to do fairly good business. The owner acquired classical music records on the black market and opened a music cafe because he wanted to use music to energize people in Hiroshima. "Musica" is Spanish for "music hall."

On New Year's Eve in 1946, the year the cafe opened, we offered a concert playing Beethoven's Ninth Symphony. The owner had obtained this record on the black market in Osaka, and only with great difficulty. I still vividly remember that day. It was snowing. The shop only had seating for 30 people. Outside the cafe, a large crowd of people stood and listened attentively to the music. Music knows no boundaries. At a time when people were short of food, it was a moving sight to see so many people healing their hearts with Beethoven's music. That Ninth Symphony record concert became a New Year's Eve tradition that was enjoyed by the local community for many years.

Musica was in the black-market area for 10 years, then moved downtown to Ebisucho in Naka Ward. It moved into a wooden three-story building and was the only music cafe in Hiroshima. At the time of the move to the new location in January 1955, I was officially appointed manager of Musica and was entrusted with all responsibilities regarding the management of the cafe. It was quite prosperous and had nearly 20 waitresses. I married one of them who was a year younger than me. Her name was Mariko, and she is still my wife.

At the time, however, her parents and relatives strongly opposed our marriage. It was probably because I was both Korean and had been exposed to the bombing near the hypocenter. Also, Mariko's family had already chosen a marriage partner for her. All of her relatives were furious and did everything they could to block our marriage.

"What a stupid business this is!" her relatives would say, attacking her. "I'm in love with him, and there is nothing stupid about that!" she answered back—an episode that her family still talk about. She also told me that there was even a rumor going around in her neighborhood that she had eloped with a Korean man. We married despite the opposition of her relatives, so her parents disowned her for some time. Despite all this, these days her relatives say, "You married the most affectionate man in our family. You must be so happy."

Toshio worked as the manager of Musica for 10 years. The cafe was increasingly popular, and the annual year-end concert became so popular it attracted as many as 200 people. Many music fans were regular attendees, including the mayor of Hiroshima and famous residents such as writers, artists, poets and students; they all enjoyed classical music during those years.

Toshio later opened his own coffee shop. After that, his life was focused on managing his coffee shop for 40 years. He has concentrated all his life on overcoming the sufferings of the atomic bombing. However, the aftereffects remain present in himself and his family.

I was exposed to the bombing in Matsubaracho, 1.7 kilometers from the hypocenter. Over the years, I have had many health problems. I have persistent diarrhea from time to time. I used to go to the hospital frequently to get vitamin shots. I have also suffered from gastric ulcers, kidney trouble and other internal disorders. I collapsed from a heart attack and have been taken by ambulance to the hospital a total of seven times. My wife is also a *hibakusha*. On the day of the bombing, she was sleeping in the basement of her boarding house. The radiation from the bombing may have had adverse effects on her as well.

Our first daughter suffered uterine cancer. Our second daughter has gone through three operations for tongue cancer and is now being treated for thyroid cancer. Experts said that the second generation would not be affected by the atomic bombing, so none of them even have an Atomic Bomb Survivor Health Book. However, the fact is, two of my daughters are suffering from cancer. I cannot help worrying that our grandchildren will develop symptoms related to the effects of the bombing.

The members of my family who returned to Korea lived truly miserable lives. My father died less than 10 years after returning to his homeland. My brother suffered a ruptured aneurysm. My younger sister had acute leukemia, and another brother developed liver cancer. They all died young, leaving my mother behind. Obviously, they were affected by radiation from the atomic bombing.

From the time I started working at Musica, I've worked in coffee shops for a total of 60 years. I came from Korea to Japan when I was four, and 80 years have passed since then. I was able to live without feeling the restrictions caused by living in a foreign country because I've been supported by the people around me. I've never experienced any Japanese making discriminatory remarks about me, nor have I been treated unfairly because I am Korean. Because I happened to live in Hiroshima, I encountered the atomic bomb, an experience very few human beings have had.

If a war were to occur again, it would eventually lead to the extinction of the human race. These days I hear growing calls for a military buildup or a national defense force. This is totally unacceptable. If a war starts, the killing will be terrible. People will kill each other with no hesitation. After the war, people like us will be left to suffer. Two or three generations will suffer.

    The absence of war is better. Peace is the best. I've lived a full and happy life. Japan is a beautiful, wonderful country. I hope that Korea, where I was born, and Japan, where I've spent most of my life, will build trust and cooperate with each other to pave the way for lasting peace, like that my wife and I have found.

    The Monument in Memory of the Korean Victims of the A-bomb stands in Hiroshima Peace Memorial Park. Every year on August 6, I pray at that monument from 4:30 to 5:00 in the morning.

Hiroatsu Taniguchi
I'm going to talk about my experience as long as I can

Born in October 1938, Hiroatsu Taniguchi was exposed to the atomic bombing in the playground of Oshiba Elementary School, 2.3 kilometers from the hypocenter in Hiroshima, when he was six years old. His mother had a son from a previous marriage. His father was serving in Dalian, China, as an airplane mechanic. While his father was away, his mother was made to feel unwelcome in her husband's house because of the stigma of having previously been divorced, so she went back to her parents' home in Oshiba with her three children and helped out at her mother's restaurant.

My mother took desperate care of me. . .

That morning, an air-raid warning sounded, and my family of five took refuge in an air-raid shelter. The warning was cleared at around 7:30. I walked to Oshiba Elementary School, which was about 10 minutes from my house. In those days, soldiers were stationed in the school, so we couldn't use the classrooms. We studied in a shack built in front of the school building. The older students were mobilized to work in factories, and the soldiers had gone out on a mission. Only younger students were left in the school. With a little free time before class started, I was playing with other first graders near the platform on the playground used for morning assembly.

Out of nowhere, I heard the faint sound of a bomber. I looked up at the sky, shading my eyes with my right hand. The summer sun was so dazzling, I squinted, when all of a sudden, a sharp flash blinded me. In the next instant, there came a deafening roar—"Ka-boom!" Just as I was squatting down as trained to do, I was carried off by the blast.

I came to in an eerie silence. I opened my eyes slightly and saw a cloud of sand enveloping everything. Ten or so children with whom I had been playing were lying or sitting on the playground crying. Our classroom shack had been completely destroyed.

One boy was standing and crying out loud. His shorts were burnt to tatters. I quickly looked at my navy blue shorts and was relieved to see that they were not damaged. However, when I looked at them later, I found that the back right side was burnt dark brown. I didn't notice it because it was in the back.

I was wearing a white open-necked shirt with short sleeves; my head and my right arm and both legs were burnt where they were not covered by my clothes.

Fortunately, my face was not burnt. That was probably because I had held my right hand over my eyes to block the sun while looking for the bomber. Most of my face was in the shade of my hand. However, my right arm was badly burnt. My head was the most seriously injured. I had close-cropped hair, which instantly burnt off, leaving my head covered with what seemed to be hot coal tar. My head must have looked terrible because when I touched it, the skin peeled off.

I started to walk toward home crying. I had lost my shoes, which were blown off by the blast, so I had to walk barefoot. My house was tilted over, and my mother was waiting for me out in front. She said that she had been watering the yard in her black polka-dot blouse. The black dots turned to burns, leaving black spots on her skin. My mother had been covered with dust and was waiting for me. I arrived home in tears, and as soon as I saw my mother I clung to her. She couldn't stop crying and saying, "I'm glad you're back! I'm so glad!" I was so fearful I kept holding onto her kimono sleeve. I followed her wherever she went.

My grandmother had been in the room on the second floor where we kept our family Buddhist altar. She was unhurt. My brother, who was three years older than me, survived in a classroom at his school and had returned home.

Many neighbors began to flee. We heard that fire had broken out in the city. Everyone headed for the hills of Mitaki, where there was no fire. In the bamboo grove there, families and friends were sitting in small groups. Some were burnt; others badly injured. A mother carrying a baby with its head hanging backward lifelessly on her back was wandering around like a sleepwalker. I couldn't tell whether the baby was alive or not. There were people whose clothes had burnt, leaving them naked and covered in soot. Some just sat down, uttering incomprehensible phrases, while others remained standing like ghosts.

Soon black rain started to fall. The coldness of the rain felt good on my burns. People bathed in the rain, faces up, opening their mouths to drink. I, too, turned my face up and went around with my mouth open to catch raindrops.

My mother came rushing over and said, "Don't leave my side without my permission!" She then took me back with her. One family picked up a piece of burnt galvanized tin roofing to keep themselves from the rain. My mother went back home to collect things we needed. Since our house was completely destroyed, however, she could find nothing more than some steamed potatoes in our restaurant.

The Taniguchi family decided to go to Hiroatsu's father's family home in Nishihara. Five family members—grandmother, mother and three boys—walked about four kilometers. Hiroatsu was forced to walk bent forward due to the twisted skin on his burns. He moved forward unsteadily and slowly.

Dead bodies were lying out in the street all along the way. We had to step around them. I saw many people who had thrust their heads into fire cisterns seeking water and died like that. At the foot of Shinjo Bridge, people had gone down to the river, where they died and were floating in the river. I was desperate to drink water and tried to go to the river several times, but every time, my mother grabbed my hand and pulled me back to her. "Don't drink the water! If you do, you'll die!" My mother never let my hand go until we got to my grandparents' house. As soon as we got there, my grandmother could no longer move. She was bedridden for three months, after which she died.

The burns I suffered were severe. In particular, the backs of my knees down to my calves, which were not covered by my shorts, were seriously burnt. My legs seemed permanently bent. I couldn't stretch them out. I slept on my back with my knees up. There were times when the back of my knee got stuck, my calf to my thigh, and peeling them apart was excruciatingly painful. My mother cut her kimono into strips and wrapped my knees.

She put medicine that looked like talcum powder on the burns. The next morning, the cloth was hard with blood and pus. Peeling the cloth off was also extremely painful. Each and every morning, I used to groan in excruciating pain.

"Peeling it off slowly hurts a lot more," my mother said as she jerked it off in a stroke. Every time I had to cry out. There was no remedy available even in hospitals. There was no other way to treat my wounds. Later, we were able to get some oiled paper from a pesticide plant, and we used that instead of the cloth to treat my wounds.

The open sores on my burnt skin smelled so horrible that my brothers kept away from me. Only my mother came to me saying, "Don't worry. You are going to get better, for sure!" She made a concoction from *dokudami* (saururaceae plants). These were believed to work as an antibiotic. She had me drink the stuff every day. My family worked hard picking the plants. Soon, all around my house the plants were gone, so my mother started learning to ride a bicycle just to go around looking for *dokudami* plants. As soon as she learned how to ride, she went to pick the plants deep in the mountains more than an hour away.

For two and a half years, my life was nothing more than repeated inflammations of the burns and the scabs. I stayed at home, sitting all the time. I used my hands and my rear end to move. Because my wounds festered so badly, I couldn't use bedding even in winter. In summer, flies gathered on my wounds, which were soon infested with maggots. My mother always removed the maggots with chopsticks. To make matters worse, my hair fell out.

Hiroatsu's father was demobilized and returned home. He was a military man by nature and always had a stern look on his face. Hiroatsu hardly ever went to school after the atomic bombing. His father always scolded him for not doing well in school. Before each meal, he made his son say his multiplication tables. By the time he finished third grade, all his scabs had fallen off. He started going to school again in the fourth grade.

Most of the houses around my grandparents' house were tilted at least a little by the blast. I had keloid burns on my right arm and legs, and people around me treated me cruelly, saying, "Hey, you stink! Look at that burn!" At that time, it was thought that A-bomb diseases were contagious. "The son of the Taniguchi family has A-bomb disease!" People often spoke ill of me behind my back, which was very distressing.

I especially disliked sports day. All the students had to wear short-sleeved shirts and shorts, so everybody saw my keloid scars. My scars had twisted up tightly, causing me to move awkwardly. No matter how much I was bullied, I never told my mother. I didn't want to make her unhappy. However, there were times when people openly abused me in front of her. My mother would remain silent with a stern look on her face, pretending she didn't hear anything.

My right hand, with which I had shaded my face from the atomic bomb, hardened into a fist; with my little finger, ring finger and middle finger curled inward, I could barely move my thumb and forefinger. When I forced my fingers to move, the skin between my little finger and ring finger tore and blood gushed out. When I tried to tear my curled, fused fingers apart, the skin would always tear. Nevertheless, I kept pulling my fingers apart after the blood and pus dried.

When I heard about skin being grafted from areas like the buttocks and thighs to replace keloid scars to make faces smooth, I went to consult a doctor about the treatment. I was told that operating on fingers was not possible because they constantly move. When I was a sixth grader, my hair finally began to grow.

"Your hair is beginning to grow, Hiroatsu!" said my mother happily. When I touched my head, I could feel the rough stubble and was overjoyed. As my burns healed, they started to itch horribly. When I scratched the skin around the scabs, pus oozed out and scabs formed again. Fortunately, I managed to get my right hand moving by the time I entered junior high school.

Since I have keloids on my right hand and the backs of my legs, the skin there does not respire. The skin in those areas is cold even in summer. I am also unable to sit cross-legged. Even today, the keloid scar on my right leg causes my skin to stretch painfully when I sit this way. I feel sluggish all the time. I get tired easily and often can hardly keep standing. I soon have to lie down to rest. On sunny days, I feel sick, as if I had sunstroke. I have suffered with these conditions to this day, ever since the bombing. I also have an irregular pulse, but I don't know if this is related to the atomic bomb.

My father's family was mean to my mother and me because we had been exposed. I couldn't stand to see them saying unpleasant things to my mother. My father's brother and other relatives had been discharged from military service and were also living in the house. Our family of five just landed there, so it was inevitable that we were treated as a burden. Several times I saw my mother watching the fire on the hearth with tears in her eyes after being bullied by my aunt. "Get out of this house!" my aunt once told us.

That was the last straw. I replied back, "My mother was in the bombing because she went to Oshiba as she couldn't go on living here. If she had never been kicked out of the house, it would never have turned out like this!"

Hiroatsu graduated from high school and started working at a shipping company. After about two years, he applied for a transfer to the Osaka branch. His request was soon accepted, so he left for Osaka alone.

My mother became ill and spent a lot of time in bed. She ended up in the hospital with liver cancer. She spent the following two years there. Due in large part to her hospitalization, I quit my job in Osaka and returned to Hiroshima. I was 21 years old at that time. When I visited my mother in the hospital, she said, "You were exposed to radiation from the atomic bomb, so take good care of yourself and live a long happy life, Hiroatsu."

"You've been the nicest to me of all my sons." This was my last conversation with her. She was only 49. For 15 years after the atomic bombing, my mother went through continuous hardship. Although she was exposed to the bomb herself, she tried desperately to do everything she could to heal my burns and cure my keloids. Soon after my mother's death, the aunt who had always been mean to her also passed away. When I was at her bedside before she died, she apologized to me, saying, "Forgive me, Hiroatsu, for having been so hard on your mother."

Hiroatsu applied for an Atomic Bomb Survivor Health Book in 1956, and has since had a physical checkup once a month.

I have been exposed to radiation, so I never know when I might get leukemia. I still can't get over the fear that I will develop some A-bomb disease. Also, I don't have any short-sleeved summer shirts. No matter how hot it is, I always wear long-sleeved shirts. I have worked for a trucking company and a taxi company, but I always found excuses not to participate in company retreats. The mere thought of taking a bath with my fellow workers made me miserable.

I never brought up the fact that I had experienced the atomic bombing. When walking with someone, I unconsciously but consistently walk on his or her right side. I always try to keep people from noticing the keloid on my right hand. Only once did I tell a coworker I became close to in Osaka that I had experienced the atomic bombing.

"What about the A-bomb disease? Isn't that contagious?" That's what he said. There must have been people who noticed the keloid scars on my hands and legs, but I never mentioned them myself.

In those days, most people married with the help of a matchmaker and arrangements made by their parents. Moreover, they referred to background investigations as "inquiries." Whenever Hiroatsu had an offer of marriage, he was refused as soon as the "inquiry" revealed that he was a hibakusha. *"I'll never be able to have an arranged marriage," thought Hiroatsu. Nevertheless, in 1966, he did get married.*

My wife was exposed to the atomic bomb in Ujina when she was 15 months old. I have never asked her anything about it. I'm afraid to ask. Even if I did, I could do nothing for her. Neither has my wife asked me anything about my experience. I have never told even my wife about my experience, and she never asked because of her sweet nature.

My wife became pregnant when she was 30 years old. I was filled with anxiety. I had heard the rumor that women exposed to radiation from the A-bomb were likely to give birth to children with disabilities. I couldn't sleep at night. When our first son was born healthy, I was so happy I wept alone.

When our second son was two, he developed herpes. He had what looked like keloid scars on his face and had to have his neck bandaged up to his head. I was horrified. It reminded me of myself.

Although I have lived in Hiroshima, I never entered the A-bomb Museum (Hiroshima Peace Memorial Museum) until I was 71 years old. I didn't want to remember. I didn't want to let anyone know my past. I avoided talking about the atomic bombing in every way possible. Every year when August 6 approached, I deliberately avoided watching the TV news.

It was when I visited a peace exhibition that I started to think I should investigate a little about the atomic bomb and peace.

I learned many things for the first time when I visited the A-bomb Museum. Japan failed to predict that the United States would drop an atomic bomb on Hiroshima. "We won! We won a battle, and another battle!" The Imperial Headquarters' announcements to the people were nothing but lies.

A week before the atomic bomb was dropped, several adults were digging an air-raid shelter near my house. I followed my mother when she went out with cups of tea to serve them. They were talking and laughing. "Hiroshima has never been hit by any air raids. This is really a good place to live!"

On the day of the bombing, the military sounded an air-raid warning because of the reconnaissance planes that had come earlier, but no such warning was issued against the bomber that dropped the atomic bomb on the city. If an air-raid warning had sounded, I would not have been on the school playground. I might not have had to suffer so much from the atomic bomb. I can't bear to think about it.

"To bring an early end to the war" was an excuse. Obviously, the US used Hiroshima and Nagasaki as sites to conduct nuclear tests. Worse still, the US dropped a uranium bomb on Hiroshima and a plutonium bomb on Nagasaki in order to assess the difference in destructive power.

The purpose of the Atomic Bomb Casualty Commission (ABCC) set up by GHQ on Hijiyama Hill was not to treat the survivors but to collect data from them. The survivors, who went there expecting medical treatment, were stripped naked, had their keloid scars photographed and their blood tested, and were then asked how their physical condition had changed. They were then sent home. I believe that the US used the A-bomb survivors as guinea pigs.

Two years ago, in front of Hiroshima Station, I was asked which train to take to Kure by a couple from Tokyo. They told me that they were temporarily evacuating to stay with their children because the radiation emitted from the Fukushima nuclear power plant accident had increased in their neighborhood due to a change of wind direction. Radiation flows with the wind. On that day in 1945, my family headed for Mount Mitaki, but thinking about it now, we were going in the same direction as the black rain and the radiation fallout.

At the urging of a member of the Hiroshima Peace Volunteers, I spoke for the first time in front of people I didn't know about my experience. My wife was there and kept her head down while I spoke. I do not know how much longer I can live, but I'm going to talk about my experience as long as I can. That's what I have decided.

People from around the world visit Hiroshima with great interest. I learned that the largest number of non-Japanese visitors are Chinese. Some time ago, my oldest son, who lives in Fukuoka, said, "The era of China is coming. You'd better learn Chinese, I guess."

Also encouraged by one of my friends, I am attending a Chinese-language course in a lifelong learning program provided by the Open University of Japan at Hiroshima University. I go almost every day. I hope that someday I will be able to talk about my experience to Chinese people in their own language.

Kaoru Hashimoto
I am determined to tell the truth

Born in October 1929, Kaoru Hashimoto was exposed to the atomic bombing on a street in the Dambara area, 2.8 kilometers from the hypocenter, when he was 15 years old.

There were seven in the Hashimoto family. His father ran a barbershop. His older brother was a civilian worker at the Army Ordnance Supply Depot in Kaita. His two older sisters both worked at a branch office of the Hiroshima Postal Savings Bureau. Kaoru was the second son and the fourth of five children.

A gun and a thousand yen in cash

When I was in my second year in middle school, a teacher told us, "Working for the military to serve the country will make your parents proud. You'll get better rations, too. You can eat what others can't!" Six or seven of the 58 students in my class joined the Volunteer Pioneer Youth Army of Manchuria, and most of the others got a job at the National Railway.

In March 1944, I graduated from school, and as of April 1, I was assigned to the Repair Team in the Ordnance Department at the Army Ordnance Supply Depot. The working conditions were privileged as the teacher had said. I always brought home food like frozen tangerines and dried horsemeat, which made my family happy.

On August 6, I was two months shy of 16. I was on the night shift and was released from work at 8:00 in the morning. I was on my way home with Hayashi, a friend of mine. When we came to an area called Dambara, we heard a deafening roar and were instantly blown to the ground by the blast. It was pitch dark.

The next thing I knew, there was no one around us. The hypocenter of the explosion was on the west side of Hijiyama Hill, and Dambara, where we were, was behind the hill. In other words, Hijiyama Hill protected us. However, the pressure of the blast from the sky was still monstrous.

Dambara Elementary School was blazing with tremendous force. Some children were trapped under the collapsed school building, crying, "Help! Help me!" Not knowing what to do, we did nothing. We just watched as the children were engulfed in flames. The children were still alive, but we could not rescue them from the fire. I am still filled with regret. The children were burnt alive in a hell on Earth, and all we could do was watch hell unfold.

I saw bodies of people who had dived into a fire cistern by the street. I saw people lying motionless on the roadside. I even saw a dead horse still standing. Some shards of glass propelled by the blast had pierced my field cap and were stuck in my head. My arms were covered in blood, but I felt no pain at the time.

In the evening of August 6, Kaoru was taken in a military truck to a cave in Nihomachi. There were hundreds of victims with white, sludgy ointment painted on them. Without receiving any emergency treatment, victims were carried in trucks to the cave one after another. They were all suffering from severe burns or bleeding from their faces and bodies. However, no children, women or fatally injured people were allowed to ride in the military trucks. Kaoru was told to help form a treatment line in the cave.

I put a white paint-like medicine that was mercurial ointment mixed with zinc oxide oil on the injured, who arrived one after another.

They were glad to receive the treatment, and said, "This will save my life." It was cool in the cave, and I found it a relatively comfortable place to stay. Even so, it was summer, so the cave was filled with the stench from the victims' festering wounds. Their bodies were so swollen they were unable to move. They lay on the ground in their own excrement.

One time a young military officer got overexcited and lost his mind. All of a sudden, he shouted out, "I'm going to kill all American soldiers!" He began to shoot his gun in the cave.

Anybody who could walk was taken to Ninoshima Island in Hiroshima Bay. Those who couldn't walk were left in the cave. They lost their hair three or four days later, and most eventually died. Even under such circumstances, people with burnt skin hanging from their bodies were continually being carried into the cave.

"Give me water! Water, please!" many cried out.

But the officer ordered us not to give them any. "If they drink water, they'll die! Don't give them water!" he said. We could do nothing but watch over them.

Many people shouted, "I don't care if I die, just give me water!" then passed away. One worker who felt pity for the injured and gave them water was hit by an officer.

Around August 10, Kaoru was ordered to dispose of corpses in the vicinity of Furue.

The job of disposing of dead bodies entitled one to receive meals. The remains were pulled up from the rivers here and there and carried in trucks. There were seven rivers in Hiroshima, and the victims jumped into the rivers because they were thirsty and hot. Most died. There were countless corpses floating in the rivers. Because the tide would take them out and then bring them back in, the corpses were not washed out to sea. This, too, was a scene from hell, with the mouth of each river full of corpses where it poured into Hiroshima Bay.

Corpses that had been in the water for a week or 10 days had swollen bellies, and their rotting flesh was spongy and easily torn. When I pulled the arm of one corpse, it came right off. I had no time to worry about the horrible smell or feel disgusted. Thinking about it now horrifies me, but we were not even given gloves. We did this work with our bare hands.

Furue is full of rice paddies. Farmers built "dig-down fields," and the ridges were 50 cm higher than the fields' surface after harvesting the crop. By laying old railroad ties over the ridges, we could line up six or seven bodies at once. The spaces between the ties helped the bodies burn well. The National Railway gave us the old ties, which we carried in a truck owned by the Ordnance Depot. Farmers nearby provided sheaves of straw.

To burn the bodies efficiently, we alternated heads and feet. We poured on the heavy oil and lit the fire. Bodies that had been soaking in water and were rotten first inflated in the heat. Then they hardened like chinaware, and "Pop!"—their heads burst open. We put a large quantity of straw over their heads to keep them from flying into the air. We would hear the heads exploding one after another as the bodies turned to ash. Senior military workers scraped together mountains of ash with rakes, then carried off the ashes and the skulls.

I cremated the dead day after day—three to four hundred bodies a day. This means I burned nearly 8,000 bodies in 20 days. A huge crowd of people who had lost their relatives gathered where I was working. Some said their mothers could not be found, and others said their children were missing.

Some said, "Give me some ashes," and took unidentified remains home with them. They used them for memorial services for their missing family members. Gradually, cremation sites increased until they filled every corner of the city. Smoke was seen rising up from each neighborhood.

The corpses decayed rapidly. If we had buried dead bodies without cremation, we would have needed far more land. A cremated body was less than one-tenth the size, so we had no choice but to burn them.

Around the time when the autumn breezes began to blow, Kaoru and his fellow civilian workers were each given an empty gun and 1,000 yen in cash. A thousand yen at that time was equivalent to about 800,000 yen today. At the end of October, Kaoru finally went home.

My mother was a nurse. She looked for tiny pieces of broken glass in my head and arms, removing them one by one with a pair of tweezers. She found about 30 pieces in all. By that time, three months had passed since the bombing. I heard that if you leave glass in your body for more than half a year, it cannot be removed.

My two sisters, both of whom worked at the Sendamachi branch office of the Hiroshima Postal Savings Bureau, were safe. In the morning of August 6, my oldest sister had arrived at Akinakano Station only to find that a button on her blouse had come off. She headed home to fix her blouse. She missed the train to work and was saved. Most of her coworkers, she told me later, were killed.

My other sister was missing for two days. We were certain that she was dead, but she came home in tatters. Her *mompe* work pants were burnt and looked like underpants. She was in the city for two days in that miserable state, but she was fortunate never to suffer from A-bomb disease.

Kaoru's work in the military ended, and he lost his job. He and his friends started dealing in black-market goods for Occupation soldiers, who gave them Lucky Strike cigarettes, the artificial sweetener saccharin and other desired products. However, his sister worried about him dealing in the black market, so she found him a new job as a live-in salesman for medical appliances.

After visiting clients, I always stopped by a noodle restaurant called Marumatsu in Matobacho on my way home. A bowl of noodles cost 15 yen. I fell in love with Emiko, who was working at the restaurant. Soon, we got married. I was 23; she was 18. Seven years had passed since the end of the war. I changed my job and became a life insurance agent. We were quite slow to be given a child, but after 11 years of marriage we had a daughter.

The Olympic Games were held in Tokyo in that year (1964), and Japan entered its era of rapid economic growth. The year after the Olympics, I thought I should make money on my own to adapt to the coming age, so I became a taxi driver. There were not many cars, and the roads were not crowded, so it was easy to drive, and I was able to keep half my day's fare after giving the company its share. I worked feverishly and made a good income. My sales performance was excellent, so the taxi company had confidence in me. I was nominated to be secretary of the union.

There was a single woman in her 40s at my taxi company. She was beautiful but seemed to be having trouble getting married.

"She was exposed to the bombing." That's what I heard. She had no keloid scars, nor was she weak, but many people at that time could not get married because they were discriminated against due to their A-bomb experience. For this reason, my sisters hesitated to receive Atomic Bomb Survivor Health Books.

I suffered burns on the back of my hand, but they neither swelled nor turned into keloids. The burnt skin looks like a bruise, though it still cuts and bleeds easily. I don't know whether this disorder has anything to do with the atomic bombing, but I also have trouble with my prostate. I still take medicine for it.

How much more pain is the atomic bomb going to cause us? Is it trying to keep us in hell? Everything I have described here is the truth about war. No matter how often people turn their faces away from me, I am determined to speak openly about my experience about the atomic bomb. I believe this is my mission, the best thing I can do for world peace.

Takanobu Hirano
I resolved to pass on the spirit of Hiroshima

Born in November 1935, Takanobu Hirano was exposed to secondary radiation when he was nine years old after entering Hiroshima a week after the atomic bombing. His house was in Zaimokucho, 300 meters from the hypocenter. His father was killed by the bomb; his mother had died of illness during the war. He was raised by his grandmother.

The Hiranos' house was located at 25 Zaimokucho, near where the Cenotaph for the A-bomb Victims now stands in the Hiroshima Peace Memorial Park. Before the atomic bombing, the area was a busy shopping district. Takanobu lived there until March 1945. His family ran a sock factory called Hirano Sock Merchants, which had six or seven sewing machines used by workers to make socks from thread.

My house was at the hypocenter

There was a tobacco store next to our house. I was often sent there to buy cigarettes for my father. He always let me keep the change, so I looked forward to this errand. Next to the tobacco store was a wooden clog store. The lady there was talkative, and whenever she saw me, she talked to me, saying, "Hello, little master." My family was wealthy, and I remember our neighbors called my sisters "Young ladies" and called me "Young master." They treated us well. I had a sister two years older, another sister two years younger and a brother four years younger than me.

On the other side of our house was a big mansion owned by a

family who ran a kimono fabric shop. The view of the garden from the second floor of their house was breathtaking. There was also a movie theater in the neighborhood, and I often watched movies through a hole in the wall.

There was Honkawa Bridge over the Honkawa River. In summer, we often dived into the river from the bridge. The water was clear, and there were crabs and shrimps on the sandy riverbed. There was a slight slope on the road to the bridge, so a horse-drawn carriage carrying a heavy load often got stuck before the bridge. Whenever we saw such a carriage on the road, we would help to push it.

On the other side of the river was Honkawa Elementary School. I went to Nakajima Elementary School, and the two schools were rivals. We would jeer at them, saying, "Honkawa is run-down and old. Its insides are worn out!" They'd call back, "Nakajima School is even worse!" This competition is one of my fond old memories.

After Takanobu's mother gave birth to her youngest son, she had difficulty recovering and was bedridden. Although the house was used for the factory and residence, his mother lived in a room in front of the house while recuperating. She passed away when Takanobu was seven, in 1943.

On the day my mother died, my teacher came to me and said, "Go home right away." When I got home, Mother took her hand out of her bed and held my hand silently. That was my final parting from my mother. I don't remember much about the days when my mother was sick or about her funeral.

Probably when I was four years old or so, my father was away from home on business, and I fell down the stairs and cut my lower lip near the right-hand corner of my mouth. My mother quickly lifted me up in her arms and hurried to a nearby clinic. I still remember vividly the warmth of my mother at that time. In later years, when I was going through a tough time, I used to look at the scar on my lip in a mirror. That would bring my mother's warmth to my mind.

After my mother's death, my father decided to marry a female relative who worked in the factory. He introduced her to us and said, "This is your new mother." She looked after my youngest brother.

During the war, we had an air-raid shelter under the living room in our house. When air-raid warnings sounded, my sisters, my brother and I quickly put on our air-raid hoods, opened up the floor and climbed down into the shelter. There we all held our breath and waited. The air-raid warnings were intense and sounded frequently. The all-clear sirens sounded calmer, and made me feel relieved even though I was merely a child.

When I was a little older, I was waiting for a bus to go back to Yachiyocho, my father's birthplace. All of a sudden, an air-raid warning sounded. All the people waiting for the bus hurried down to the air-raid shelter at the Western Drill Ground nearby. I jumped in with them. With a blanket covering us, we all sat still. I lifted one end of the blanket and looked up at the sky through a gap in the shelter. I saw B-29 bombers flying in formation, and antiaircraft guns busily firing toward the bombers. Not one of the shells hit a B-29. The bullets totally failed to reach the bombers. The B-29s flew magnificently away. Even as a child, that made me wonder if Japan was actually going to win the war.

In March 1945, when the war got more intense, the four children in the Hirano family were evacuated to their grandmother's house in Yachiyocho.

We had not been close to our grandmother, so we felt quite nervous at her house. The four of us huddled together all the time. When people feel insecure, the loneliness of not having a mother is beyond words.

Our grandmother's house had no electricity. At night, we had to carry a lantern when we went to the outhouse. We also needed it when taking baths. This was inconvenient, and that also made us uneasy. Even during the war, the Yachiyocho area was a laid-back place. There were three boys about my age next door. In summer, we used to go swimming in the river. One of my aunts and our younger cousin also lived at our grandmother's house. She took good care of us like a mother.

Meanwhile, Takanobu's father and stepmother lived together in the factory-house in Hiroshima. Hearing the sad news of many cities being destroyed by air raids, Takanobu's father decided to evacuate the factory to the countryside. He found a factory site in Yachiyocho and started to move things there. Takanobu's uncle went to pick up some luggage by horse-drawn carriage in the early morning of August 6. Takanobu's father usually went right back into the factory after seeing people off at the entrance. On that particular day, however, he watched until his brother turned the corner of the street, as if reluctant to see him go. Perhaps he had a feeling that it would be the last time he would see him.

On the day before the atomic bomb was dropped, my father returned to Zaimokucho. I was later told that before leaving, he said, "I've got a little more work to do."

On the morning of August 6, I was playing in an empty lot in front of the house with the boys from next door.

"Wham!"

"Boooom!"

A tremendous rumbling came out of the ground. I looked to the south and saw a giant mushroom cloud rising high. Since our grandmother's house had no electricity, she had no radio. I only heard a rumor that something serious had happened in the area of Kabe. I went to bed as usual that night.

The following day, I heard the news from a neighbor. "It seems Hiroshima has been destroyed!" That evening, my sisters and I started for Route 54 to meet our father when he came home. We left my youngest brother with our grandmother. My older sister led my younger sister by the hand. Yachiyocho was about 30 kilometers from the city center, and very few trucks were running on the road. Feeling tired, both of my sisters squatted on the road.

When we saw a truck approaching from a distance, we got up and peered inside. The truck was carrying a lot of injured people. Some were bandaged; some were burnt and sooty. Every time a truck passed by, we strained our eyes, hoping that it would pull over and our father would get off. We waited for him until it got dark. He didn't come home that night. Our grandmother tried to put a brave face on the situation: "Don't worry. He'll soon be back!"

The next day and the day after that, my sisters and I went to Route 54 to welcome him home, but he never came back. On the fourth day, my grandmother and the sister of my stepmother went to Zaimokucho. They told me they soon recognized the site of Hirano Sock Merchants because of the burnt sewing machines and other machinery. They also found my father's body on the staircase.

Takanobu's grandmother asked the relief workers to dispose of his father's body. His stepmother and her other sister had gone out early on the morning of August 6. They remain missing. His grandmother turned back to Yachiyocho.

A week later, on August 14, my grandmother, my sister and I got a ride from a truck to go to Hiroshima, and went back to our house in Zaimokucho. I will never forget how shocked I was when I got off the truck. The town had been reduced to a field of ashes. The tobacco shop and the clog shop were gone. I had never seen such a sight. I couldn't stop my knees from shaking.

I saw a dead horse floating on the river. There were almost no people in the neighborhood. We looked for a burnt sewing machine and entered the house, and there were the ashes of cremated remains heaped up on a burnt galvanized iron sheet.

"Soldiers cremated the body for us," our grandmother said quietly. I looked around and found a burnt kettle on the ground. We put the ashes into the kettle, and I carried it as we went home. To this day I still treasure the kettle. I resolved to keep it for the rest of my life.

My grandmother, my sisters, my brother and I held a memorial service for my father in Zaimokucho on August 19. Two months later, my uncle's wife remarried, took her son and left, saying: "My husband has been missing since he was drafted into the military." This was shocking news to me, for she had cared for us like a mother at our grandmother's house. "She, too, has left me," I said to myself, feeling abandoned.

Our grandmother was very old. Besides her, there were only the four of us left—two sisters, a younger brother and me. Helplessness filled my heart. I felt I had nobody to rely on.

If we had not had our grandmother, we would have had no choice but to live as A-bomb orphans. We are still very grateful to our grandmother. The four of us continued to live with her. Now that I think about it, our grandmother grew her own rice and vegetables but had no other source of income.

Back then, everyone was hungry all the time. We mixed minced radish in a small amount of rice to make our food go further. Day after day, we only ate a small amount of rice mixed with chopped radish or sweet potato. Since we had no shoes, we wore sandals to school. When it rained, sandals splashed mud on our clothes, so we were always barefoot on rainy days.

This is a story I heard long afterwards. One day, an elementary school teacher came to our house and wanted to adopt my younger sister. My older sister firmly opposed the offer, saying, "I don't want to part from my sister or brothers at any cost!" Our grandmother objected, too, and said, "I'll take care of my grandchildren myself." This is how my younger sister was able to remain in the house.

After that, Takanobu graduated from junior high school. He apprenticed himself to a barber when he was 15.

There was a barbershop on the national highway. When I passed by the shop, it was always brightly lit and looked so beautiful. Since we used lamps and lanterns at that time, my heart danced at the sight of the shop's bright electric lights. That was why I wanted to become a barber.

After serving his apprenticeship at the barber's for four years, Takanobu worked there without pay for a year. When he was 20, he returned to Yachiyocho, where he opened a barbershop. He spent the money he had made from his job to marry off his two sisters.

Soon after I started working as a barber, I met a boy at the nearby lumber shop whose owner I made friends with. My friend said, "He's a war orphan. I'm thinking of hiring him." The boy was 15 or 16, and always had a lonely expression on his face. I now think that without our grandmother, my sisters, brother and I would have met the same fate.

Several years later, when Takanobu was 26, he married a woman introduced to him by one of his friends. She was two years younger and was a hairdresser. After getting married, they built a beauty salon and barber shop along the national highway, where they both worked. After three years of marriage, they had a son.

Four years after our marriage when I was in high spirits enjoying my family life, in 1965, I suddenly got a backache. Then, I had a slight fever for a while. My family doctor said, "I have no idea what disease this is." He eventually referred me to the Hiroshima University Hospital. At the hospital I was diagnosed with tuberculosis and was told that I would be admitted to the hospital as soon as a bed became available. I was worried because I had a son to look after. Instead of being admitted, I went to the hospital regularly as an outpatient and took streptomycin.

Although Takanobu recovered, people in the neighborhood found out about his disease. As a result, he could no longer work as a barber. His wife continued to run the beauty shop, and he started working at an aluminum window frame company run by his wife's brother. He later opened his own window frame business, which he managed for 20 years. "A-bomb survivors have mixed feelings," he says. Almost 70 years since the atomic bombing, he feels it has constantly tortured him.

A part of me says, "Leave me alone," while another part of me says, "I need to tell people about the suffering I've experienced." I have been tormented by these conflicting emotions. As a matter of fact, when I got married, I didn't tell my wife that I was a *hibakusha*. I was afraid to talk about it. "I will never tell anyone all my life," I thought. In those days, it was said that Hiroshima would be bare of vegetation for the next 75 years. When the atomic bomb was dropped, I was in Yachiyocho, a town not directly affected by the bombing. I was exposed to secondary radiation when I went to gather my father's ashes. I thought that unless I mentioned it, nobody would notice.

Despite this, three years after our marriage, my wife became pregnant with our first son. She was diagnosed with placenta previa at the hospital in Yoshidacho, and was told that the hospital could not handle the case. We somehow managed to get a referral to the

Hiroshima Prefectural Hospital, where she gave birth. The baby was born two months premature, weighing 1,800 grams.

I was restless for days, thinking, "Is it because I was exposed?"

When our son was one and a half years old, he had a hernia. I could not bear to see him suffer from so many physical disorders, so I confessed to my wife that immediately after the atomic bombing, on August 14, I went to Zaimokucho, which was near the hypocenter. She simply said, "Don't worry." Fortunately, our son grew up healthy without any serious illness.

I decided to apply for an Atomic Bomb Survivor Health Book, although it took me a long time to do so. People who had entered the hypocenter area within two weeks of the atomic bombing were recognized as "entry victims." The Health Book allowed free physical checkups. I needed a witness to prove that I entered the city. My grandmother had already passed away, so I looked for the sister of my stepmother. I met her and persuaded her to become my witness.

I have suffered a sharp ringing in my ears since I was young. I often get dizzy. I went to see a brain surgeon, who said he had no idea what caused the condition and couldn't prescribe any medication. I can't help but think that it's because I entered the bombed area. When I'm not feeling well, I get so worried that I can't sleep.

Sometimes my son ran a fever or got a nosebleed because of the heat. This is not a big deal for most children, but with my son, I wondered in fear if it was related to radiation. The slightest thing made me uneasy. My heart freezes with fear even about things that don't seem to upset others.

My older sister also married without telling her husband that she had been exposed to radiation. "If I talk about my experience, I may not be able to get married," she said. Since then, she and I have never talked about Zaimokucho. We both wanted to keep it a secret as much as possible. It saddens me to think about how much she suffered without being able to talk to anyone.

Probably many people in Fukushima are now experiencing the same grief my sister and I have gone through. I wonder if some of them will have to endure the same pain in the future. This is why I cannot consider the suffering of people in Fukushima to be "someone else's problem."

Soon I will turn 80. I have come to believe that I have to pass on the spirit of Hiroshima to the generations to come. Last year, I read in the newspaper that Hiroshima City had launched a project to train younger people to convey the experiences of the A-bomb victims. I was immediately interested in the project and applied. My testimony was recorded and released on a DVD entitled "The testimony of Hiroshima: The atomic bomb survivors tell their story." In my community I was president of the development association for my local district for four years and am now a board member. I am also a member of the executive committee of the Yachiyo Sports Association. Spreading hope in our local community, I intend to devote the rest of my life to peace.

Shoso Kawamoto
No more A-bomb orphans

Born in March 1934, Shoso Kawamoto entered Hiroshima three days after the atomic bombing from an evacuation site in Kamisugi, returning to his home in Shioyacho. He was 11 years old. Five members of his family died or went missing, making him an A-bomb orphan.

Shoso was born the eldest son in a family of seven in Shioyacho, 600 meters from the hypocenter. In April 1945, all the sixth graders from Fukuromachi Elementary School were sent to four villages for school evacuation. His group went to Kamisugi Village. A total of 45 boys and 32 girls stayed at a temple called Zentoku-ji.

No choice but to live as a street child

A meal at the temple was a bowl of rice, *miso* soup and some pickled vegetables. It was not enough for growing children, so we were hungry all the time. At lunchtime, the lunchboxes local students opened looked like feasts to me. Fully packed with white rice, they made me envious. I sometimes bartered for some, saying, "For some of your lunch, I'll give you a pencil and an eraser too!" I wanted anything I could put in my mouth. Children from farms in the area told me which plants were edible. I even tried raw wheat, pulling off the kernels and rubbing them between my hands. I picked soybeans growing on the roadside near rice paddies. It wasn't about the taste. I just wanted something to eat, something to stave off hunger.

What I liked best was Japanese leopard frog. You pulled the legs wide apart and the skin easily peeled off. The cook deep-fried it for us. It tasted like white chicken meat and was a precious source of protein for me. I believe that I was able to build my body thanks to those frogs. I also ate locusts, grasshoppers, anything that could be eaten.

At the temple, we didn't have time to study. Instead, we had to fill bamboo tubes with resin from pine trees by scraping the bark and also collect pine root oil. This oil was used for airplane fuel. We cultivated unused land, planting potatoes and sweet potatoes.

On August 6, we had been working in our field since early that morning planting vegetables. Then, I noticed the sky looking so odd. A gigantic column of white cloud was rising in the direction of Hiroshima City. I had never seen such a sight, so I was eager to know what was happening. "The way the clouds are forming is not normal," I said to myself.

At that time we were more than 50 kilometers away from the city, so we did not see the flash or hear the roar, but how the clouds were forming bothered me greatly. Our teachers had clearly heard news from the village office by evening, but they didn't tell us what had happened in Hiroshima.

Later, I heard different stories from families who came to pick up their children. Even when I heard that Hiroshima was totally destroyed by a "special" bomb, the reality did not hit me. Many families came for their children and took them away, eventually leaving only a few of my classmates and me.

On August 9, my sister, who was five years older than me, finally came to the temple from Hiroshima City to pick me up. As soon as she saw my face, she burst into tears. She said that she had visited the site of our house in Shioyacho the day after the bombing and had found the burnt remains of what appeared to be our mother, younger sister and brother. She found them holding onto each other in the living room. Although their faces were burnt black and were difficult to recognize, she was sure the bodies were those of our family members because of where she found them. Our father and eighth-grade sister had been out helping to demolish houses for a fire break and were missing.

Shoso and his sister returned to burned-out Hiroshima. Their house had burnt to the ground. So, with the boxes of their family's ashes, they were passed from one relative to another. None of their relatives could afford to keep them. Eventually his sister, who had just turned 16, rented a room, and they moved in.

When my sister and I stood on the platform at Hiroshima Station, I was stunned. The sight from there was beyond belief. No buildings stood in front of us. I could look over the city out to the islands in the Seto Inland Sea. And the whole city was dead silent. It made me feel sick. My sister rented a room in the building where she worked, so we started living there together. My sister worked for the management bureau of the National Railway. I had nothing to do, so I walked around the streets every day. There were many orphans in the city. Having lost their parents, they had nowhere to go. Some of them were my classmates from Fukuromachi Elementary School. We went to the fire-ravaged sites to collect iron scrap and cigarette butts.

Hot meals were provided twice a week. I desperately wanted to make friends, so at soup kitchens I often traded places with orphans standing in the back of the line. I collected iron scrap with them. I gradually became accepted by the orphans. It was easy to tell whether a child was a "street orphan" or not by looking at his or her clothes. Street orphans wore clothes that were obviously different from the children who had parents or lived in institutions.

At night, street orphans had no place to go, so they slept under bridges, in corners of burned-out buildings and in air-raid shelters. They slept together in groups of five or six, with their clothes on. But the groups did not mean they were friends or comrades. They were collections of individuals gathering because it was better to sleep together than separately. In the morning, they went their separate ways looking for food.

Street orphans targeted open-air food markets trying to get food, particularly stalls run by women or elderly people. A street orphan would make off with a rice cake. While the shopkeeper chased after that orphan, others would appear and instantly steal the remaining rice cakes. Stealing was a frantic struggle. Having food in hand was often dangerous. An orphan with food became a target for other orphans, who would immediately try to grab the food. So stealing and eating had to be done at the same time. Older orphans would even pry open the mouths of the younger ones to take food before it could be swallowed. The term "hungry little devils" described them perfectly.

About four months after the atomic bombing, Shoso's sister fell sick. Blisters on her feet burst and bled continually. Her hair fell out. A week or so later, she died. Shoso was then taken in by the village mayor of Numata in February the following year. Before the bombing, about 8,600 elementary school students in Hiroshima were evacuated to the countryside. Of those, 2,700 became orphans, and only 700 were admitted into orphanages. The exact figures are unknown, but it is reasonable to think that at least 2,000 orphans were left abandoned to become street children.

I was the only one in my family of six to survive. People around me tried to help me get accepted by an orphanage, but those facilities were full to overflowing. I couldn't even go to an orphanage. And then the month after the atomic bombing, the powerful Typhoon

Makurazaki hit Hiroshima, washing away many of the street children who were sleeping under bridges.

The people who took care of most of the neglected street children were young gangsters. They built two-story shacks, where they lived upstairs and the street children slept downstairs, crowded together like livestock. The gangsters provided the children with food and shelter, in return for which the children had to work and pay kickbacks. Only orphans who were teenagers or older were able to form groups with leaders that could live on their own, as in the *manga* and movie *Barefoot Gen*. The younger children could only commit petty crimes like pickpocketing, so they could not make it on their own.

The gangsters gave the children work. The children were divided into groups of five and provided with shoeshine kits. Two of the five children worked as shoeshine boys, with the other three recruiting customers. They returned to the shack at night and gave the money they made to the gangsters. The group that made the least amount of money was replaced with another group and was sometime made to go without meals. For this reason, all the children worked hard, and the groups would often fight with each other.

Besides shining shoes there was plenty of other work. For example, they sold glasses of methanol diluted 10-to-1 with water for 10 yen each. They sold Philopon (methamphetamine) and "rebuilt" cigarettes made from cigarette butts that Occupation soldiers threw down on the streets. The gangsters taught the children how to work, then pocketed all the money. Even so, the children didn't run away because they were given food and a place to sleep. This was how they managed to survive.

Not many know these things. The stories of the orphans abandoned to the streets are never told. When people hear the word "orphan," they think of children whose parents have died and who are in orphanages. The fact is, in Hiroshima, the street children greatly outnumbered orphans in institutions.

The city was full of street children, who died one after another, starting with the younger ones. When older children caught younger ones with food in their hands, they snatched it away from them. I even heard about a small child who was mumbling, so a bigger child held him down and opened his mouth only to find he was sucking pebbles. If a child fell ill and lay unconscious on the street, nobody paid any attention. As soon as a child died, other children stripped off his or her clothes, which is why most children found dead on the street were naked. On the other hand, orphans taken in by gangsters survived.

Eventually Shoso's uncle wanted to take him in. All the orphanages were full, but he didn't want to stay with this uncle. At the end of February 1946, he was placed in the custody of the Kawanaka Soy Sauce Store in Numata. The shop owner was the village mayor, and Numata was where his grandparents on his father's side had lived.

"We can't afford to send you to junior high school, but we'll give you food if you help out around here. We'll build you a house in the future," I was told. Under these conditions I was allowed to live in the house of the Kawanaka Soy Sauce Store. Since I had nowhere else to go and didn't want to live with my uncle, I worked hard at the shop. I did everything I could, from looking after cows early in the morning, to mowing, cutting rice stubble in the paddies and farming. I also learned how to brew soy sauce. I worked there for 10 years without taking a day off. When I was 23 years old, as promised, they built me a house of my own. I also became leader of the local youth association.

I then fell in love with a girl from the village and asked her to marry me. Her parents, however, strongly opposed our marriage, saying: "You were in Hiroshima at that time, weren't you? Those who were there were contaminated with radiation. You probably won't live long, and if our daughter marries you, she will give birth to a disabled child. We can't allow you to marry her!"

This made my blood boil. "There's no point in having my own house if I can't marry anyone. From now on, I'm going to live my life the way I want to," I said to myself.

Shoso ran away from the village in anger and returned to Hiroshima. Visiting the city for the first time in 12 years, he found that it had changed completely. By chance, he met a man who had been a year younger than him in elementary school and had also been an orphan. This man was a "full-fledged gangster."

I met a friend on the street with whom I had stayed at the temple. He was swaggering along in his territory with some young men in tow. Since I had a driver's license, I soon got a job at a trucking company because this friend put in a good word for me. At night I went into town and frequented the local gambling house. I was attracted to the gang because of my friend's influence, so I asked him if I could join. He said, "You're not cut out to be a gangster. You're too nice, so no." Sometime later, my friend was killed in a fight.

I led a rebellious life for about 10 years. Then one day, when I was 30 or so, I was fined 2,000 yen for a traffic violation, and I couldn't get the money. I felt miserable. I no longer had the will to live. I couldn't be bothered to borrow money to pay a fine. I began to believe my life was not worth living. "I'm going to kill myself!" I thought, "But I don't want to die in Hiroshima. I'll go someplace where nobody knows me and die there." I decided to leave the city.

I only had 640 yen with me and could only make it to the next prefecture, Okayama. I got off at Okayama Station and started to walk. Still wondering which way to go, I saw a noodle shop with a notice saying: "Live-in Help Wanted."

"No one in Okayama knows me. Maybe I can start my life again," I thought. I went in and asked the owner to hire me. "If you're really serious about working here, you're hired," he said. I was hired on the spot. I worked hard at that shop. I ended up working in Okayama for 30 years, and even started a small food company with about 50 employees. Around that time, convenience stores were popping up across the country, and our prepared food and boxed lunches sold well in them.

One day, when I was 60, an employee told me I had a phone call from Hiroshima. I had not called or written to anyone in Hiroshima for decades, so I was sure nobody knew where I was.

I answered the phone and heard a cheerful voice say, "Hey, Kawamoto! I'm glad you're alive! We were worried about you. We've been looking for you!" It was one of my friends from when I had stayed at the temple. "Come home, Kawamoto! Let's hold a 50th-anniversary memorial service." Hearing the voice of an old friend brought back a lot of memories. "I'll spend the rest of my life in Hiroshima," I said to myself. I decided to go back.

Shoso put his affairs in order, closing down his company, and returned to Hiroshima at the age of 70. In Hiroshima, he visited the Hiroshima Peace Memorial Museum and was astonished to find a paucity of information about street children. Although the museum featured a wide variety of exhibits and displays on the atomic bombing, there was only one photo of a boy shining shoes, with one line stating, "It is said that there were 2,000 to 6,500 orphans living in the city." Shoso has been addressing the issue of "A-bomb orphans" head-on since then, utilizing his own experience.

After returning to Hiroshima, I visited the Hiroshima Peace Memorial Museum, where I was surprised to find that there was almost no material on A-bomb orphans. For the children who were thrown out on the streets because they were unable to get into an orphanage, the biggest problem was food. Most had no choice but to rely on gangsters, because they simply couldn't live by themselves. These circumstances have been completely ignored by the museum. I have no desire to glorify gangs. I do not approve of them. However, we must not deny the facts—orphans on the streets were associated with and cared for by gangs. This was how they survived.

I now work as a Peace Volunteer. I tell visitors to the Hiroshima Peace Memorial Museum about my experience and the orphans living on the streets. I have been criticized for my story by some of my classmates from Fukuromachi Elementary School, including some of those who encouraged me to return to Hiroshima from Okayama. Some have objected to what I'm doing:

"I'm married with children and grandchildren. They are dimly aware that I was an orphan, but they don't really know how I survived. I'm afraid that my children and grandchildren will find out about my awful past because of your talk."

"You've got nothing to worry about because you don't have a family. Think about former orphans who have children and grandchildren. Think how they feel. Please stop telling that story."

After I was rejected as a marriage partner because of the atomic bomb, I never got married because I didn't want to be rejected again. My classmates, however, are mostly married with children and grandchildren.

One of my classmates said, "I have never told even my children about how I survived those days. I don't think I can. I was 10. I had no one to depend on, so I had to find ways to live on my own. I did what I had to do to live. I have even snatched food violently away from a stranger. This was how I survived."

My classmates are afraid that if I speak, their children will hear my story and be tormented thinking, "What sort of terrible things did my Grandpa do?" They may all want to forget the past, but it's impossible. We cannot ignore the past. I have to tell the truth even if it's painful, because children in the future must understand what war was really like.

Many of the orphans who managed to survive were those who were placed in orphanages. This fact is also important. Many of them were able to continue their education because of those orphanages. Many were able to make plans for their future. In contrast, the orphans who were thrown out into the streets were forced to live like livestock. This fact is not known to the world; it has been forgotten. The undeniable fact is that many orphans survived in the care of gangsters.

This is not a matter of good or evil. This is simply the reality, the way orphans on the streets lived as a result of the war and the atomic bombing. Talking about the past is painful for me and also for those that listen. But this pain is a real aspect of war. As a person who has survived the cruelty of war, I believe I'm now obligated to speak about my experience. I need to convey the facts to the future so we will create no more A-bomb orphans.

Kiyoshi Ito

I pray for peace so the children's laughter will continue

Born in March 1937, Kiyoshi Ito escaped direct exposure to the atomic bombing because he had been evacuated to Miyoshi City. His parents, who lived in Komachi, 900 meters from the hypocenter, were killed by the atomic bomb, leaving him an A-bomb orphan. He spent his childhood being passed from one relative to another. He worked at the Shimonoseki City Office in Yamaguchi Prefecture, returning to Hiroshima after retiring.

Passed from one relative to another

Although our family had always been well-off, we found ourselves living in dire need by 1945. I was eight at that time. Sweets were very hard to come by. Once I saw an article in the newspaper that talked about children being delighted to receive plenty of sweets at the temple to which they had been evacuated. I remember that this article gave me an irresistible urge to eat something sweet. I was in second grade. Although evacuation was optional, I decided to join the evacuation program. I couldn't get this newspaper story out of my mind.

My friends and I were evacuated to a temple in Miyoshi City. Some of them were homesick and cried on their beds under the mosquito netting. Much to my disappointment, the newspaper story about plenty of sweets turned out to be a lie. We were served small portions of *miso* soup, pickled radish and rice mixed with barley. We were always hungry. At night, some of my friends and I would sneak into the temple kitchen and steal uncooked rice. We nibbled on it in bed to keep the hunger pangs away.

"I think we were evacuated from the city around June," says Kiyoshi, adding that he remembers he and his friends helping to plant rice out there. "That day" came while he was living at the evacuation site.

Even after August 6, we were not told about the *"pika-don"* (flash-boom, the common name for the bomb). Our teacher said only, "I went to Hiroshima to see your parents. They said they'll come get you soon. Let's wait."

Several days later, my friends' parents and families began arriving to pick them up, but nobody came for me. Watching them leave one after the other made me feel lonely and uneasy.

By late August, only three children were left. I was one. A few days later, Tei, my cousin, suddenly turned up with a bag of rice and some canned food. He cooked rice and served me canned beans and meat. I was relieved that he finally had come for me. Because of the tasty rice and the feeling of happiness he brought, I no longer felt anxious. He didn't mention the atomic bombing, and I was too excited to ask him about my parents.

Tei took me to his parents' home in Kure City. He later told me that he had visited my home two days after the atomic bombing and found the bones of my father, mother and older brother in the living room. Their bones were still where they had been sitting.

It was not until the beginning of September that I learned the truth about what had happened. Tei and my older brother, Toshi, who was in Kyoto at university, took me to Hiroshima. We arrived at Hiroshima Station. I cannot describe the terror I felt when I saw the city. My legs gave way, and I lost the power of thought. My parents' house and Kokutaiji Temple next door had disappeared without a trace. Only the remains of the temple pond could be seen. We were unable to hold a funeral for our parents. For some time, I couldn't believe they were dead.

I started living at Tei's parents' house, but I felt there was no place for me. Tei died of pulmonary emphysema at the age of 69. He may have become sick because he went to gather the remains of my parents and became an indirect victim of the bomb. I lived at his house for only about three months.

Soon afterwards, my brother Toshi took me to Ofuna in Kanagawa Prefecture. We traveled on tightly packed trains. I found myself at our Uncle Kenzo's house. He was my father's brother and worked for the National Railway. He was an honest man. Although he had five growing children, he never bought rice on the black market. His family of eight, including myself, shared a small amount of rationed rice. We didn't have enough to eat. There were times when we ate almost nothing for a week. My five cousins and I lay down in a corner of the room, because if we moved, we got hungry. We were all malnourished. Uncle Kenzo's voice sounded like my father's. "I'm going to talk like your father, so close your eyes," he once said. I closed my eyes and he said, "How are you doing?" He sounded exactly like my father. I burst into tears. While I was staying with my uncle, I couldn't go to school.

In April 1946, Kiyoshi had to move to Shimonoseki in Yamaguchi Prefecture, where he lived with his mother's brother. His uncle ran a construction company and had four children. Kiyoshi had never met this side of his family, so he was meeting his cousins for the first time.

My uncle's family had no problems economically, but I felt as if I had been tossed into a house of strangers. I was always alone. Each of the four children had a private tutor, though almost no households could afford to hire tutors back then. My cousins looked like they were having fun with their tutors. Watching them from the corner of my eye, I always felt jealous. I once saw my uncle's wife and her children happily eating sweet bean cakes in the living room when I got up to use the bathroom in the middle of the night. I felt completely alienated, and gradually became subservient.

They had a housemaid named Otoki. She probably felt sorry for me, so when I came home from school, she always invited me to her room. However, I didn't like being in the "maid's room" all the time. It hurt to think that the others knew that I felt like I wasn't welcome. This was why I always stayed at school until dark.

I couldn't say what I wanted to at home, so I behaved badly at school as a reaction. Every day I would pick a fight, take somebody's lunch, or have "sword fights" with measuring sticks in home economics, often breaking them. My teacher once said, "Don't come to school anymore."

On sports days I had a particularly tough time. My friends ate lunch with their parents during the break. Since I had no parents and no lunch, I had to kill time in a classroom by myself until lunch break ended.

In the fall of 1946, Kiyoshi's oldest brother Takeshi returned to Japan from China, having been discharged from the military. Takeshi discovered that his parents' home in Hiroshima was gone. He started searching for his family and finally found his way to Shimonoseki. He took his brother in.

Takeshi took me in, and soon, he got married. Now in fourth grade, I lived with the newlyweds. Takeshi often hit me. I think it was because he was hot-blooded and violent after coming back from the military, but it was also out of frustration and concern about his wife's situation. Meanwhile, I became a rebel. Once I stole an apple from a Buddhist altar inside the house next door. Takeshi found out and beat me with a bamboo stick until it split into pieces. However, I did not hate him for beating me. The sense of alienation I had felt at my relatives' house had been much harder on me emotionally than his beatings.

My brother's parents-in-law manufactured *udon* noodles. When I was in junior high school, I worked at the factory and lived with other workers on the second floor. I was living on my own for the first time in my life. I woke up at three every morning and worked all day. I went to night school for high school and junior college.

After the atomic bombing, I had been passed around from one relative to another. I was taken care of, but nowhere was ever home to me. I couldn't even open a cabinet without permission, nor could I vent my anger and frustration to anyone.

Takeshi told me once when I was in high school, "You may think you're no different from others, but you are. You've grown up without things tangible and intangible that you were supposed to get from your parents. Always keep that in mind, and work hard to overcome it."

It was not until later that I understood what he meant. I never thought about my mother until I became an adult. Some may think me coldhearted, but back then, all I could do was make it through the day. I didn't have the time to reminisce about the past.

After graduating from junior college, I was employed by the Shimonoseki City Office, where I worked until retirement in 1997. My wife and I came back to Hiroshima, and we now live an ordinary but happy life together in Kita Hiroshimacho. Composing *senryu* poems is my favorite pastime. Every day I hear children laughing as they play on the jungle gym and the slide in the park next to our house. During the war, no children were laughing.

One day I suddenly realized that peace can be defined as a society in which we can hear the laughter of children. I hardly went to school at all when I was in second and third grade. I was an A-bomb orphan, so I feel that I missed out on my childhood.

This is why I hope that children today will cherish and maintain peace. I pray for peace, that is, for the laughter of children to continue. I feel strongly that I should contribute to that peace by telling my story about the horrors of war and the tragedy of the atomic bombing.

> A child's smiling face / Always tells us / The importance of peace
> Looking back / I find the joy of peace / in the thorny path of life

Tadayoshi Tashima
No matter what, war is wrong

Born in May 1939, Tadayoshi Tashima avoided direct exposure to the atomic bombing after being evacuated to Nakasu, seven kilometers from the Hiroshima hypocenter, at the age of six. However, he lost his grandmother, father, younger brother and younger sister who were in Hiroshima. He was brought up by his mother, who survived the atomic bomb. He worked at Toyo Industries (Mazda today) and several other companies.

The atomic bomb killed my grandmother, father, brother and sister

I was six years old, the oldest of three siblings. My sister Hiroko was five; my brother Akio was three. My parents sent me to live with my father's parents in Nakasu one year before the atomic bombing. They may have been hoping to keep at least their oldest son in a safe place. The war was becoming more intense, and a cousin my age lived with us as well.

The Tashima family lived in Hirose Kitamachi. Their house was scheduled to be demolished to make way for a fire break to prevent the spread of fires resulting from incendiary bombs. On August 6, Tadayoshi's parents were moving their furniture and belongings out of the house. His little brother was at his grandmother's house at Takajomachi. Only his sister was with his parents.

My family in Nakasu had just finished breakfast, and I was playing on my uncle's lap in the room with the Buddhist altar. I neither saw the flash nor heard a loud sound, but all the doors in the house were blown off. Some houses in Nakasu were destroyed, but no residents were hurt. That night, the Nakasu area was flooded with people fleeing from Hiroshima. Some were Nakasu residents who had been demolishing houses in the city. Others were Hiroshima residents who had relatives in Nakasu and were taking refuge. They all had badly burnt faces and bodies and were wearing tattered clothes.

My parents and my sister were among them.

"Oh no, ghosts!" I shouted without thinking.

My mother had been exposed to the heat ray from the front, so her face was hideously burnt. The right half of her face was burnt, its skin peeling, and her right ear had melted off. Her hands were also severely burnt. My kind, gentle mother had changed beyond recognition. If she had not been with my father, I would not have recognized her. My father, too, was seriously burnt on his back, and my sister had a hole about the size of a bean in her forehead. Strangely, it was not bleeding, and she wasn't crying.

Their hair and faces were dirty, and their clothes were tattered. They said that on the way they had swum across a river with their clothes on because a bridge had collapsed. They were exposed in the morning and arrived at my uncle's house around 5:00 in the evening. That meant they had walked for more than nine hours.

The following day, Tadayoshi, his uncle and his mother headed for Takajomachi where his grandmother and his brother were. Takajomachi was right by the hypocenter. Most of the town was burnt out. And at the fire-devastated site of his grandmother's house were the burnt bodies of an adult and a child. They were forced to the conclusion that these bodies were his grandmother and his brother. He was overcome with grief.

The burns my father suffered were so severe he couldn't lie on his back. He lay on his stomach, groaning, "It hurts! It hurts!" On August 9, he died, at the age of 34. On the bank of the Yasukawa River, some members of the local fire brigade and my uncle piled up some wood scraps and cremated my father's body. It took long hours. My sister had no injury except for the hole in her forehead, but she gradually stopped moving. She died on August 16.

My mother started to complain that she wasn't feeling well. She lost her appetite and spent more and more time lying down. Our relatives brought her some *dokudami* plants (saururaceae). They told her, "*Dokudami* plants are good for your health." She often drank a concoction made from *dokudami* by boiling the plant in a kettle of water. Soon, my mother's hair fell out, and she was bald. She lost the hair she was using to hide her keloid scars.

Tadashi, her younger brother, often visited her and encouraged her. "I'll avenge this tragedy. I promise! There's nothing to worry about!"

Her life was utterly transformed by the atomic bombing. In pictures of her as a young woman, she looks very beautiful. My daughters take pride in the few pictures that are left of my mother. My mother was only about 30 years old when she experienced the atomic bombing. She was still young. She must have gone through tremendous pain.

For about a year, my mother and I stayed at my grandparents' house. When she wasn't feeling well and had to stay in bed, my aunt looked after her. I saw my mother weeping late at night several times. After she became well enough to leave her bed, she began to put on light makeup in front of a mirror.

Eventually, my mother's hair began to grow back. She grew her hair long on the right side to cover her keloids. She tried to hide them as much as possible. No matter how many years pass, once skin turns into a keloid scar, it will never become normal skin.

Later on, my mother began to wear glasses, but she didn't have a right ear. She fixed her glasses to her right temple with a hairpin.

Before long, Tadayoshi's mother started working as a housekeeper at a food-processing store in Nakahiromachi. The following year, Tadayoshi started elementary school. Every day his mother commuted to Nakahiromachi from Nakasu, and Tadayoshi walked 20 minutes to Osu Elementary School. Later on, Tadayoshi and his mother were given some land in Furuichi that belonged to a relative. In those days, workers built makeshift shacks from wood scrap and burnt galvanized iron sheets. They built a hut with a six-tatami-mat room and a three-tatami-mat kitchen. Finally, mother and child started their lives on their own.

My mother was a housekeeper, so she left home early in the morning. She came home when she finished cleaning up after dinner at her employer's home. She would get home late at night. I was often by myself at home. I ate alone and went to bed alone. I used to be scolded by my mother frequently. She yelled at me to "take in the laundry!" or "do the dishes!" I did little to help with the housework. Mostly I would just hang around and do what I wanted to. After coming home, she would angrily say, "Why didn't you do what I told you?" My mother must have been so disappointed.

I never heard my mother hold a grudge or complain. One night, I saw her sitting up on her bedding speaking quietly to herself: "War is wrong. No matter what, war is wrong."

Eventually, their lives reached a turning point. As Tadayoshi's mother was honest and hardworking, the owner of the store was concerned about her. "There's a man who comes here to repair our processing machine. He lost his wife and baby, but he has small children and is having a hard time raising them. Why don't you get remarried?" he asked her. Tadayoshi's mother remarried through this introduction by the storeowner.

When I was a fifth grader, my mother married a man with four boys and a girl. Three of the stepbrothers were much older than me, but my stepsister was the same age as my late sister, and the youngest stepbrother was the same age as my late brother.

On New Year's Day in 1951, I met my stepfather and his family for the first time. We met at Koi Station, and then went to Miyajima Island.

"We're going to be a family," he told us and took a souvenir picture. In the picture, my mother has her hair hanging over the right side of her face to hide her keloids. What I thought of my mother's remarriage was, "She is no longer just my mother. I shouldn't be too dependent on her." I now had a sister a year younger and a brother three years younger than me.

After her remarriage, my mother and I moved to my stepfather's house in Kure. He was a farmer and had two black calves, which he was raising to sell the meat. When I came home from school, I cut grass to feed the calves. They also ate straw, so I chopped straw into small pieces and boiled it in an iron pot before I fed them. Sometimes I replaced straw soiled with dung with new straw, and the calves jumped for joy. I helped my stepfather plant the rice paddies, harvest rice and cut trees in the hills for firewood. My mother and stepfather weeded the terraced paddies and worked on the farm every day.

My stepgrandfather also lived in the house. He was well built, but an older man who already had a bent posture. He was a stonecutter who built stone walls for many years, which was probably hard on his back. Soon after the marriage, he became bedridden. Besides doing unfamiliar farm work, Tadayoshi's mother looked after her father-in-law for seven years. He liked her very much, and often called out her name saying, "Miyoko, Miyoko."

After graduating from junior high, I apprenticed myself to a master craftsman making wooden molds for casting metal. I lived and worked at his house. I wanted to become independent, saying to myself, "I am the one who will carry on the family name!" I had almost no memories of my father, but I knew that he had been a wooden mold craftsman. I was sent to live with my uncle when I was five, and even when we lived together, my mother was always working, so I have few memories of her despite living with her for 15 years.

There was an auto manufacturer called Toyo Industries (Mazda) in Hiroshima. They manufactured a cast model before creating a car engine. My job was to make wood molds to pour the cast into. I served my apprenticeship for eight years, starting when I was 15. I had a tough time learning the skills. In the world of craftsmen, an apprentice is never praised. He is yelled at all day, sometimes for no reason. About 10 craftsmen worked in the shop. In the morning, I had to be at the shop before they arrived. I did all the minor chores, from sharpening the teeth of band saws to boiling glue. I worked like a dog. Although my life was hard, I was served meals, provided with a space to sleep and given a small allowance. That was enough for me.

During my apprenticeship, I was sometimes allowed to return home to Kure. Whenever I came home, my grandfather would say, "If you want to marry someone, marry Kazuko." Kazuko was my stepfather's daughter. She was nice to my mother and me, so I gradually fell for her. I asked her to the movies on my days off. When I was 21, Kazuko and I held our wedding at the community center in Kure City. My family and relatives, the company president and three colleagues were there. It was a simple but touching reception. "Make a happy family!" my mother admonished us.

After the wedding, my mother improved physically and lived to be 76. She died of heart disease. I do not know if it was related to the atomic bombing, but if it hadn't been for that war or the atomic bomb, she would have lived a completely different life because of her beautiful face. Even during a string of bad luck, I never once heard her complain or even look downcast. I believe she was a good mother-in-law to my wife. And while she was taking care of my bedridden grandfather, she fed him spoonful by spoonful, patiently waiting for him to swallow each one.

My mother sent my wife to a dressmaking school, even though she herself was struggling to make ends meet. She always said, "Say what you want to say tomorrow." This was a phrase she had learned from my grandmother. I think this helped her endure all the hardships over the years. Even today my wife says, "Your mother did her best to do for me what my mother would have done if she had lived. I'm deeply grateful to her. When I think of her, tears come to my eyes even now. Living with her since I was in fourth grade, I am proud that I had such a wonderful mother-in-law."

Part 3

Nagasaki August 9, 1945
Telling the Story of Nagasaki Seventy Summers Later
Testimonies of men and women from Nagasaki

Tsugiya Umebayashi
My family was exposed in Hiroshima, my grandmother and I in Nagasaki

Born in December 1934, Tsugiya Umebayashi was exposed to the atomic bombing at the age of 10 while playing in a river in Hinodemachi, 4.5 kilometers from the Nagasaki hypocenter. His parents and siblings were exposed in Hiroshima.

In 1944, Tsugiya was a fourth grader at Hiroshima Municipal Kanon Elementary School. He lived in Kanon Shinmachi, several kilometers from what became the Hiroshima hypocenter. His father, who had previously worked at Mitsubishi Shipbuilding's Nagasaki shipyard, had been transferred to Hiroshima and moved his family there.

Tsugiya was the third son, and was 10 years old. He had three sisters, aged eight, seven and less than a year, and a four-year-old brother.

When air raids on the mainland intensified, evacuations of schoolchildren began. Those who had relatives in the countryside were sent to "family evacuations." Those who didn't were sent to "group evacuations" with other students.

The smell of dead bodies everywhere

As an evacuee, I was separated from my parents and sent to a temple in Saijo, Hiba County, a rural part of Hiroshima Prefecture. My first experience of life away from my family was terribly lonely. In addition, we never had enough food so I was always hungry.

A typical meal was rice gruel with a few mountain vegetables like Japanese butterbur, bracken and fern fiddleheads picked in the mountains. But after eating, I was still hungry. I often tore the skin off a stick of knotweed and nibbled its sour inner stem. I also remember one sunny day crushing lice that were crawling in lines along the seams of my shirt with the tip of my fingernail.

Letters to our parents were censored by the teachers. We were told not to complain or even say, "I miss my home," because our parents would worry about us.

All I had to look forward to was gifts sent occasionally by my parents. The gift was usually dry bread, which I shared with friends who didn't get gifts from home.

Tsugiya's grandmother lived in Nagasaki and sent a letter asking his parents to send her one of her grandchildren, saying she was lonely. His parents decided to send Tsugiya because he was away from home anyway. Tsugiya's two months of "group evacuation" would end and change to "family evacuation." He went off to live in Nagasaki.

August 9, 1945, began with a clear, sunny morning. I was playing in a river near a shelter dug by people in my neighborhood. It was just upstream of the Shiinoki River. Because the river suddenly widened at that spot, it was also called Gourd River. I was catching river shrimp with two boys in my neighborhood.

An air-raid warning that morning had kept me waiting impatiently at home. When the warning was cleared, we met up and headed for the river. Gourd River was shallow, with the water only coming up to our knees. When we put our net below the bank and stirred up the water, the river shrimp swam into the net. We were having great fun.

We were completely concentrating on our enjoyable task when suddenly there was a flash like a tremendous bolt of lightning. We rushed into the shelter in a panic and were there by the time we heard the tremendous booooom.

So much dirt fell from the ceiling of the shelter that I was buried. We called it a shelter, but it was actually just a tunnel dug by neighborhood volunteers. It always looked like it could collapse any time.

I couldn't move because of fear and the dirt. I stayed still for a long time. The mothers of the boys I was with came looking for us and dug us out.

We went outside and looked around for the first time. I'd probably been buried in the shelter for about an hour. The summer sky was so dark it could have been night. Fires were springing up here and there and spreading quickly.

Tsugiya's grandmother came to the shelter looking for him, and they went home together. On the way, they walked through roof tiles that had fallen from houses. Broken glass was everywhere, and furniture was scattered around on the road.

There are many hills in Nagasaki. Because Hinodemachi was sheltered behind Boom Hill, our house was still standing. We called it "Boom Hill" because a cannon at the summit always boomed to let us know it was noon. A steel tower on Nabe Kanmuri Hill stood facing Boom Hill a few kilometers away. When the boom sounded from Boom Hill, a large iron ball in that tower would slide to the bottom. If not for Boom Hill, those of us at Gourd River would have been directly exposed to the flash and blast. We would have been blown away.

I heard that a similar bomb had fallen on Hiroshima a few days earlier, and I had immediately worried about my parents and siblings. When we heard the rumor that Hiroshima had been completely destroyed, I couldn't sit still, I was so full of anxiety. My grandma and I decided to go to Nagasaki Station. Because they had lived in Nagasaki until quite recently, we thought they would surely come to Nagasaki to stay with Grandma. The houses in Hinodemachi had been spared, thanks to Boom Hill, so many people who had family members there went there to seek help.

We headed for Nagasaki Station following the streetcar tracks. From Hinodemachi, we passed Ishibashi streetcar stop. As we went toward Dejima and Ohato, the damage to houses became more obvious. Some buildings were blown away, leaving no trace of their original form. After a while, we couldn't even tell where we were walking. Debris was everywhere and we couldn't see the road.

A cart lay on its side. The horse that had been pulling it had been burnt to death. Corpses were lying all around us.

When we arrived at what we thought was Nagasaki Station, we were stunned. The station building was gone, completely burnt away, with no trains in sight. Almost everything around the station was burnt. The steel skeletons of buildings were left standing, but twisted like taffy.

The railway was not going to be fixed any time soon. We learned that the trains were stopped at Michino-o, two stations away. There was nothing we could do, so we just went home. The following day, there was still nothing we could do but worry if we stayed at home waiting, so we went back to the ruins of the station. This time, we saw a streetcar all burnt and smoldering.

A person in a shirt dyed with blood appeared to be wandering in a daze. A woman carrying a child on her back was asking everyone if her family was safe. Some people were just standing vacantly in front of collapsed homes. They had probably come from the countryside to find their relatives. The whole city looked eerily desolate.

People with "Relief" armbands carried corpses, and fire brigade members were finding scraps of wood in order to burn them. Surrounding them were people standing in shock, watching the flames consume their loved ones. They had no more tears to shed because they had already cried their last tears.

Tsugiya's grandmother fell ill on August 13. They gave up going back to the station. The following afternoon, on the 14th, his parents arrived from Hiroshima, bringing his brother and three sisters, all just as they were following the atomic bombing.

They had departed from Miyajima, located west of Hiroshima, but the trains were in turmoil because of the bombing. It took four days to get to Michino-o station. From there, his father carried Tsugiya's injured brother on his back. They had walked all the way through the burnt plain of Nagasaki.

Rather than joy, I first felt tremendous surprise. My parents and siblings were standing in front of me. My grandma was so happy she cooked all the rice she had saved, and all the potatoes. I still remember that day whenever I eat a potato.

The dining table had been so quiet with just my grandma and myself. Now we had a cheerful, lively family, with my father, mother and grandma all talking in loud voices, rejoicing at being safe and with each other again.

In Hiroshima, the whole family had been trapped under the house. Fortunately, my father had been at home getting ready to go to work. He helped the others one by one, pulling them out from under the collapsed house.

My sisters were just scratched, but my younger brother had suffered a serious injury when a beam fell on his back. My parents, sisters and brother were exposed to the bombing in Hiroshima; my grandma and I in Nagasaki. And yet, we had suffered little damage and were alive. We all celebrated our good fortune.

Later on, Tsugiya and his three sisters evacuated to Futsucho in Minami Shimabara, which was his father's hometown. They took the train just after service was restored. His mother remained at his grandmother's house together with his injured brother. His father took Tsugiya and his sisters to his parents' house and then he left them there, returning to his workplace in Hiroshima.

From the window of the train I saw the burnt bodies of people who had been working on their farms. They were still lying there abandoned, though almost two weeks had passed since the atomic bombing. I noticed white foam around the mouth of a charred body. Later I realized that foam must have been maggots.

Inside the train it was also gruesome. In the hottest days of summer, burnt arms and legs soon rotted, attracting swarms of flies. The flies just kept coming, even though people did their best to chase them away. One person's wound was just covered with white maggots. It seemed his mother was picking them out with chopsticks. I heard him say, "When the maggots move, it hurts a lot."

Another person was doing nothing but vomiting blood into a washbowl. Others had lost their hair in the explosion. I couldn't tell if they were male or female. And the terrible stench was making me sick. The smell of burnt flesh, mixed with the smell of dead bodies. The smell of a dead body is peculiar, indescribable and horrible. And that smell was everywhere for the rest of that year.

After six months, Tsugiya and his sisters left Minami Shimabara and went back to Nagasaki. His brother contracted spinal tuberculosis after the wound on his back became infected. His mother stayed in the hospital all day to care for him. Tsugiya visited the hospital every day to deliver meals to his mother.

My brother also had a burn on his left arm, which got infected and was slow to heal. He got tuberculosis of the spine, which deformed his backbone. However, his condition did not degenerate further, and he is still alive and well.

My three sisters who were exposed to the atomic bombing

in Hiroshima have been in poor health. They have never been diagnosed with any specific illnesses, so they don't know what is wrong, but they are always in poor physical condition. They spend more days in bed as they get older. Their health seems to be deteriorating slowly but steadily.

I suffered from the effects of the atomic bombing the whole time I lived in Minami Shimabara. I was always tired and could hardly get up. I frequently had to lie down quickly. I was bleeding from my gums, and my mouth always felt bad. These symptoms continued for some time even after I came back to Nagasaki. I got high blood pressure early on and was unable to go without medicine.

I graduated from the Faculty of Education at Nagasaki University. I became a teacher at Doinokubi Elementary School in Nagasaki City in April 1957 and taught for seven years. I then worked for many years at the Nagasaki Peace Hall. I am now retired and in good shape.

Ryoko Iwanaga
Always standing next to death

Born in May 1928, Ryoko Iwanaga was exposed to the atomic bombing at Bunkyomachi, 1.1 kilometers from the hypocenter in Nagasaki. She was 17 and was seriously injured. After recovering, she became a nurse's assistant at a clinic, and then worked for the post office and got married. She is still fighting physical conditions officially recognized as caused by the atomic bombing.

After graduating from Nagasaki Prefectural Girls High School, Ryoko was assigned to an office job related to weapons manufacturing. She was in the volunteer corps of the Design Section, Engineering Department II, Mitsubishi Ordnance Works in Bunkyomachi. Her office was in the corner of a large factory building where her job was to record manufacturing times.

Her home was at Fukahori, 12 kilometers from the hypocenter. Ryoko left home early that morning, taking a ferry leaving at 6:00 a.m. She arrived at Ohato Wharf after a one-hour boat ride. From there, she took a streetcar to her office.

Soon after she arrived, at around 8:30, an air-raid warning sounded. She took refuge with fellow workers on the hill behind the factory. When the warning was lifted, she went back to the factory.

Countless glass shards pierced my body

I went back to the factory and resumed work. Suddenly, I heard the buzzing sound of airplanes.

"What? Another air raid!" At that instant, I saw an intense flash just as a tremendous blast struck. If I had stayed on the hill, I would have died instantly, as it was completely stripped bare.

When the flash came, I immediately threw myself to the concrete floor. I don't really remember what happened after that. One memory I do have is of Ms. Ueda, an older worker, who called my name and helped me stand up. Her face was right in front of my eyes. I saw her again by chance a month later in a first-aid station set up in Shinkozen Elementary School. She had no obvious injuries to her face or body, but I found out that she died a week after that.

I was covered in blood due to the glass that the blast blew into my whole body—my arms, my back, even some in my face. I had dropped down onto my stomach, so my front was protected. The glass from the skylight above me had blown down and pierced my back and arms. My right elbow was ripped open: it looked like a pomegranate. I heard that the worker sitting right next to me died with a window frame stuck in their back.

I knew I had to get out. I went out of the back door of the factory. I heard later that those who ran out the front entrance facing the hypocenter suffered much more from secondary exposure.

Just outside the back door was a stretch of rice fields. One of my sandals slipped off in the mud, but I just kept running.

As I walked through debris that was burning hot and smoldering, I met Miss Nishi, a classmate. She found a shoe along the way and I put it on. The shoe belonged to a small child whose foot was half the size of mine, but I had no other choice.

Miss Nishi appeared to be without injury, but she had to sit down frequently and throw up. All I could do was flee. I really don't remember most of what was happening around me. I do remember someone standing on the road yelling, "Don't sleep! Don't drink water!"

Along the way, Miss Nishi was able to get a ride on a young man's back. Because of the glass shards stuck into her back and both arms, Ryoko was unable to grip anything, so she couldn't be carried on anyone's back.

A lady living in the neighborhood saw her volunteer corps armband and informed her school. Soon, two teachers pulling a cart came to pick her up. Seeing the cart, several students joined them, and the group headed for the school together. Ryoko's legs were uninjured, so she knelt on a straw mat in the cart, keeping her body upright and making sure not to let anything press on the glass.

Coming close to the school, several more students joined the group, and they all went into a classroom together. They gathered in the "etiquette room," a tatami mat room where they had studied the tea ceremony and flower arrangement. They spent the night there as a group. Once in a while they heard the sound of a B-29. Frightened, they huddled against each other. All the others lay down as if they had simply fallen over, but Ryoko couldn't lie down to sleep because of the glass shards. She sat on her knees or with her feet out in front of her all night, waiting for daybreak.

The next morning, since I was still bleeding badly, a teacher took me to the first-aid station in the elementary school nearby, saying, "You should at least get some first aid." But when we arrived at the first-aid station, we were shocked. It was filled with people whose skin and clothes were burnt and tattered so they were nearly naked.

Thinking, "I'm better off than they are," I seemed to gain energy. But it was clear I would get no treatment, so I returned to the school.

Around that time, Ryoko's family in Fukahori was getting the news that Nagasaki had been completely destroyed by the same new type of bomb that destroyed Hiroshima. Some were crying, certain that Ryoko had been killed by the bomb.

The names of people who were staying at the school were displayed on a sign at the school the next day. A neighbor saw the sign and told Ryoko's parents she was there. Ryoko's father, who worked for the fire brigade, and her uncle, who was a policeman, went to the school with *a stretcher. Ryoko was taken on the stretcher to the ferry and got home on the night of the 10th. She was on the verge of death. She was barely conscious and couldn't speak.*

We feared there might be another air raid, so we took refuge in a shelter. We spread some straw mats there and rested on them. My youngest sister (aged nine) stayed with me all the time and took care of me. I was really on the brink of death.

My hair was sticking out in all directions like a bird's nest. The small pieces of glass still sticking into my head were sparkling. Countless tiny pieces of glass were in my head and face. I was badly cut in at least 38 places. The blood running down onto my school uniform dried and made the cloth stiff. It stuck to my body. Taking that cloth off my wounds was so painful I thought my skin was being torn off. My sister felt so sorry for me. She cut very carefully with scissors and took the cloth off.

She told me there was a 15-centimeter scar on my back where a big piece of glass had stabbed me like a knife. She said she could see all the way down to the bone. My sister pulled as much glass out as she could, but some was left deep in my body, where it remained for a long time.

Years later, the remaining pieces would start to hurt. Each time I felt this pain, I had to go to the hospital and have a doctor cut open my healed wounds to pick out another piece. He was getting pieces that were small, like grains of rice. I had about seven such pieces removed, but I still have tingling and scraping feelings around my knee, even after 70 years.

The most difficult thing was not being able to lie on my back. In fact, I had to keep both of my arms elevated all the time, or blood gushed from my elbows. We piled *futons* under my left side, which had fewer wounds, and I slept leaning over the pile of *futons* with my arms over my head.

My sister spoon-fed me rice gruel and water. She wiped the blood and sweat from my face and body, constantly changing the water in the washbowl. She was a loving nurse, but those were days of hell to me.

There was no medicine, of course. I only got Mercurochrome for my wounds. When the gashes on my elbows closed and made scabs, my elbows wouldn't bend. To keep that from happening, the doctor forced my elbows to bend. When the healed scabs broke and my skin ripped open, blood flowed out again. My bent elbows were tied to my chest, then forced to straighten up the next day. The same procedure continued for more than a week, until I finally was able to bend and extend my elbows at will.

August 15. The war ends.

With no medicines available other than Mercurochrome for the wounds, Ryoko's strength gradually declined. Her hair fell out in handfuls, and her gums bled every day. Red spots appeared on her arms and thighs. It was said that when these "spots of death" appeared, the patient would die.

Ryoko became so weak she couldn't even drink water. Her family heard that Shinkozen Elementary School had become a first-aid station where a doctor from the University Hospital was treating survivors. They decided to take Ryoko there. Even so, everyone believed there was no hope for her. Even the local doctor had told them to give up.

I, too, thought, "I guess I'll never go home." I gave the dolls I had treasured since I was small, along with some beautiful colored papers I had saved, to my sisters and brothers, saying, "Please share these when I die."

The day I left for the first-aid station I was carried on a wooden door. As I lay there, I looked carefully around my home, thinking this would be the last time I would see it.

I was the eldest child. I had three younger sisters and two younger brothers. When my siblings sent me off, they were all crying. I have a dim memory of neighbors seeing me off along the road.

Although it was called a first-aid station, it was just an elementary school. There was nothing like a bed, just straw mats spread out on the floor. My family had brought a *futon*. They laid it out and laid me on it.

I was assigned to a classroom on the second floor and put by a window. At one point I happened to look outside and see a truck parked in front of the school. Dead bodies were being carried out on doors and loaded onto the truck. There was a pile of half-naked corpses on the bed of the truck. When they moved a body that had just been put onto the truck, I saw its head, more like a skull, roll down away from the body. I was terrified, thinking that was going to happen to me.

Less than an hour after I arrived at the first-aid station, we were informed that a US hospital ship had arrived at the port with a load of medical supplies. They decided to start by treating me and others who had just arrived.

In my case, treatment meant blood transfusions. Every day, I received more blood and grew stronger. I was soon on the path to recovery. I went home on the 45th day. When they saw me come walking home, my parents and all the family came out to welcome me with amazement.

From the time we first took refuge in the shelter, my hair had been falling out. Soon I was bald. Even after I returned home, my hair kept falling out. It grew back, but was like baby hair. I felt so sad whenever I saw my head. I couldn't go out in public.

I had wanted to be an elementary school teacher. I remember talking once with a classmate in my neighborhood, saying, "We'll be teachers together." When I heard that she had become a teacher, I knew I should be glad for her, but the truth is, I felt bitter regret.

Ryoko recuperated at home for a year. She was later hired as a nurse's assistant at a relative's clinic. Two years later, she got a job at the post office. After working for two years for the post office, in 1951, she got married. The marriage was arranged by her mother's friend. Ryoko was 23 years old.

Maybe this was only around me, but it seemed that people I knew did not consider the effects of radiation much of a problem. Therefore, I had not spoken about my exposure to my husband and had not asked him about his. I learned only later that he was also a *hibakusha*. He had been working in the torpedo test facility of the Mitsubishi Ordnance Plant at Dozaki. On the day of the bombing, he entered the city from Dozaki and was disposing of corpses. Thus, he was an "entry victim."

At one point, he told me, "The stench was so bad I couldn't do the disposal work without drinking alcohol." According to him, a massive amount of expensive whisky and brandy was hidden by the military in his plant.

My husband constantly complained that his body was itching. I always suspected it was due to radiation. He passed away in 2002.

My father, a member of the fire brigade who went near the hypocenter many times for relief activities, died of gallbladder cancer. My youngest brother is always in and out of the hospital because of colorectal and gastric cancer. My youngest sister, the one who took such good care of me, suffers from an irregular pulse, hypertrophy of the heart and angina.

I obtained official recognition of my atomic bomb disease when I fell ill in 2006. I had a high fever of unknown cause for about a week. I was hospitalized with an irregular pulse in 2011. Right before leaving the hospital, I was found to have colorectal cancer. Six months later, I had an operation for skin cancer.

Then I was hospitalized with heart failure in the summer of 2014.

The examination revealed that I had a disease of the heart valve. Because of my age, the doctors are investigating whether or not I should have an operation.

A body exposed to radiation is always standing next to death. I have made it for these 70 years despite having been given up for lost, but my battle with radiation continues.

Masahiro Tanigawa
Inscribing the names of the victims in the register each year

Born in December 1937, Masahiro Tanigawa was exposed to the atomic bombing near his home in Nishikoshima, four kilometers from the Nagasaki hypocenter, when he was seven years old. He worked for Nagasaki City Hall while studying at night school to get his high school graduation equivalent. After graduating, he continued to work there, and was often called on to write certificates and other documents requiring good penmanship. After retiring, he began writing diplomas for schools. He still enters into the "Register of A-bomb Victims" the names of those who died during the previous year. The Register is placed in a symbolic coffin each year on the A-bomb memorial day.

Masahiro was the seventh of nine siblings (five older brothers, one older sister and two younger sisters). His mother had four children with a previous husband, remarried and had five children with Masahiro's father, who worked for the customs office in Nagasaki.

Masahiro's oldest brother was serving in the military; his second oldest brother was killed in combat; the third oldest worked as a firefighter in Nagasaki, and the fourth oldest had died of illness in 1941. Masahiro was seven years old and a second grader at Sako Elementary School. He, his sixth-grade brother and younger sisters (aged five and two) were always together, usually playing happily.

While catching dragonflies for my sisters

That day, my mother went out early to help our neighbors dig a shelter, part of their "labor service." I was with my three siblings at home because an air-raid warning had sounded. After a while the warning cleared, so we talked for a while about what to do and decided to go find our mother. We headed for the place we thought she was working.

The shelter was being dug at a site about 200 meters from our house. The digging was done by women because the men had all gone off to military service. They used a hoe to loosen the earth, packed it into bamboo baskets and carried the baskets outside. We had some time before lunch, so I was in an empty lot nearby, catching dragonflies for my sisters.

Suddenly, a flash like a bolt of lightning filled the sky. We were terrified and ran into the shelter where our mother was. We heard nothing.

Someone shouted, "It's a bomb!"

Fortunately, none of us was injured, but injured people soon began coming into the shelter. Everyone was saying, "Nagasaki is gone."

When I went out, I saw the Nagasaki Prefectural Government Building burning and a black cloud hanging over the front of the station.

Someone said, "It's too dangerous to go out now. You'd better stay here for a while." So I stayed there with my mother and my siblings until evening. Some went home, worried about their homes.

My father came to the shelter that evening. He had a white curtain wound around his head like a turban; it was bright red with blood. He had been injured at his workplace by glass shards blown through the air by the blast.

When night fell, Masahiro, his parents and siblings went home. Their house was not even tilted. No roof tiles were blown away. It was fine.

His third oldest brother, who worked at a fire station two kilometers from the hypocenter, had been blown through the air but was not seriously injured. He immediately went out to do rescue work in the

Urakami area. He received permission from his boss to confirm his family's safety that night and went home. Having confirmed his family was safe, greatly relieved, he went back to join the rescue work.

My brother and his team were helping to dispose of the vast number of corpses that littered the area. I remember that a site near my home where the Kannai Market had been before the bombing was used for cremation. Corpses were lined up there waiting their turn. Most were brought in almost naked. While they were waiting, the bodies were covered with summer kimonos or other clothes. People felt sorry to see them just lying there naked.

Workers brought pillars and beams from fallen houses and laid them in a cross-pair pattern like building a campfire. They laid the bodies on the piles of wood and kept them burning night and day. I still can't forget the light from those flames and the continual stench of burning bodies.

They cremated many bodies at once, so relatives would stand in rows around the fire waiting for the flames to die down. They didn't really know whose ashes were whose, but they all put some in boxes and took them home.

After a few days a rumor flew around town. "The Occupation army is landing. Women and children will be massacred." People in my neighborhood fled to their relatives' homes. My family decided to evacuate to Nishi Arie, where some distant relatives of my mother lived.

Nagasaki Station was burnt out and no trains were running, but six of my family set off toward evening on the 14th. We walked all night and finally arrived at Isahaya where trains would be available at dawn on the 15th.

We were allowed to rest in a temple nearby. The temple was overflowing with escaping people. I will never forget how delicious the rice ball I was given was.

I heard the Emperor's announcement of the end of the war at that temple.

We went from Isahaya to Nishi Arie by train.

My mother's relatives were the main branch of the family and so they had a large farmhouse. I played with my sisters in their huge yard.

They had already accepted many families from elsewhere, so they said there was no place for us. We stayed there one night and returned to our home in Nagasaki. I remember my father being in a very bad mood in the train going home.

The city right after the bombing was a ruin. It was full of debris, with smoke still rising from the smoldering remains. I saw corpses charred so badly even the gender was unrecognizable. One person's arm was torn off but barely held onto the body by skin. I saw a mother wandering in a daze holding her dead baby. Some people were struggling to push their internal organs back into their torsos. Later I heard that people like those I saw were all over the city. Many simply fell to the ground moaning, "Water, I need water."

At first I thought we had less damage in Nishikoshima just because we were four kilometers from the hypocenter. But our area was actually behind a small hill. Many of the houses were shielded by that hill, which is why so many were undamaged. Other neighborhoods also four kilometers away were badly damaged because the blast hit them directly.

Later, my brother the firefighter who was doing rescue work told us, "We headed for the Urakami District to help. Streetcar cables were hanging down. Houses, schools and factory buildings were collapsed or burning. Water pipes were broken, so we couldn't fight the fire or do much of anything." That brother died of lung cancer. The brother who had been with me died of heart disease. It's strange that my parents, my sisters and I have apparently had no aftereffects from the atomic bombing.

Because Masahiro's brothers had died, his father suggested that he get an Atomic Bomb Survivor Health Book. He applied in his mid-20s. To get the Health Book, he needed two people to testify that he had been in the bombing. It had been nearly 20 years, and the neighbors in his old neighborhood had moved away. No one was left who knew Masahiro as a child. He had a hard time finding people to testify for him, but he eventually succeeded.

Masahiro went to night school to get his high school graduation equivalent and worked at City Hall during the day. He stayed on at City Hall after graduating. Masahiro loved calligraphy. He had never studied it formally at school, but he was often assigned to write certificates because his handwriting was so beautiful. After retiring, he got requests from local associations to write certificates of commendation and from schools to write diplomas.

His wife is from Saikai City and not a hibakusha. Still, no one on her side of the family opposed marriage with a hibakusha.

I write the names of those who passed away during the previous year into the "Register of A-bomb Victims" which is placed in the symbolic coffin each year on Nagasaki Day (August 9). I have been doing this since 2006, at the request of Nagasaki City.

When I began writing these lists, I visited my brother (the fifth son) in the hospital where he was waiting for a heart operation. I told him what I was doing, and he encouraged me, "That's an important task, so do your best."

Soon after that conversation, his surgery was suddenly scheduled and carried out, but he died two weeks later. I never thought I would be writing my own brother's name on that list in the first year I started the job.

From the day I received that writing request to this day, I always visit the Atomic Bomb Museum a few days before I start writing. Looking at the exhibits, I think about the victims. I pray sincerely,

"Please let my calligraphy embody my desire for peace and my prayer for the peaceful repose of their souls."

I write the names, age at death and date of death for each of the departed, and what I write will be preserved forever. Naturally, I am absolutely determined to write as carefully as I can.

Every year on August 9, when the list is placed safely in the coffin, I feel a relief that comes from the bottom of my heart.

Yasuko Nakao
"The atomic bomb is contagious"

Born in July 1939, Yasuko Nakao was exposed to the atomic bomb while playing with children in her neighborhood near Nishizaka Elementary School, 1.8 kilometers from the hypocenter in Nagasaki.

Yasuko was the third of five girls. Her sisters were 12, 10, 4 and 3 years old. They lived near Nishizaka Elementary School. The sisters were always together, happy and having fun. Their house was surrounded by fields at the foot of a hill. There was a bomb shelter near the top of the hill; they had to climb steep stone steps beside the school to get up to it. Her father worked for an ordnance factory and was seldom home.

Such was our terror, we couldn't make a sound

In those days, a yellow alert would sound, then quickly become an air-raid warning. Air raids came in the middle of the night. B-29s flew over in formation and sprinkled red-hot incendiary bombs. As soon as an incendiary bomb hit, the ground would instantly burst into flames.

At first, when an air-raid warning sounded, the whole family put on air-raid hoods. I would carry a backpack stuffed with the family's Buddhist memorial tablets, my older sisters each took one of my younger sisters, and we all fled to the shelter. Later, we stopped going to the shelter because my mother was pregnant. She could barely get to the top of the hill, and we were afraid that we would burn to death before we got to the shelter. We decided, "If we're going to die, we'll all die together!" After that, we never took refuge in the shelter at night. We stayed at home, huddled around our mother.

On August 9, my mother went out early in the morning with our neighbors to work on the shelter on the top of the hill. All the adults from every house were mobilized to work on the shelter, and I think about a dozen children were left at home.

That morning an air-raid warning sounded. My oldest sister took us to the shelter, but the warning changed to a yellow alert, so we left the shelter and went home. I was playing in an empty lot in front of my home with other neighborhood children.

Soon after 11:00 a.m., all of a sudden everything turned pure white in front of my eyes, then pitch black. When I thought about it later, I realized that the flash from the atomic bomb was so intense I couldn't see anything at all for a while.

As I gradually became able to see the scene around me, everything had changed. Houses had collapsed. Roof tiles had blown away. Sliding paper doors, window frames and even pickle jars that had been in a kitchen were scattered outside.

I realized that I, too, had been blown some distance by the blast. My second oldest sister was bleeding. It looked like something blown through the air had hit her head. Maybe she was too stunned, but she didn't even cry out in pain. None of the children I had been playing with was crying. No one was able to make a sound due to the extreme horror. We couldn't even cry.

My oldest sister and other older children who saw the completely transformed landscape around us led us toward the shelter on top of the hill where my mother and the neighbors were working. The road was blocked by debris from fallen buildings. We could hardly walk.

On the way, we saw a man who seemed to be stirring the water in a small irrigation reservoir with a bamboo stick and crying.

I asked him, "What are you doing?"

He said, "My son and I were working in the field, and now he's gone."

I learned later that the child had been thrown into the reservoir and struck the bottom forcefully.

Fighting our way around the debris, we finally arrived at the shelter after almost an hour, though it usually took about 10 minutes. By the time we arrived, our mother was nowhere to be seen. Later we learned that, despite her big belly with the unborn baby, she and some others had been carrying large logs with which to support the ceiling of the shelter to keep it from falling down.

We found her climbing the stone steps from the vacant lot next to the school. She said she had been blown all the way down to a ditch by the blast. However, she had no serious injuries and did not lose the baby. As soon as my younger sisters saw our mother, they clung to her and, for the first time since the bomb exploded, started crying.

Because of Nagasaki's hills and valleys, we couldn't see the area around the hypocenter. We didn't know what had happened.

That evening, black smoke rose up from the area near Nagasaki Station. The flames sped fiercely up the slope. The remaining houses started burning one after another. By nightfall, the whole area was a sea of fire.

People in the shelter were muttering desperately. "The house is burning! My house is burning!" When the fire spread to Nishizaka Elementary School, a heavy sigh echoed through the shelter.

Eventually, even our house on top of the hill was enveloped in flames. We watched our house burn from a field in front of the shelter. The fire burned bright red, making the night as bright as day. We could do nothing but watch in a daze.

Because their house had burnt down, Yasuko and her family stayed in the shelter for some time. The shelter was filled with people, leaving no space to stretch out. Yasuko and her older sisters leaned on their mother, being careful not to push on her belly. Her younger sisters rested on their mother's lap.

In the evening when it got cool, some people left the shelter, but being afraid a B-29 might come at any moment, they lay down in a field or under a tree just to stretch their bodies. It was the height of summer, and eggplants, tomatoes and sweet potatoes grew in the fields. Because they had no way to cook anything, they ate them raw. Yasuko looks back at that time, saying, "It's horrifying that we ate food so covered by radiation."

It took their father two days to find them. He had been working at the ordnance factory, and they were sure he was dead. They were deep in grief at his loss when, to their surprise, he somehow managed to get back to them despite a severe leg injury.

Their father described what he had seen on his way back. People roaming around begging for water. People washed away down the Urakami River. A baby still sucking at the breast of his dead mother. People whose skin was hideously burnt and in tatters, even their gender unrecognizable, groaning, "Hot! I'm so hot!" He described a living hell.

Yasuko's grandmother's house was further up the hill. Fortunately, her house was shielded by a road and a cliff, so the fire didn't claim it. Since her grandmother's house had escaped the fire, they moved in there after her father came back. Twenty relatives from four families who had lived in Nagasaki sought shelter there and lived under one roof for some time.

I learned the war had ended from the Emperor's announcement of Japan's surrender, which was broadcast on August 15, but I couldn't understand the meaning of "the end of the war." Overall, it seemed the adults were feeling relief that the B-29s would not be coming anymore.

I believe it was the day after the end of the war. I had not uttered a scream or cry at the time of the atomic bombing, but when a thunderclap sounded even though it wasn't raining, I was so scared that I jumped up and screamed. The adults around me also thought an enemy plane had come. Even my father clasped his youngest daughter to his side and rushed out of the house.

At the end of August, my whole family boarded a ship from the port at Ohato to go to my uncle's house. Today, we can go there in an hour by car, but in those days there was no road. We had to go by ferry, and there was no direct ferry. We changed boats several times. The boats got smaller and smaller until the last one, a rowboat, landed with only my family on board.

There were many injured victims on the bigger boats. During the war, many students were mobilized from faraway islands to Nagasaki City. Those students were exposed to the atomic bombing, and their parents or relatives came to Nagasaki to take them home. They were taken on board without sufficient treatment, and their wounds were open burns, festering and drawing swarms of flies.

Some of them were already dead. I'm sure the parents at least wanted to have their loved ones buried on their home island. Corpses were wrapped in blankets and laid on stretchers. I felt pity for them to some extent, but I couldn't bear that horrible smell. All I wanted was to get out of that boat as soon as possible.

We finally arrived at my uncle's house, but we were treated badly because we had been exposed to the atomic bombing. My uncle's family lived in a rural area far from Nagasaki City. No one had been exposed, and no one understood our suffering. They hated my family because they thought the effects of the atomic bomb were contagious. They worried about what the other villagers might think.

Not only did they refuse to let us into their house, they didn't let us into the empty annex either. We were given a shed filled with farm equipment and fertilizer. We borrowed some fields around the shed and planted vegetables on our own to have something to eat.

Our father had a job in Nagasaki and soon went back to work. Once we became an all-female household, the discrimination went from bad to terrible.

The Dondo Festival was the finale of the New Year's celebrations. This big event in the village featured the burning of ornaments displayed during the New Year holidays. Feeling the excitement, my younger sisters and I were eager to go out. The family told us, "Don't leave the shed while village people are at the festival." I begged my mother, saying I wanted to go to the festival. She looked sad and said, "We owe them our lives, so let's forget about it."

My oldest sister had gone several times to see what was going on at the festival and finally confirmed that all the villagers were gone. She took us to the site, but the fire had already gone out. It was just coals and ash.

There was a beautiful beach right behind our shed, and when it got dark and the other people left, our oldest sister took us to dig for shellfish. The villagers had already dug the shellfish thoroughly, so there were almost none left. But our younger sisters were happy playing with sand and digging for small shells. I also felt some brief enjoyment. We found some beautiful empty shells and took them home to play with.

Meanwhile, we got a new brother in October. People around us were still thinking that exposure to the atomic bombing was like a contagious disease. My mother delivered our brother by herself in the shed with no help from any midwife or nurse.

My sisters, who were 12 and 10, helped with the delivery by boiling water and collecting cloth rags according to her directions. Our brother was given the name Hatsuo because he was the first boy in our family. We five sisters took every opportunity to surround him, touch him and stroke him. Even though our mother scolded us, we couldn't stay away from him.

The following year, Yasuko's father built a shack in the city, so the family went back to Nagasaki. In April, eight months after the atomic bombing, Nagasaki was still a burnt plain.

I started at Nishizaka Elementary School in 1946. It was called a school, but it was a hastily constructed wooden building with few classrooms and not enough of anything. First and second graders shared a room, one in the morning, the other in the afternoon. Sometimes we were taught while sitting on the stone steps outside.

During this time of severe shortages, Yasuko's father managed to find a paper carp streamer to celebrate Boy's Day in May for Hatsuo. He put it up in front of the house. The colorful banner streaming in the wind was a great source of pride for Hatsuo's sisters, even though they were girls. In addition, for the New Year holiday, her parents made new dresses for all five sisters. They bought battledores and shuttlecocks for a game played on New Year's Day. Each of them received ones of almost the same size and pattern, to avoid fighting. The girls joyfully compared what they had received.

My brother Hatsuo started to walk holding onto furniture when he was about a year old. But after he walked two or three steps, he would fall heavily on his bottom. I remember thinking that was strange. He developed big boils on both sides of his belly. They swelled up big and red. Soon they broke and discharged pus. He screamed loud and long because of the pain. I felt so sorry to see such big boils on such a small body.

He was taken to a hospital where the doctor opened his boils. After cleaning out the pus they filled them with gauze, but the openings of the wounds were like gaping holes. They looked very painful.

The doctor said, "He won't live to be 10 years old." Before long, his boils were completely healed, but his backbone remained bent due to the aftereffects. He also developed myocardial infarction, cerebral infarction and other illnesses one after another. I have often thought this could have been due to in utero exposure.

After graduating from school I took various jobs. My last job was making Chinese sweets. I worked there until I was 68.

My husband is also a *hibakusha*, but I didn't worry about his exposure when we got married. There was a time when rumor had it that A-bomb survivors would have deformed babies. Since my sisters had healthy babies, I didn't worry when I was pregnant. My children and grandchildren are all fine.

My father, oldest and second oldest sisters died of heart disease. My mother died of liver and pancreatic cancer. My youngest sister died of uterine and colorectal cancer. My brother, who developed so many diseases and was told that he wouldn't live until 10, is doing well. My younger sister and I had no major illnesses and are healthy today.

We must never allow our children, grandchildren or any of the generations to come to suffer the pain that the *hibakusha* have experienced.

Masaki Morimoto
1,500 students reduced to 100

Born in April 1933, Masaki Morimoto was exposed to the atomic bombing while swimming in an irrigation reservoir in Shiroyamamachi, 1.2 kilometers from the hypocenter in Nagasaki. He was 12. He was one of fewer than 100 out of around 1,500 students at Shiroyama Elementary School who survived.

That morning, about 9 a.m., Masaki, a sixth grader at Shiroyama Elementary School, went to a nearby reservoir to swim with 10 friends from his neighborhood. It was already a hot, humid day, so all 10 boys were swimming in skimpy loincloths.

I want to tell my story for the sake of my classmates

We were about to go home. We had been swimming energetically, so we were tired and hungry. Some were putting on shirts and trousers. A few of us were about to climb up to the top of the bank, when a fifth grader pointed up at the sky and yelled, "Wow, a parachute bomb! Look at that!"

Others ran up the bank, saying, "What is it?" A strange three-umbrella parachute was riding on the wind, coming closer and closer out of the sky over the Nagasaki Shipyard. When it was right above the wooded area near us, everything turned pure white and I lost consciousness. I remember feeling as if I were in a white cloud.

When I came to, I was in the irrigation reservoir. I must have been blown down the bank and into the water. I was quite lucky to have fallen into the water. My body was instantly soaked in water, which countered the burns. Also, I had turned my face away, so it was spared. However, I did have burns on my head, belly, arms and legs.

My chest felt too hot. I put my hand where it hurt, and the skin stuck to my hand. Much of the skin on my chest peeled right off. My clothes were burnt to tatters, and the skin on my arms had nearly all peeled off. When I looked up the bank, I saw only two or three of my friends. I heard later that seven of us died in less than a week.

Masaki staggered home alone from the reservoir to his house in Shiroyama. On his way, he saw houses flattened as if they had been stamped on. These smashed houses lined the road. So much debris was scattered around, he could hardly find places to step. He often didn't even know if he was walking on the ground or on smashed roofs.

I finally got home, but the house had been knocked over by the blast. I couldn't find a way in. I stood in a daze in front of my house, feeling the strength draining out of me. People barely able to move were taking refuge in a shelter near my house, and I started walking toward it. I had been walking barefoot, and all of a sudden, I couldn't walk anymore. I looked down at my feet and found the base of my right big toe split open. The toe was just dangling, almost torn off.

I held my big toe on and, crawling, I made it to the shelter. Some others came crawling in by themselves. Others came in on someone's back or in someone's arms. The survivors in our shelter were pitiful—one in particular. His eyeballs were nearly out of their sockets, leaving big open holes on his face. Two days later, his eyeball sockets were full of maggots wriggling in and out through the holes in the sockets.

Another one had glass shards piercing her whole body. There was nothing any of us could do to help. I couldn't stand the smell and moaning. I crawled out, found a dry streambed in front of the shelter, and lay there for two days.

After a while, my father came looking for me. As soon as he found me, he scolded me, saying, "I told you to come to the field. Why didn't you come?" My father had cultivated some land on a hillside to plant potatoes. I had gone to help him the day before, but the day of the bombing my friends came by my house, so I went swimming instead.

Later, I learned that my mother was unconscious. A beam in our collapsed house had hit her head.

My father collected usable pillars and beams from our broken house and leaned them against trees in front of our house. He made a space about big enough to lay three tatami mats and let me lie down there. My burns suppurated, with pus oozing from the open wounds.

We had lots of bees that summer. Bees flew over to drink my pus.

If I drove them away, they stung me before leaving. That was quite painful, so I couldn't really drive away bees or flies. As a result, I was soon infested with maggots. Maggots crawling around my wounds and bees coming to drink my pus—I was a living corpse. I was completely miserable.

My big toe was fixed tightly with relative ease. We rubbed it with potato vines. However, the burns from my chest to belly were much harder to cure than I expected.

About a week after the bombing, a relief station was created in an open space on the grounds of Shiroyama Elementary School. Masaki's father carried him on his back to the school. Finally, he was able to get something like medical treatment.

They put a kind of oil on my burns and used a big triangular cloth instead of a bandage. They put it on my stomach like a waistband, tying it behind my back. This was a terrible mistake. The cloth became solid with bloody pus and adhered to my wounds. It was nearly impossible to peel off. They soaked it in water starting at the edge and peeled it off slowly during the next three days. The skin from my chest to my belly peeled completely off after all. A liquid oozed from my bare red flesh, but we decided to let my skin dry out naturally without any bandage.

Strangely, I didn't feel much pain or sorrow. I had no feeling to see the bodies of my friends. I think my nerves were just completely paralyzed.

Masaki's father thought it was too pitiful to lay him down more or less on the ground outside, even in the three-tatami-mat space. He was temporarily moved to his uncle's house in Kawaramachi, where his two older sisters were already being cared for. Two months later, Masaki's father, who had some carpentry skills, built a shack out of scraps from their crushed house. Masaki returned to this two six-mat room shack.

During this period, I struggled not only with the burns from chest to belly but also with chronic diarrhea and the loss of my hair. My father bought Chinese herbal medicine for me that cost 50 yen (equivalent to between $500 and $1,000 today). He had me take it, saying, "Don't waste this valuable medicine." It was bitter and difficult to drink, but it had marvelous effects. It was expensive, so I took it only once a day, but first my diarrhea and hair loss stopped, then my consciousness grew clear again. I didn't apply any ointment, and yet my chest and belly improved rapidly, forming scabs. My burns began to improve. Still, my chest and belly looked like a turtle's stomach. The scabs all over them became extremely itchy and I could hardly stand it.

By November that year, my scabs were nearly gone, and I received notice that my school would reopen. I went to school and found out that nearly all my classmates were dead. Of the 1,500 students that had been enrolled at Shiroyama Elementary School, fewer than 100 had survived.

We began receiving lessons in a room rented from Inasa Elementary School, located three kilometers from our school. The following spring all the sixth graders graduated. We graduates numbered 14.

That summer, my oldest sister, who had stayed at our uncle's house in Kawaramachi, died of A-bomb disease. Another older sister who had had no injuries at all died of leukemia in 1951.

In 1968, 23 years after the bombing, the first Shiroyama Elementary School reunion was organized by a TV station. The 14 who had graduated together were down to nine. Classmates continued to die year after year; there are scarcely any of us left today.

If I were asked for memories of Shiroyama Elementary School, I would have to say that lessons stopped even before the summer holiday and we mostly had days off. Thus, I really have very few memories. One thing I do recall is that our schoolyard turned into a farm. I clearly remember growing peas and potatoes.

When he was 17, thanks to a recommendation from a neighbor, Masaki got a job at the Civil Engineering Department of Nagasaki City Hall, where he worked for 30 years. He then became a security guard there for 14 years.

Masaki married in 1957. His wife was two years older than him and came from Futsucho. They had two daughters and have had a happy marriage. He developed prostate cancer when he was 73, but recovered.

Among my best memories are the times when my wife would put our very small daughter on her back, then get onto the back of my motorbike and we would ride into downtown Nagasaki on my days off.

Because I was blown into a reservoir, I could easily have died that day. And yet, here I am, still alive. I'm deeply grateful for this. I decided to tell my A-bomb story for future generations primarily on behalf of my many classmates at Shiroyama Elementary School who have gone ahead before me.

Mitsuko Iwamoto
The atomic bomb shows no mercy to women

Born in March 1937, Mitsuko Iwamoto was exposed to the atomic bombing near her home, 500 meters from the hypocenter in Nagasaki. She was eight and suffered serious burns. Her parents and sister died, leaving her completely alone. She suffered from extreme anemia, but got married when she was 27. She survived three dangerous deliveries with heavy blood loss and the near death of one of the babies.

Mitsuko's father was a policeman. He had died while serving in Korea several years before the bombing. Her mother was raising Mitsuko (aged eight) and her sister (six) while working for Mitsubishi Steel Works. Mitsuko's aunt and her three daughters also lived with them because her husband was a soldier serving in the Philippines.

I never told my husband about my exposure

I was a third grader at Shiroyama Elementary School. I have no fun memories of school: school events like trips and sports meetings were canceled. My classroom was on the third floor. Whenever an air-raid warning sounded, we had to run down to the first floor to the shelter. My only memory is of rushing down the stairs every time the warning sounded.

My house was near Hachiman Shrine, a 15-minute walk to the school for us children. We went to school in a group, walking behind the school building. The roots from trees spread across this small lane, and when it rained, the lane soon got muddy. It was quite a difficult walk on rainy days. When we arrived at school, older students would be watching us from the upstairs windows. They would shout, "Your arms weren't swinging together, and you weren't marching in time." They made us start over, marching in single file. That drove me crazy.

It was summer vacation. I was playing with my friends, two sisters from next door. I looked up as the airplanes flew over us. I saw them drop something black. The next instant, there was a tremendous flash, and we were blown off our feet by the blast.

A huge apricot tree fell over. I was lying on the ground with a root of the tree pressing down on my neck. I had serious burns over the right half of my body. The two sisters I had been playing with were trapped by the tree's branches. All three of us managed to get away from the tree and take refuge on the hillside.

The hill soon filled with people taking refuge there. Many didn't even look like human beings. Their arms and chests were burnt and covered with reddish sores. Mitsuko and her two friends went to a shelter, but it was full. They sat down by a spring that trickled by in front of the shelter and waited for daybreak. The next morning, one of the sisters was dead. Of the students enrolled at Shiroyama Elementary School, 93 percent died in the atomic bombing.

My mother had been at Mitsubishi Steel Works and fled to an evacuation site in Nagayo. The next day, she went to my uncle's house to get my sister and bring her home. It had been decided that my uncle would adopt my sister, so she was frequently sent to his house. When my mother reached his house, it was gone. It was nothing but a heartbreaking mountain of smoldering debris filled with an unbearable stench. My mother looked desperately for my sister in the burnt ruins, but in vain.

It seems my sister was blown away by the blast and incinerated somewhere by the fire. My mother stuffed some earth from the ruins into a pot in lieu of her ashes and brought the pot home.

Mitsuko's aunt had been hanging out the wash in front of the house. She suffered serious burns from head to toe. Miraculously, she was still alive. Mitsuko's mother borrowed a cart from a neighbor and laid her completely burnt sister in it. Then she put Mitsuko and her cousins at the other end of the cart. They headed for the relief station at Shinkozen Elementary School.

The relief station was so full of injured victims there was no space even to walk. But their house was gone and they had been living in a shelter, so they stayed in the school.

My aunt's burns were so bad she had maggots crawling all over her. My mother would pick them out of her wounds one by one with a twig. My aunt soon died, and my mother cremated her sister by herself. When my mother came home with my aunt's ashes, one of my cousins had died. She had to go back again to cremate her.

I was able to walk a little, but my right leg didn't bend at all. I crawled in order to move about the house. My mother often carried me on her back and took me to get massages. The massages on my rigid right leg were so painful I couldn't stand it. I cried and screamed, but my mother pressed me down, saying, "You have to bear this, Mitsuko! This is your only hope of ever walking normally!" For years, I shivered with fright just hearing the word "massage." But I am extremely grateful to my mother. Thanks to her, I am able to walk.

After the atomic bombing, Mitsuko and her mother lived with her uncle on Hisaka, one of the Goto Islands. When they arrived on the island, Mitsuko was barely conscious. She looked like a corpse. Her hair had fallen out, and she was nothing but skin and bone. All she did was moan, "I'm dying! It's killing me!" Seeing her in such agony, people said she'd suffer less if she could just die quickly. People around her were always thinking, "Will it be today or tomorrow?" But Mitsuko clung to life.

I was confined to bed. I couldn't even go to the bathroom without my mother holding me like a baby. One day when I had finished a bowel movement and was on my way back from the yard to my room, still being supported by my mother, something gushed out of my body.

My mother thought it was urine and scolded me. When we looked more carefully, a swelling in my groin had broken open, and something like pus had poured out. My mother later said, "I wonder if the gas you breathed from the atomic bomb collected there."

The scar from that wound is still a large indentation. I also had swellings on my knee and ankle. I had them cut and the pus discharged at a hospital. After that, I began improving quickly day by day. By April the next year I was ready to start the third grade again.

I entered an elementary school on Hisaka Island, but I was bullied. I was called "red spider lily." My hair didn't grow back for a long time, and when it finally came in, it was kinky, kind of dancing on my head. I was ashamed and sad, a miserable young girl.

Her mother remarried soon after Mitsuko went back to school. Her stepfather was the husband of her late aunt. He had lost his wife and three daughters, so he was alone. He returned from the Philippines to his house on Hisaka Island. Mitsuko liked him very much. Her mother had declared she would never marry again, but seeing Mitsuko being so happy with him, and he with her, she decided to marry him.

They had four boys and girls. But then one day, my mother suddenly fell ill while working on the farm. She passed away on the way to the hospital in Fukue. Her youngest child was still nursing. It had been 10 years since the bombing, but the cause was A-bomb disease.

I was 18 at the time. I had a stepfamily from my mother's remarriage, but in a sense I was suddenly truly alone. Worse yet, my stepfather developed gangrene and couldn't move. I was forced to take care of my four younger siblings and do all the housework. Plus, I had to do the farm work my mother had been doing.

I would drop my two brothers off at nursery school and pull the three-year-old along by his hand. I would put the nursing baby and lunchbox together in a big basket and carry them on my back. I took them with me to the potato field or the rice field.

I had the three-year-old boy watch the baby while I planted seedlings or potato cuttings. I had no milk, of course, so I softened some potatoes in my mouth and fed that to the baby. I was literally their surrogate mother.

The days wore on. I worked so hard I was completely exhausted by evening. My only break was taking firewood to my relatives' house where they let me take a bath. Soothing my little siblings as they cried for their mother, I wanted to cry myself. To make matters even more unbearable, my relationship with my stepfather's mother was bad and got worse as time went by.

Her uncle on her father's side was living in Nagasaki and felt sorry for Mitsuko. He invited her to stay with him. Although she was worried about leaving her siblings, she knew she was on the edge, physically and emotionally. She decided to leave the house, entrusting the children to her stepfather's mother.

Just when I thought, "Finally, I can start my own life," I had to go to the Atomic Bomb Hospital regularly. My exposure and too much hard work had given me extreme anemia. I tired easily and often got dizzy just standing up. It was hard even to get to the hospital.

When I reached that age, my uncle brought me an offer of marriage. However, I had heard the rumor that A-bomb survivors have deformed babies, so I had decided I would never marry. But when I was 27, my uncle pushed me very hard, so I got married to an electrical engineer. Soon after we got married, my mother-in-law, who lived in Saga, visited us. She had heard something about me and asked directly, "You were in the atomic bombing, weren't you?" I admitted it honestly. My mother-in-law said nothing, but I could see in her face that she was upset.

I thought my husband would say something about it that night, but he didn't. I don't know if his mother didn't tell him or if she told him but he didn't mention it. Therefore I left it alone. I never told my husband that I was an A-bomb survivor.

When I was pregnant with my first child, I was more nervous about the baby's health than I was joyful about becoming a mother. It was agony every day. What if my baby were deformed? I had been exposed outside, unshielded. Anything could happen. My thoughts went round in circles, and grew darker and darker. I couldn't sleep at night and lost my appetite. All I did was pray continually that my baby would be born with no defects.

When the time came, I was still in a state of high anxiety. I gave birth in January 1965 at a private clinic. The doctor was a woman, so I immediately grabbed her and asked, "Is there anything abnormal about my child? Does it have all its fingers and toes?"

She replied, "You have a healthy boy." The anxiety that had bothered me so much melted away immediately. But since I had been so anxious for so long, I felt all the strength in my body drain out of me, and my joy was short-lived. Eight hours after the delivery, I felt something clammy below the waist. I was hemorrhaging badly.

When I had been going to the Atomic Bomb Hospital, I had been worried about anemia. Now, I was diagnosed with leukemia and hemophilia, characterized by an increase in red blood cells.

Immediately they prepared a blood transfusion. I was attached to a tube and stayed in the clinic for more than a week.

Despite my poor overall health, my breasts swelled normally, and I experienced the great joy of motherhood, holding my son in my arms as he nursed eagerly.

Mitsuko was saved from death by a blood transfusion after her first delivery, but she confronted crises with each subsequent birth. She chose the well-equipped City Hospital for her second delivery, but again, she suffered massive bleeding and was in a critical condition due to anemia.

Because of that experience, I went to the even better-equipped University Hospital for the delivery of my second daughter. However, the baby stayed in the birth canal too long. She was born unconscious and not breathing. I felt so sorry for her and apologized to her, crying, "I'm sorry my pushing was so weak! Please, please don't die!"

The nurse slapped the baby many times and finally she let out her first cry. When I heard her voice, I was so happy I almost jumped out of the bed to hold her.

The atomic bomb is especially cruel to women. Some were denied marriage because they were hibakusha. *Others gave up on marriage, or if they got married, they gave up on having children because of the rumor that they would give birth to deformed babies. Many who got pregnant endured hellish days due to anxiety. And, like Mitsuko, many risked their lives each time they gave birth. The atomic bomb inflicts terrible suffering on mothers, whose natural role is to nurture new life.*

Isao Yoshida
66,000 signatures demanding the abolition of nuclear weapons

Born in August 1940, Isao Yoshida was four years old when he was exposed to the atomic bombing in his home at Nakashinmachi, 3.9 kilometers from the Nagasaki hypocenter. After graduating from junior high school, he worked in restaurants and a cafe and then opened a Chinese restaurant. He married and had a son and three daughters. He had never told anyone about his A-bomb experience until, after reading second Soka Gakkai president Josei Toda's 1957 Declaration Calling for the Abolition of Nuclear Weapons, he decided he could not remain silent any longer.

Isao was the second son of parents who managed a china shop. His father died young; his older brother died when Isao was two. His mother was in her mid-20s and, taking his grandmother's advice, remarried. Isao went to live with his grandmother. Three years later, 15 days before Isao turned five, the atomic bomb was dropped on Nagasaki.

"A blank for 48 years! I turned my back on the atomic bombing for that long."

I was at home at Nakashinmachi near Hollander Slope, 3.9 kilometers from the hypocenter. My grandmother was doing her wash at a community well. I was playing next to her when she suddenly shouted, "Enemy planes! Get indoors!"

Rushing in through our back door, I turned and glanced back up at the sky. I remember the shiny American plane. Just as my grandmother entered the back door with the wash, the world outside of our window was brilliantly illuminated by a bright light. I didn't hear anything like an explosion, but a strong wind shook the sliding paper doors causing the house to rattle.

I stood still for a while. For some reason, I started to worry about my desk. I went upstairs and found the window glass shattered. A chest and bookcase had fallen over. My room was enveloped in thick smoke that was swirling up as if somebody had turned over a charcoal grill.

"Let's run for the shelter," Grandma said to me in a daze. I left the house holding her hand. The sky was cloudy and dark, like twilight. I learned later that the atomic cloud had covered the whole sky, blocking the sunlight.

On our way through the dim light to the air-raid shelter located halfway up a hill about 40 to 50 meters from our house, I couldn't think of anything but my thirst.

"I want some water! Give me water!" I said. A soldier came over and gave me his canteen. I can still remember how delicious that water was.

We made our way, pushing aside debris from fallen houses. I saw a galvanized sheet swinging and about to fall from the roof of a collapsed house. Suddenly, it dropped and fell right toward me. I escaped a direct hit, but the edge scratched my mouth, making a deep cut 2.5 centimeters long. Blood gushed out.

My grandmother handed me the cotton towel that had been covering her head. I pressed it down on my cut crying, "It hurts! It hurts!" We finally reached the shelter. I still carry the scar from that cut.

When I turned back and looked out from the entrance to the shelter, I saw red flames rising up all around the railway station. The fire was spreading very rapidly. By the next day, it had burnt a third of our neighborhood.

There were so many people in the shelter it was impossible to move. The smell of sweat and burns made me sick. Still, people naked from the waist up and others burnt and blistered all over were carried in on wooden doors one after the next. I remember round slices of cucumber being placed on red skin. They used cucumbers as an emergency treatment for burns because that was all they had.

We stayed in the shelter that night and returned home the next day. Our house and the houses in our immediate area escaped the fire. I continued to live with my grandmother and entered Nita Elementary School a year and a half later.

Soon after Isao entered elementary school, his grandmother fell ill. The following year, he was sent to his aunt's house in Gamagori, Aichi Prefecture. Isao lived there from second grade to his second year in junior high school. His aunt and her husband had no child of their own, and they took loving care of Isao. But having moved to a completely new place, he developed the strong feeling that he was all alone. He felt he would have to live his life by himself.

Disorders due to radiation were generally called "A-bomb disease," and two of the eleven certified disorders were applicable to me. One is spondylosis deformans, an inflammation of the spinal joints. Mine gets worse every year. Another is reduced white blood cell count. My main symptom is scabs all over my body. A crop of pimples or sores develops somewhere on my body, on my head, face, chest, back and so on. They suppurate and ooze pus, then produce scabs. The pain and itchiness drive me crazy. In Nagasaki when I was younger and then in Gamagori, this caused me to get bullied at school. They called me "Scab Boy!"

That bullying was one reason I decided to get rid of my A-bomb experience. By "get rid" I didn't mean not talking about it: I simply decided the whole thing had nothing to do with me. Once I cut my relationship to the atomic bombing, I had no problem seeing TV reports or newspaper articles regarding the annual ceremonies on August 9. I was not just enduring the pain. I actually made it go away. The bombing was something that had nothing to do with me. I believe this was partly made possible by not living in Nagasaki from the second grade of elementary school until the second year in junior high school. I was living with my aunt in Aichi Prefecture when I convinced myself that my A-bomb exposure had gone away.

I don't remember if it was candy or sweet cake, but I remember wanting something sweet. I took some money from my foster father's wallet to buy some sweets. He knew I stole his money, but he didn't say anything.

His kindness made me feel bad. It made me decide to work so I could buy what I wanted with my own money. When I was a first-year student in junior high school, I started delivering newspapers. I was very happy when I bought the boots I wanted so much with my first paycheck.

Just before Isao started his third year of junior high, his foster father retired, and the family fell on hard times. Isao was sent to live with another of his father's sisters. Their house was on Gunkanjima Island in Nagasaki Prefecture.

Gunkanjima Island was a coalmine for Mitsubishi Shipbuilding and was thriving due to the postwar restoration boom. His new home was on the seventh floor of a high-rise building, which were quite rare at that time. Isao completed junior high school on Gunkanjima Island and got a live-in job at a bakery in Nagasaki City.

His job was to operate a machine that cut bread dough, loaf by loaf. After three months, he pushed some dough into the machine with his finger extended too far into the machine. He suffered a serious injury that took part of his left index finger.

He was moved to the cake section and worked there for a while. Then he heard from his grandmother that his father had always wanted to open a cafe, a wish Isao discovered he shared.

He started to work at a cafe in Nagasaki and then went to Tokyo to study the cafe business. Starting at a coffee stand at Takashimaya Department Store, he studied for three years in Tokyo. He had promised his grandmother he would go back to Nagasaki after three years, but there was no job for him when he returned. He worked at several places including a Chinese noodle stand, and finally got a job at a Chinese restaurant in Nagasaki. There he trained himself as a cook and later opened his own restaurant.

Now that he had his own business, a relative introduced him to a young woman as a prospective marriage partner. He was very busy because he had just opened his restaurant, but he went on two dates with her. The third time he met her was at their wedding ceremony at her parents' house in Shimabara. Because he had decided he had no relationship whatsoever to the atomic bombing, he didn't tell her about his exposure, even after she became his wife.

I will never forget that when she was about to give birth to our first son, all of a sudden, I was filled with anxiety. I remembered that I had been exposed to the atomic bombing, so I thought, "What if the baby's deformed?" I had never told my wife about my exposure, so my anxiety just grew and grew, one sleepless night after the next.

On the day of the birth, I stood in front of the delivery room, praying, "Please let our baby be born normal." I was so relieved to find out that the baby had no defects. After that, I applied for an Atomic Bomb Survivor Health Book just in case something happened to my health.

We were blessed with one boy and three girls, but I was still determined never to tell anyone about my exposure.

My first daughter married when I was 53. The full text of Josei Toda's Declaration Calling for the Abolition of Nuclear Weapons was displayed on the second floor at the Soka Gakkai community center where my daughter's wedding ceremony took place. The display was the size of a tatami mat (about 3 x 6 feet), and I was casually looking at it when my eyes were drawn to a certain part of the text. "Even if a country should conquer the world through the use of nuclear weapons, the conquerors must be viewed as devils, as evil incarnate." Before I knew what I was doing, I was writing the whole text in my notebook.

The Declaration concluded as follows: "I believe it is the mission of every member of the youth division in Japan to disseminate this idea throughout the globe." What if we were to change the words "member of the youth division" to "A-bomb survivors"? It was at that moment that I thought again about the atomic bombing experience I had concealed for 48 years, ever since I was five years old. It rose up within me, and I determined, "I can't stay silent. I have to raise my voice!"

As soon as I got home, I made a phone call to City Hall and requested the phone numbers of the four survivors' organizations I had heard were in Nagasaki City. I called all of them and ended up applying for membership of the Nagasaki Atomic Bomb Survivors Council because its secretary, Mr. Yamada, was so kind to me.

I attended my first sit-in demonstration, convened by the Citizens' Group to Protest Nuclear Testing, the next Sunday in the Nagasaki Peace Park. I have continued such activities, and my 43rd sit-in demonstration was to protest the third underground nuclear test by North Korea in 2013.

I didn't mean to hide my activities from my family, but thinking that they were not important enough to mention, I kept silent. Then, during one of the sit-ins, I appeared on TV. My wife was watching the news and said, "Hey, that's my husband! What's he doing there?"

That is when my four children learned what I was doing. Now they know they are second-generation *hibakusha*, and I hope they will eventually become active. At the moment, they are not as interested as I am. I certainly expect my grandchildren to do something.

"A blank for 48 years! I turned my back on the atomic bombing for that long." This feeling grew into a great source of irritation, and I began thinking, "I have to fill that blank."

One day, I received an invitation from a person I was with at a sit-in. "We're going to deliver petitions opposing nuclear tests to the embassies of nuclear-weapon states in Tokyo. Why don't you come with us?"

"Yes, please take me along." I immediately decided to join that group.

I went to Tokyo many times, delivering petitions against nuclear testing to the US, Russian and other embassies, and the Japanese Ministry of Foreign Affairs.

In Nagasaki, one of our annual nuclear weapons abolition activities is the High School Students Signature Campaign. The committee that directs that campaign selects Hiroshima-Nagasaki Peace Messengers to deliver the signed petitions to UN Headquarters in New York.

In 1999, I was invited to go to UN Headquarters. I ended up being appointed delegation leader and went to the UN with three high school Peace Messengers on November 15, 1999. We visited Under-Secretary-General Jayantha Dhanapala and gave him 66,048 signatures on petitions calling for the elimination of nuclear weapons. Mr. Dhanapala told us that he was genuinely grateful for our action. Peace Messengers also deliver signatures to the UN Office at Geneva.

I visited UN Headquarters in New York in 2005, 2008 and 2010. When we visited in 2005, we observed the Nuclear Non-Proliferation Treaty Review Conference, and met with a group of NGOs in New York. Some of the delegates stressed how important it was to hear survivors of the atomic bombings of Hiroshima and

Nagasaki speak. "We want to hear directly from *hibakusha*. We want you to speak."

On May 5 that year, we toured the National Museum of the US Air Force in Dayton, Ohio. The B-29 *Bockscar*, which dropped the atomic bomb on Nagasaki, was displayed, all polished and shiny. "This is the one that dropped the bomb! This plane caused all those casualties!" I was speechless. My body shivered with anger.

The Nagasaki Peace Ceremony on August 9, 2012, was attended by Clifton Truman Daniel, grandson of President Truman, the man who ordered the dropping of the atomic bombs. Clifton is promoting the abolition of nuclear weapons. I met him by chance, and we pledged to work together to eliminate nuclear weapons. That "historic handshake" to move beyond our tragic past is an unforgettable memory for me.

I hold firmly in my mind the humanism and absolute pacifism contained in Josei Toda's Declaration Calling for the Abolition of Nuclear Weapons. That document changed my life. As a person who experienced an atomic bombing, I am determined to continue working as hard as I can for the total abolition of nuclear weapons.

Yuriyo Hama
I hid my A-bomb exposure from my husband

Born in October 1935, Yuriyo Hama was exposed to the atomic bombing at home in Inasamachi, two kilometers from the hypocenter in Nagasaki. She was nine years old. After losing her mother to the atomic bombing, she and her older siblings had to make a living by themselves. She married at 22, and was often confined to bed due to poor health, but gave birth to a healthy girl.

Yuriyo was the fourth of seven children, three boys and four girls. Her eldest sister was 15, her eldest brother was 13, and she was nine at the time of the bombing. Her father had been sent to Saipan; her mother lived with the children in Inasamachi. Her eldest sister and brother commuted to the Mitsubishi shipyard for labor service.

I picked up my mother's ashes and put them in a broken bowl

Because my mother was physically weak, she always called me to her side and made me help her take care of things. She always said, "Girls must be modest."

August 9, 1945, 11:02 a.m.

A yellow alert had cleared, and the whole city was silent, quiet enough to be eerie.

That morning we had received some rations from the neighborhood association. Each family got two handfuls of *adzuki* beans. My mother had put a pot on the kitchen stove and was cooking sweet bean soup using saccharin instead of sugar. In those days we hardly ever got sweets, so even a single mouthful of sweet bean soup per person was a great treat. We were eagerly looking forward to it being ready.

Finally, my mother said, "It's ready, but it's hot, so I'll let you eat it later when it cools down." In that instant, the flash struck us, followed by a tremendous booooming blast.

The house tilted over but stayed standing. My mother, my siblings and I were all blown off our feet by the blast. The sweet bean soup flew in all directions. I could see straight out of the house and saw lots of clothes flying through the air like kites.

My seven-year-old brother had been taking a nap on the veranda. He was seriously burnt all over his body. Looking for someplace cool, I had been lying next to him. But as the sun rose higher, it was getting hot on the veranda so I had woken up and gone inside. My brother had especially terrible burns on his face and arms. My mother was distraught when she saw him so grotesquely transformed.

My sister and brother came home from labor service that evening. We decided to go to my uncle's house in my mother's hometown, Sotome, Nishi Sonogi County. We waited for daybreak. Her hometown was eight kilometers from our house in Inasamachi.

My eldest sister carried our burnt brother on her back. On the way she frequently asked, "Are you still alive?" "Are you still alive?" She only started walking again when she knew he was breathing.

When we came to Ohashi Bridge over the Urakami River, we saw a crowd of people who looked like seals. They were completely black with soot. Most of them were mumbling something about water. They walked right into the river and were washed away.

My brother was thirsty and kept weakly gasping, "Water, water!" We had heard that if we gave him water, he would die. We managed to soothe him along the way and finally arrived at my uncle's house.

As soon as we arrived, my mother said, "I'm worried about our house in Inasamachi," and went back to take care of the damaged house. She must have breathed in a lot of radioactive gas. When the four of us older children went home to Inasamachi a few days later, black spots had appeared on my mother's face. Those spots spread day after day to her entire body. Her lips turned purple. She kept gulping water, saying, "I'm tired! I'm tired!" Then, on August 16, one week after the bombing, she died, pregnant with her eighth child.

Right before she died she kept saying, "Just a small amount would be fine, but I want to eat white rice." "I don't want to die. Where's my husband? Hasn't he come back yet?" She grasped my hand and opened her eyes so wide it seemed her eyeballs would jump out, and died. She was 33 years old. She was a fair-skinned, small and quiet woman.

My uncle and four of us children cremated my mother's corpse early in the afternoon the next day. My uncle didn't want to let us see him lighting the fire under my mother. He told us to stay away. After a while, when the fire was burning, he called us to him.

I was so sad to see my mother's body burning, and it was frightening as well. We kept piling on the wood to make it burn faster. It probably took three or four hours. I remember it took quite a long time. We picked some of the ashes and the remaining bone and put them into a broken bowl we had found in the rubble. What had been my mother's body several hours earlier was now just a bowlful of ash and bone.

When we came back to my uncle's house holding the ashes in a bowl, my younger brothers and sisters asked, "Where did Mommy go?" "When will she be back?" My oldest sister sobbed and squeezed them tight but remained silent.

Yuriyo's burnt brother (aged seven), her youngest brother (five) and youngest sister (three) stayed at her uncle's house at Sotome for some time. *The four older siblings had to live by themselves in the broken-down house in Inasamachi. They had no electricity or water. Like Hiroshima's many street children, they lived a harsh life. They managed to survive by going out, each with a different group, to look for food. When things got too bad, her eldest sister or brother went to their uncle's house at Sotome and got some sweet potatoes. It was difficult to make fire at home, so they just washed them and ate them raw.*

The water system at our house was broken, so my oldest brother told me to go out and get water from a tap in the ruins. I went out, and there was a man standing in front of our house. The man stared at me and said, "Are you Yuriyo?" It was my father. My father had come back from the bloody battlefields of Saipan. We had heard all the Japanese had died there, so we were amazed.

Besides, he looked like a different man. He had a beard and a sword at his side. He wore a combat cap and looked like a general. Rather than joy, fear and surprise came first.

My father asked, "Where's your mother?"

I replied, "She's dead." He didn't say anything. He just looked down and stood still. After a while, he burst into tears, as if a dam inside him had broken. He was screaming, "I will kill all those big-noses from the US! Give me back my wife!"

Yuriyo's father repaired their tilted house. When they ran out of food, he went to his brother-in-law's house in Sotome and got potatoes to give the children something to eat. That miserable life continued for over a year.

Eventually, Yuriyo's father got a job at the Mitsubishi shipyard through his brother's introduction. However, he began drinking more and more heavily to distract himself from the loneliness and grief of having lost his wife. He started to stay out drinking and began missing work due to hangovers. After a few months, he was fired. It became increasingly difficult for the family to get by.

The year of the atomic bombing was a good one for summer oranges. My siblings and I stole oranges wherever we could. That was how we kept from starving.

Maybe because we were stealing oranges, whenever something was missing in my neighborhood, my neighbors immediately blamed me and my siblings. We all cried about this and said, "If our mother were here, we wouldn't be attacked like this."

My younger brother who had been terribly burnt in the bombing got sores all over his body. His face was so swollen he couldn't even open his eyes. He was suffering terribly and saying, "I can't see. I can't see. It's so painful!" His arms and the backs of his hands were infested with maggots. Bloody pus oozed out of the sores, the suppuration hollowed out his flesh and smelled terrible.

I had heard that potato juice was good for burns, so I started visiting our relatives in Sotome to get potatoes. I grated them and applied the juice to my brother's burns. Whenever I put juice on him he shrieked, "It stings!" "It hurts!" I felt so sorry for him, but thanks to the potatoes he was doing fairly well in a year and a half. He returned to elementary school, having missed two years.

However, the keloid scars on his head and down onto his face were ugly. I have to admit that a person seeing him for the first time would be repulsed. I think that's why he gradually stopped going out. It seems the children in our neighborhood bullied him and called him "A-bomb kid."

Still, that brother got married in 1958 when he was 20. Now he is blessed with five children and is leading a happy life. However, he hides his scars by wearing long-sleeved shirts even in summer. And he never fails to wear gloves to hide the keloids running up his hands.

After graduating from junior high school, I got a job at a mandarin orange canning plant in Inasamachi. I was often too weak to work due to anemia. I didn't want to be a burden on the company, so

I quit. My physical condition was such that it took me two or three times as long to do household chores compared to a healthy housewife.

In 1958, the same year as my brother, I got married to a sardine fisherman after being introduced by a friend of my father's. I was 22. I was quite anxious about my health, but I married without telling my husband about my A-bomb experience. In those days, rumor had it that a woman who had inhaled the gas from the A-bomb would give birth to deformed babies. In many cases, when a woman was found to be a survivor, she was divorced. I decided never to tell him, no matter what.

My honeymoon, which was supposed to be one of the happiest times of my life, brought me misery. Day after day I couldn't get out of bed because of dizziness and nausea. I wanted to cook for my husband. I got up and stood in the kitchen, but the blood drained from my head. Everything went black. I felt dizzy and fell to the floor.

I went to a doctor, who said, "You have extreme anemia. The cause is unknown."

Despite my poor health and instability, I very much wanted to have a child. Soon, I was pregnant. One day my husband said, "I've heard that atomic bomb survivors deliver black babies." I wondered where he had heard that rumor. Then he asked, "Are you a *hibakusha*?"

In that instant, the memory of the atomic bombing 13 years earlier came flooding back. I was speechless. I have no idea how I answered him.

I knew he was asking not because he doubted me but because he was worried. Like all parents, he worried about having a healthy baby. I was painfully aware of his anxiety. Still, I had no choice but to keep hiding my exposure. If I had told him I was a *hibakusha*, he would have been even more anxious. I kept it to myself. However, I felt very guilty about not telling him. That guilt was worse than the anxiety about the baby. I had many sleepless nights.

My husband, who knew nothing about me and the A-bomb, was so kind and considerate when I was pregnant. He treated me like I was his treasure, saying, "You just rest in bed."

To meet my husband's expectations, I prayed wholeheartedly for a healthy baby. I thought I would die if my baby were born black. During that time, I often thought about the fetus that died with my mother.

On March 23, 1959, the baby came with an unexpectedly easy delivery, given my health. That baby, born despite my emotional instability and internal conflict, was a healthy, chubby girl with normal white skin.

When I heard the wife of our landlord, who attended my delivery, say, "It's a beautiful girl! She resembles her father!" I was overwhelmed with joy. I sobbed out loud.

Teruko Yamaguchi
Without my mother's ashes, I couldn't believe she was dead

Born in October 1928, Teruko Yamaguchi was exposed to the atomic bombing at her home below Sumiyoshi Shrine, 1.8 kilometers from the hypocenter in Nagasaki.

Teruko's parents ran a laundry in Iwakawamachi. As the war got worse, food was strictly controlled through a rationing system. Her parents bought a house with rice fields and gardens beneath Sumiyoshi Shrine. They had Teruko (aged 16) and her older sister running the laundry together with a hired cleaner, while they grew potatoes and rice for food.

Teruko was the seventh of nine children: four boys and five girls. The second and third sons were fighting in Burma (Myanmar). The second daughter was married and living in Shanghai. Teruko lived in the house beneath Sumiyoshi Shrine with her parents, her other siblings, two of her oldest sister's children and two cousins.

An intense air raid took place on August 1. Thinking it was dangerous to keep the laundry going, they decided to move to the house under the shrine. Beginning in early August, they transported their belongings little by little on a cart.

We children scratched our father's "unbearably itchy" burn scars

We had planned to fetch more stuff and bring it over on August 9, but we were so tired we stayed at the new house and decided to air out the clothes we had brought previously.

I was peeling potatoes in the kitchen for lunch. My sixth-grade cousin and his older brother who was in high school said,

"A parachute is coming down!" I thought, "That'll be coming down slow." I continued peeling a potato until it was finished. Just as I was about to leave the house to see the parachute, a sulfur smell and blue smoke drifted in. I quickly turned back into the house and grabbed the edge of the well in the earthen-floored kitchen area.

I saw no light and heard no sound. The shock was so strong I had no idea what could possibly have happened. When I looked around, I saw all the glass windows broken and the inside of our house a chaotic jumble.

I was so terrified, my legs wouldn't support me. I couldn't stand up, so I crawled out. I found the two boys who had called to me earlier about the parachute. They had been transformed into the most grotesque figures. Their clothes were burnt, and they were half naked. Their faces, arms and other places where their skin had been exposed were badly burnt. The skin had peeled right off, showing the bare red flesh below.

A firefighter was going around, saying, "Don't give water to the ones with burns!"

I took the boys into the house and attempted to lay them down, but they had burns all over their bodies, so they couldn't lie down. I had them sit down on the earthen floor and tried to give them some sort of treatment. They kept saying, "I need water!" I knew I shouldn't give them water, so I went out to the garden and picked a cucumber. I peeled it and gave that to them.

If I had not finished peeling that last potato and had rushed out to see the parachute, I would have been in the same state as my cousins. In fact, if we had gone to the old house as planned to get more of our belongings, we would have been killed instantly because our house was in Iwakawamachi, not more than 500 meters from the hypocenter.

My cousins couldn't control themselves and drank lots of water from the well during the night. The next morning their faces and bodies were swollen up hard like big bladders. A few days later, my oldest sister and her husband took them to the relief station at Michino-o Elementary School. On August 11, the younger one passed away, followed by the older one on the 17th.

My father was outside like my cousins. He was blown about two meters by the blast and dropped into the eggplant garden. He had been hunched over weeding a field in front of our house, so he had serious burns on his back.

Many houses near Sumiyoshi Shrine had thatched roofs. Fire spread from a storehouse to the nearby house, then from one house to the next through the whole area.

The house Teruko and her family were in was some distance from the others and had tile roofing on both its storehouse and the main house. They escaped the fire. Their house was the only one in the area that didn't burn. However, the inside was so damaged that the family went to a shelter.

We couldn't enter the shelter because of the intense stench of burns and corpses. I could see survivors hugging each other, rejoicing with tears in the shelter. I also heard the voices of people calling out loudly the names of their children and other missing family members. The next day rice balls were served, but we had no appetite. Hardly anyone ate them.

My younger brother had been going to Nagasaki Commercial School, but classes had been canceled, and his classroom had become a weapons manufacturing plant. He was working there at the time of the bombing. Thanks to the training he'd received every day, he threw himself instantly to the floor. However, numerous pieces of window glass shattered by the blast stuck into his back. The classmate working next to him died instantly because his abdomen was burst open.

My brother was treated by his coworkers and walked all the way home along the streetcar tracks. He arrived with a bandage wrapped all around him. On his way, survivors suffering from burns had reached out to him, saying, "Please, give me water! Water, please!" They grabbed his ankles. He said, "I'll get some water for you, so let me go." Then he ran away from them.

My father and younger brother went to Ikeda Hospital in Shimabara for treatment. On their way, the burns on my father's neck, back and legs where cucumber slices had been placed were covered with hundreds of white maggots. They rented a house in front of the hospital and concentrated on getting some treatment.

My mother had been missing since that day. She had wondered if the house at Iwakawamachi had been damaged by the conventional air raid on August 1. She had gone to check on the house and take some eggplants and cucumbers from our farm to a friend's house near Sanno Shrine. It was not until September that I learned what had happened to her.

The husband of a friend of Teruko's mother, Mr. Kondo, was working for Mitsubishi Ordnance Works. When he rushed home immediately after the bombing, he found his youngest daughter (aged five) trapped under the collapsed house. He was unable to pull his daughter out of the rubble despite his best efforts.

While trying to get her out, he asked, "Who was here?" She replied, "Brother, sister and me. And Mommy and Mrs. Inoue (Teruko's mother)." Thus, Teruko found out later that her mother had died in the Kondos' house.

Because I didn't have my mother's ashes and didn't see her body, I couldn't accept her death for a long time. Whenever I heard footsteps in the middle of the night, I woke up thinking, "There's my mother!"

When she didn't come home for years, I had to accept that she was gone. That's when I thought, "I wonder if she died at the Kondos' place?" I heard that Mr. Kondo, who was left all alone, became mentally unbalanced and passed away.

Six months after the bombing, two aunts visited us from Osaka, and we had a narrow escape. Although our house had been spared from the fire, it was leaning badly. I said, "Please come in and rest." But they were scared and showed no inclination to enter. I put cups of cold barley tea on a tray and served it to them as they stood outside.

Even as we stood there, our house collapsed with a roar. Looking from aunt to aunt, I trembled so severely my teeth chattered.

After our house was flattened, my sister and I were sent to our aunt's house in Kitaarima on the Shimabara peninsula. My brothers moved to the house my father was still renting, to receive treatment.

The wound on my father's back had hardened, and the scar around it rose up to the thickness of fingers. It even looked as if fingers were spread out and reaching out from the opening. When his body warmed up under the covers at night, the scar got so itchy he could hardly stand it. Each child took turns rubbing his back all night.

Neighbors who lived near the house beneath Sumiyoshi Shrine visited us in Shimabara. They asked us to sell them the beams and pillars of our house, as it had collapsed and was uninhabitable. Soon after we gave our consent, the house vanished with no trace of its original form.

That fall those neighbors near Sumiyoshi Shrine visited us again. This time, they said our rice field had produced a fine crop, and they wanted to buy our rice.

We went to the field and found the seedlings my parents had planted in spring ripening abundantly despite complete neglect. We harvested 13 large bags of rice (780 kg).

In March the following year, I took a graduation exam at the Girls Commercial School and graduated. I went to the school to get the diploma. There, for the first time, I found out that many of my classmates had died.

After coming back from Shimabara, four of us children reopened the Inoue Laundry near Meganebashi Bridge.

At 18, I married a man who was in the same business. My eldest brother introduced him to me. Two years later, we opened our own laundry in Heiwamachi and we were eventually blessed with six children.

My father's burns healed, but he died on January 1, 1951, due to tuberculosis. I had extreme anemia. I used to faint often, but it's better now.

My brother, who looked like a hedgehog because of all the glass piercing his back, still often says, "Something is back there again! Something is hurting me." He goes to the hospital and has the area cut open. A piece of glass is found, and when they remove it, a wart-like scar forms. My brother's back is covered with such warts.

The atomic bombing left scars in both mind and body that never disappear.

Kwon Sun-gun

Praying for fellow Koreans killed by the atomic bombing

Born in January 1926 in Andong, Korea, Kwon Sun-gun was exposed to the atomic bombing in Asahimachi, 1.8 kilometers from the hypocenter in Nagasaki. She and her husband ran construction camps, sold scrap iron and eventually opened a Korean barbecue restaurant, which became successful and expanded into a three-story building. She is currently an advisory board member for the Korean Residents Union in Japan Women's Group, Nagasaki Chapter. Her late husband was the local leader of the Korean Residents Union in Japan and chairman of the Nagasaki Commercial Credit Union.

My husband said, "My love, I'll go on ahead"

My mother and I arrived in Kyoto when I was four. My father had come to Japan before us. When he was young, my father was a bit irresponsible, and casually went wherever he wanted to go. Every time he moved, my mother and I followed him. We moved from place to place in Japan, from Yokkaichi to Gifu, Nagoya to Sasebo.

We lived in Kyoto until I was in the fourth grade. We were so poor we couldn't even buy rice. Because we couldn't afford to make rice balls to take on school trips for lunch, I was unable to go on them. In school I was insulted. "You smell like garlic!" "Stupid Korean!"

My mother came to school one rainy day wearing a traditional Korean costume, a *ch'ima chogori*, to bring me an umbrella. I avoided her and went home alone. I was afraid of being insulted even more by my classmates. I apologized to her when I got home. I will never forget my mother's sad face as she said, "These are the only clothes I have."

We moved to Sasebo, Nagasaki Prefecture, when I was 15, the year my sister was born. I went to Ainoura Higher Elementary School in Sasebo. My mother was in poor health and said, "Please take the baby with you to school."

When my sister cried during a lesson, I would leave the classroom and try to pacify her in the corridor. Other children walking by us would say, "*Yarashika, yarashika.*" I didn't understand Japanese well and thought they were making fun of us. Later, I learned they were saying, "She's cute," in Nagasaki dialect.

My father went back to Korea and recruited laborers for construction work in Japan. He opened a construction camp in Nagasaki. Five or six day-laborers at a time would stay in our bunkhouse with its galvanized tin roof.

To tell the truth, I wanted to continue my studies and become a nurse, but my parents wanted me to quit school to help them prepare meals for the laborers.

My father's work camps were mainly on Koyagi Island. Honson was the main community on Koyagi Island, and many Korean forced laborers worked there. They had to work night and day on intensive construction rush jobs. I worked with them.

Koyagi Island was a tough worksite for me. There was no water on the island, so we had to bring it in from Nagasaki by boat. One of my tasks as a cook was to carry water from the boat in two big buckets hanging on both ends of a shoulder pole. I did this over and over. It was extremely hard work for my 15-year-old body.

At 18, I married a man who was doing office work under my father. His name was Cho Yon-sik, and he was 11 years older than me. We made a new home on Koyagi Island. Later my husband said, quite seriously, "You are short. I bet that's because you carried all that water when you were still growing."

My husband later quit my father's company and set up his own. One reason was because my father enjoyed drinking after work, whereas my husband never touched a drop of alcohol. My husband built a new camp in Kosedo, taking in nine laborers.

Around that time, Allied air raids were intensifying. Houses throughout the city required repair, so Sun-gun's husband got plenty of work. He soon had several construction camps housing over 30 laborers. They had no children, so Sun-gun took care of the laborers, going to the camps with her husband.

On August 9, I went to the Inasa Bridge camp in Asahimachi to prepare lunch. My husband came in, and just as I was serving him tea, we heard a tremendous boooom. I went outside and saw black smoke rapidly spreading across the sky. Then, it turned pitch black.

When the darkness lifted, crowds of badly burnt people were walking single file in front of the bunkhouse. Fires broke out everywhere. I saw horses, cows and many human bodies floating in the Urakami River.

With no means of transportation, Sun-gun and her husband walked over the hill and back to Kosedo. The next day, her husband visited his construction camps, including the one in Matsuyamamachi, right near the hypocenter. All the camps were gone without a trace. He found no laborers. He didn't know if they had been burnt to death, buried under debris or had run away.

Of his 30 laborers, only two were ever found. Both had died and were identified on a municipal ferry where they had been traveling from Ohato to a worksite.

Daily, my husband made the rounds of all the construction camps, looking for our laborers. The only ones he ever found out about were the two on the boat.

It was said that 70,000 Koreans were in the Nagasaki area at that time. Of that number, 20,000 were exposed to the atomic bombing, and 10,000 were killed. I am sure that many of those laborers had been forced to come to Japan.

The situation of my fellow Koreans after the bombing was tragic. Most who survived the bombing had no place to go. Many came to our house, begging for something to eat. Many Koreans with no place to go, including forced laborers, stole radishes from farms or were given potatoes, which they sold near Harusame Bridge. They built shacks in that area, which quickly became a Korean settlement. Maybe because so many Japanese men were away at the war, I noticed a number of Japanese women had fallen in love with Korean men and were living with them near the bridge.

Our family had a very hard time, too. My husband received work from the Construction Cooperative Union and worked without his laborers to clean up the ruins of the atomic bombing. My parents went back to Korea after the war ended, in October.

We couldn't run construction camps any more, so my husband and I purchased sports shoes from a wholesaler in Kobe and sold them in Nagasaki. That was not enough to feed us, so we brewed and sold illegal Korean rice wine. However, we were discovered and policemen came to our house. My husband escaped to Osaka, but I was left behind. I was arrested and subjected to merciless interrogation. I never wavered in claiming ignorance and denied any involvement. At last the policeman questioning me was so impressed he said, "You are really tough!"

Sun-gun's husband later returned, and the couple started a scrap iron business that involved collecting scrap in a cart and selling it to a trader in Sasebo. In 1963, after saving enough money, they opened a small Korean restaurant called Arirang House. At that time Korean barbecue was virtually unknown in Japan.

My husband resigned as the local chief of the Korean Residents Union in Japan to become chairman of the Nagasaki Commercial Credit Union. He said, "I can't be of any help at the restaurant, so you run it however you like!" I worked hard by myself, and it paid off. We were able to expand the restaurant, eventually having a three-story building serving Korean barbecue. We were so successful that we were able to do wedding receptions in our big hall on the third floor.

My husband was not the only one devoted to the Korean community. I joined the Korean Residents Union in Japan Women's Group in 1952 and am still on the advisory board.

Since about 1959, I have often been asked, "Why don't you obtain an Atomic Bomb Survivor Health Book?" I had heard that being a *hibakusha* would have a bad influence on a business like ours, so I was reluctant to get the book. My husband also said, "If we get the Health Book, it will be on our record forever. Let's not do it."

However, my husband developed a problem in his throat in 1971. We heard that if he had a Health Book, he could get medical treatment for free. We applied for the Health Book, and he was identified as a "Residual Radiation-Exposed Patient."

In 1983, my husband told me he had a dull pain that wouldn't go away. We visited a clinic nearby, but his condition didn't get better. We visited the Atomic Bomb Hospital, and he was immediately admitted. The doctor said, "His cancer has spread from the pancreas to the liver. There is nothing we can do." I couldn't tell my husband. I just said, "There seems to be a problem in your stomach."

It was painful to watch my husband's face get thinner and thinner. Whenever I came home from the hospital and was alone, I cried. About four months after being admitted to the hospital, he passed away. It was around three in the morning. "My love, I'll go on ahead of you." He said this barely audibly in Korean and closed his eyes.

After he died, my sister Hideko, who was 15 years younger than I and four years old at the time of the bombing, contracted multiple myeloma. My youngest sister Matsuko, who was just one at the time, underwent surgery for leg pain of unknown cause.

On the day of the bombing, our mother had got off a streetcar, pulling Hideko by the hand and carrying Matsuko on her back. Just before they entered a laundry in front of Nagasaki Station, the atomic bomb exploded. They were exposed outside and directly but at a distance of about 2.3 kilometers from the hypocenter.

Almost all the survivors suffer from deep anxiety. "When will I develop symptoms?" Personally, my knees get numb when I sit on them, and I can't stand up afterwards. I can't help wondering if it's due to the atomic bombing.

Every year on August 9, the day of the Nagasaki Peace Ceremony, I attend the ceremony wearing the traditional *ch'ima chogori*. I have a deep feeling of solidarity with my fellow Koreans who rest here and their families who cannot come to the ceremony. I pray for all of them, and I want to pray for them in my national costume.

On August 5, 2010, as a Korean atomic bomb survivor living in Japan, I met United Nations Secretary-General Ban Ki-moon, who came to attend the Peace Ceremony. That meeting was not in his original schedule, but about 30 of us who attended the ceremony greeted him in the peace study room in the Atomic Bomb Museum. When he saw me in my *ch'ima chogori*, he quickly came over and shook my hand.

"Welcome to Nagasaki," I said in Korean, and he smiled at me. Later, speaking in the hypocenter park, the Secretary-General told us he would do his best to abolish nuclear weapons. His words made a deep impression on me.

Nobuharu Takahira
I would still prefer not to remember...

Born in December 1928, Nobuharu Takahira was exposed to the atomic bombing at the Mitsubishi Electric factory near Nagasaki Port, 3 kilometers from the hypocenter in Nagasaki. He was 16. His health deteriorated after exposure, and his life has been filled with great anxiety. He was assigned to Mitsubishi Electric for "labor service" and worked there until he retired.

Nobuharu was a second-year student at Nita Higher Elementary School, and was going to graduate in four months. His job was to connect rotating parts to fixed parts in ship motors. This was his official "labor service."

Anxiety was the deeper pain

It was a perfectly clear day. Nobuharu heard the buzzing B-29 bombers and looked toward the sky from a factory window, but he didn't see anything.

While looking out the window, I noticed the clock over the entrance to the factory and was just looking to see what time it was. In that instant a pure white flash came in horizontally through the window. As soon as I turned my face toward the flash, I heard a tremendous boooom!

I pressed my ears with my thumbs and my eyes with my index and middle fingers and threw myself to the ground. We had been drilled to do this to protect our eyes and ears. As we worked, a civilian employee would suddenly shout, "Down!!" and we would have to get into that posture as quickly as possible. Because of this training, I was able to take quick action.

Just as I got into the posture, window glass from the high factory ceiling came crashing down with a roar. I wore a combat cap and work uniform, so my head and body were protected. Still, a sharp glass fragment struck the back of my right ear. I felt warm blood flowing onto my face. What if the glass fragment had been slightly to the left? It might have struck my carotid artery. I shudder to think of it. I still have the scar from that cut.

When Nobuharu raised his head, he saw the roof had been totally blown off by the blast. The factory building had been reduced to an iron frame. He was looking outside as dust and dirt from the factory billowed high into the sky.

The other side of the factory was a wooden building for female workers. A volunteer corps from Kumamoto Girls School had come for training in making searchlights. Because their building was wooden, many workers were killed.

I saw my coworkers at the factory running toward the shelter behind the factory. We called it a shelter, but it was just a hole scooped out of the rocky slope of the hillside. It had been used as a test site for large turbine generators. Over 1,200 factory workers rushed there all at once.

Many who had been working in the factory were bleeding, like me, due to injuries from glass shards or other objects hurled by the blast. Those who had been working outside were in worse condition. Their hair was scorched and frizzy, their skin hideously burnt, and their clothes in tatters. Even though it was midsummer, most people in the shelter were shivering and saying, "I'm cold."

The sights I saw when I left the factory to go home were too horrible to believe. Among the people rushing to escape faster than others was a person tottering unsteadily, looking exactly like a terribly burnt ghost. A woman clung tightly to her dead baby, yelling in delirium. People like these were everywhere. I finally reached Inasa Bridge.

Probably because it was almost noon and so many households had been preparing lunch, fires quickly broke out here and there, spreading rapidly. The entire Urakami area was soon a sea of fire. Wooden homes were the first to go. Concrete buildings were blazing by evening.

I saw a streetcar with its whole top blown off. Its passengers lay dead, piled on top of one another on the streetcar floor. Streetcar rails were raised and twisted like roller coaster rails. Terribly burnt cows and horses lay toppled in the road.

I wanted to get home, but I thought it might be dangerous to cross Inasa Bridge. I decided to cross the river by municipal ferry. I turned around and headed for a pier, thinking I could get a ride to Ohato Wharf.

At the pier, they said they couldn't launch the boat because the captain had run away. While we were speaking, an enemy plane appeared and fired its machine gun fiercely in our direction. We all ran this way and that to escape from this unexpected strafing. Some hid under the pier. Others threw themselves on the floor. There's no way to miss a white summer shirt, but nobody was shot. I still wonder why.

The enemy plane left, but the ferry captain never came back. I was irritated, but when I think about it now, what followed was like a cartoon.

At that time, besides the municipal ferry, which was like a bus service, quite a few people had bought and used *tenmasen* as their means of transport. A *tenmasen* was a boat rowed with a single oar in the back, like a sampan or gondola. Creak... Creak... Given the tension around us at that moment, the *tenmasen* appeared utterly foolish, but people worried about what had happened in Nagasaki were arriving on one.

When the passengers got out, those of us on the pier started fighting to get on board. The boat soon filled up with five or six people, but there was no one to row it. One of us took the oar and started rowing based on his imagination of how to row a *tenmasen*.

When we got to the middle of the river, the same enemy plane came back. Now we were in a panic. The *tenmasen* was just slightly bigger than a rowboat, and there was no place to hide.

"Hurry up! What are you doing, idiot?"

"Turn right!"

Everyone was complaining and blaming the rower, but he was a beginner and was in a complete panic. He seemed to hit his wrist on something. His watchband broke and the watch dropped into the water. He tried to grab the sinking watch. Thrusting himself forward, he fell into the water himself. We pulled him out of the water, while watching the enemy plane closely. As we did so, the oar slipped off the oarlock. We were left with no choice but to float helplessly wherever the river would take us.

The enemy plane flew high into the sky. It seemed to turn off its engine. It grew quiet, then flew back down in a fast dive. It came back at a height where they could clearly see our boat. The machine gun began firing as the plane buzzed the surface of the water, then climbed high again.

We were under attack, so naturally, screaming and chaos filled the boat. We all wondered why a boat stopped in the middle of a harbor with no oar should be the target of an enemy plane. Then we discovered that the oar was attached to the boat by a string, so we used the string to pull the oar back.

When I talk about it now, it's ridiculous, even funny, but there, on the border between life and death, we were completely out of our minds. I shrank myself as small as possible and concentrated on praying for safe passage to Ohato.

I will never forget the sound of that machine gun firing bullets into the water with a *pyun-pyun* sound. Perhaps the gunner was upset, or a beginner, but miraculously, no one was shot. We arrived safely in Ohato. From there, I took a long detour home to Kamikoshima.

On the way home I saw the area behind Ohato (now the Nagasaki Prefectural Government Building). The entire area was a sea of fire. The fire burned continuously for three days and three nights. Then, heavy rain fell for a few days. In Kamikoshima we had normal heavy rain, but I heard some places had black rain.

When I got home, I found all the window glass shattered, but other than that, the house was undamaged. My mother had died a few years earlier, and my younger brother also had died from tuberculosis when he was small. Therefore, I lived with my father, who worked for a printing company.

I arrived home in the evening. My father, who was saved by a shelter, came home later that night. He was overjoyed to see me, saying, "I heard the city was totally destroyed by a new type of bomb. I was sure you were dead."

The Mitsubishi Electric factory was destroyed; no operations were possible. It remained closed for more than two years. When it reopened, Nobuharu returned to work and stayed until retirement.

I got married in 1953. My company often held parties in a certain *champon* restaurant. (*Champon* is a Nagasaki specialty, like ramen noodles.) In that restaurant a certain young woman lived and worked. The proprietress of the restaurant knew my uncle, and the two of them would talk about me marrying her.

My future wife's mother said, "Even if he's poor, I want your husband to be healthy." I looked a bit pale, so they made me submit a certificate of health. My mother-in-law knew I was a *hibakusha*. According to my wife, when our first son was born, her mother came into the hospital and surreptitiously counted our son's fingers and toes. Sure enough, she had been worried.

I was inside the factory and didn't breathe the "radioactive gas." I was convinced there was no reason for me to be affected. As far as I was concerned, the only aftereffect of the atomic bombing was the scar behind my ear where I had been cut by a glass fragment. However, a medical checkup I had when the factory reopened found that I had a stomach ulcer. Around that time, my health deteriorated. I frequently had diarrhea. I carried with me a medicine for intestinal disorders and took it often. My thyroid gland was weak, and whenever I got sick, my throat would swell up.

I do not want to talk much about my anxiety. It is something you simply cannot understand if you were not exposed. It's so cruel. When I get even slightly sick, I get a stinging pain near my stomach. I feel fear, wondering if I've finally come down with some terrible disease. More than burns and injuries, I think the primary suffering of survivors is our anxiety, the lack of normal peace of mind. I have lived with this anxiety for 70 years.

Even my wife asked me why I haven't talked about my exposure to the atomic bombing through all these years. The fact is, I didn't want to remember. But soon after my daughter entered high school, she said her class had to write essays to pass on the atomic bombing, and asked me to tell my story. I turned her down at first, but in the end, I decided to tell her.

To tell the truth, I would still prefer not to remember.

Fusae Fukushita
I entered the city right after the bombing

Born in September 1930, Fusae Fukushita was 14 when she was exposed to the atomic bombing at the Mizunoura Mitsubishi shipyard, three kilometers from the hypocenter in Nagasaki.

Fusae had graduated from higher elementary school in the Shimabara Peninsula and entered Kazusa Youth School in her neighborhood. She was one of only two students from that school assigned to a munitions company in Nagasaki. Employed as an apprentice, she moved into a dormitory. Fusae went to school one day and the Mizunoura Mitsubishi shipyard the next. She was apprenticed to learn technical drawing, but had many miscellaneous tasks. One was to go to the dining hall in the next building around 11 a.m. to get lunch and bring it back for her section chief. This usually consisted of bread and a side dish, which she carried over to her section.

Those who survived died early, tormented by A-bomb diseases

I had come to Nagasaki from Kazusa four months earlier. That day I was on the sixth floor of the office building at the shipyard. At 11 a.m., I had just started walking toward the exit to get lunch for my section chief when I heard an enormous explosion. The glass in the windows of two separate walls broke at the same time, and the shattered glass flew toward me. I was well trained to hit the floor quickly, and I had made myself wear a long sleeve blouse despite the heat of summer, so I was lucky and did not have any injuries.

Everyone in the office was shocked and rushed to be the first one into the shelter. I went down the stairs, being jostled by the crowd all the way to a shelter. There I saw people covered in blood due to flying glass, but I didn't see any with burns.

The previous day in the elevator I had seen a coworker in the Drafting Section with his arm in a sling. I asked, "What happened?" He replied, "I went to Hiroshima for a business trip, and it was hit by a new type of bomb." That meant he encountered two atomic bombings.

Fusae stayed in the shelter near her office until evening. Thinking it must be okay by now, she went out to find a sea of fire on the other side of the river near the Prefectural Government Building. She couldn't imagine what had happened.

Her dormitory was in Komabamachi near the hypocenter. She tried to get back there, but all transportation was stopped. Normally, she would have taken a boat from Mizunoura, where the shipyard was, to Ohato, then gone back to the dormitory by streetcar.

With no sign of any boats or streetcars, she decided to walk through Inasamachi to her dormitory. She left the shelter around 5:00 in the evening and arrived at the dormitory after 7:00.

The further she advanced into the city, the more badly damaged the houses were. When she reached the area near Mitsubishi Steel Works, charred corpses were everywhere. Streetcar rails were lifted and bent like bows pointing toward the sky. The Steel Works buildings were nothing but skeletons.

It took me two hours to get to the dormitory, and it was gone without a trace. The whole area was a burnt plain as far as I could see. A few fellow workers who had arrived before me were trying to get their bearings. "Wasn't it about here?" Everything was so completely changed.

Our dormitory was a one-story house in a row of about 10 similar houses standing together. Residents from various companies lived together in these houses. Shipyard workers shared one house, ordnance workers shared another, and so on. As I recall, 100 to 200 young women lived in those dormitories. They came from the Goto Islands and the Shimabara Peninsula. Some had graduated from school; others were labor service volunteers from girls' schools. Those girls were going to a large facility in Maruomachi every other day to study. I was among those who went to study.

We studied every other day, but every day we first went to our workplaces in the morning at the regular time, then headed for Maruomachi. When an air-raid warning sounded while we were studying at Maruomachi, we were supposed to take refuge in a nearby shelter. When studying, I felt differently about the warnings than when I was at work. I didn't go to the shelter when the alarms sounded because I was so used to hearing them near the end of my study sessions. I was especially reluctant to do so when it was hot.

Fusae generally left the dormitory at 7:00 in the morning, commuted to the shipyard and then returned in the evening. Her workplace didn't have a night shift, but some companies did. The dorms had cooks, and all the residents ate in a single dining hall.

The food shortage in Shimabara where I grew up was not that bad, so eating the gruel mixed with soybean dregs and weeds the dormitory served was painful to me.

Three women lived together in a six-tatami-mat room. On our days off, we all hung our wash in the yard. We had a dorm mother and a superintendent, but they supervised all 10 houses. I didn't even know where they lived.

When I arrived at what I assumed were the ruins of our dormitory, all 10 houses had vanished. Even the trees around the dormitories were completely burnt to the ground. I could see Shiroyama Elementary School and Chinzei Gakuin Junior High School up on the hillside. I used these two schools as landmarks in my effort to confirm where my dormitory had stood.

A number of other residents who worked for the Ordnance Works came back to those ruins, but no one said a word. I heard later that our housemother and superintendent were reduced to skeletons where they sat in their chairs. All who had been in the dormitory due to being on the night shift were killed instantly.

As I stood there in a daze, a person with an armband saying, "Subsection Chief, Mitsubishi," told us, "This area is dangerous. You should go to Togitsu (a town north of Nagasaki)." I had just come to Nagasaki four months earlier and had no idea where Togitsu was. Of the 10 of us standing there, one knew where Togitsu was. We walked off following her.

When we came to Ohashi Bridge next to Komabamachi, most of the bridge was blown away leaving only the naked iron frame spanning the river. We crawled cross the bridge frame. Looking down, I saw a crowd of injured victims who had come to the river seeking water. They were groaning and begging for help. Many fell into the river; many of those were washed away.

The victims I saw near the Mitsubishi Steel Works were dead, so I had a feeling something like resignation; I didn't care that much. But here, people were screaming and struggling desperately. I couldn't help but feel terribly sorry for them, but there was nothing we could do. We just kept walking silently toward Togitsu.

We finally reached Togitsu in the middle of the night. We had not eaten anything since noon. The villagers gave us some rice balls, and I still remember how good they tasted. We were taken into a big house. When I was able to lie down under a mosquito net, I finally felt a sense of relief.

The next day, they said, "Those who came from Shimabara

should go home." I went to Michino-o Station. Again, I saw a lot of injured people in the square behind the station, and their numbers increased even as I watched.

One person's clothes were tattered and full of blood. Another's hair had taken the shape of the helmet he wore, and his exposed ears and neck were burnt badly. It was so grotesque, I had to turn my eyes away.

I was allowed to ride the train, but I failed to get all the way home that day. I spent the night in the train at Shimabara Station, arriving at my home in Kazusa the next day.

My mother told me the family had been saying, "Fusae must be dead. How can we find her body?" The family told me they could see the mushroom cloud from Kazusa, and Nagasaki had burned all night.

Many of my friends died. Many of those who survived initially died in great pain from A-bomb disease. Nearly all survivors live in anxiety, knowing they could develop symptoms at any time.

I took lessons in dressmaking in Kazusa. When I was 20, I returned to Nagasaki with a friend. I worked for an insurance company for 26 years until retirement. At 30, I married a man I was introduced to by an acquaintance. He had come from Kumamoto Prefecture and was working for a fruit and vegetable company. He was 10 years older than me and cared for me very well.

When I was pregnant with our first daughter, I was a bit nervous. But then I heard my husband say, "I wonder if our baby will be born with deformed feet or something. I hope our baby will be healthy." I knew he was worried about the effects of the bombing.

We have two daughters. When our first daughter was in elementary school, she had a health checkup, and the doctor said she had a tendency toward anemia. When she's healthy, I don't worry much. But when she has any kind of problem, I can't help thinking, "Maybe this is because of. . ." I hate thinking like this.

On the day of the bombing, I knew nothing at all about radiation. Otherwise we would not have gone to the ruins of the dormitory in Komabamachi near the hypocenter immediately after the bombing. I first learned about "entry exposure" when I heard that soldiers who had entered the hypocenter to clear debris developed diseases of unknown origin. They were sent to the University Hospital, and many died.

I didn't know how to interpret this information, so I made myself believe that the effects of radiation don't all manifest immediately; they come out over time. When we went to the hypocenter immediately after the bombing, the radioactive gas had yet to be fully generated. I don't know if this makes any scientific sense, but without believing this, I would not have been able to confront my fate.

Yasuko Tasaki
Pain and grief expressed through *waka* poems

Yasuko Tasaki was born in November 1945. She was exposed to the atomic bombing in utero; her mother had been in Nishiyamamachi, three kilometers from the Nagasaki hypocenter. Her parents divorced when she was a toddler. Because of recurring infant tuberculosis, she developed renal tuberculosis. She got married at 27.

My anger at my father for divorcing my sick mother

I am an in utero survivor. My Atomic Bomb Survivor Health Book states: "Age at exposure: Fetus"; "Place of exposure: Shimo Nishiyamamachi, Nagasaki City, three kilometers from hypocenter"; "Situation immediately after exposure: Entered hypocenter area in mother's womb; mother was looking for great-grandfather who had gone to Iwakawamachi, one kilometer from hypocenter."

My mother, Nuiko Kunitake, was 20; I had been in her womb for seven months. The air-raid warning was lifted. My mother was sewing baby clothes for me and chatting with her mother-in-law.

Yasuko was later told: "A lightning-like flash ran through the sky, followed by a tremendous roar. A cabinet, other furniture and a beam from the ceiling fell down. Your mother protected her fetus, instinctively laying down on her stomach."

In the midst of confusion and chaos, her mother was informed that her grandfather, who lived in Nagasaki, was missing. The next day she went out with her mother-in-law to look for him. Yasuko's mother walked with her big belly from her house near Suwa Shrine straight through the hypocenter area to her relative's house in Iwakawamachi. Neither she nor her mother-in-law had any idea about something called "radiation."

My great-grandfather eventually came home, but he soon began complaining about his health. He died of an unknown illness in June the next year.

My mother had been one of the healthiest children around. She never took a single day off from school, from elementary school right through high school. But two days after she delivered me, she felt weak. When she gave birth to my brother in January 1948, she suffered extreme anemia, heart problems and hypotension, and eventually contracted tuberculosis.

After struggling at home, she went to a tuberculosis sanatorium in Tagami for long-term treatment.

My newborn brother was the heir to succeed my father, so he was taken to live with our father's family. Not yet three years old, I was taken to my mother's parents' house in Isahaya. The two of us lived completely separate lives after that.

I grew up not knowing my father. By the time I was old enough to understand the situation, my parents were divorced, and my mother was in the sanatorium. I never had a conversation about my father with my mother. She never mentioned him, and I didn't ask. However, over the years I always harbored a deep anger toward my father who had divorced my mother when she was ill.

To tell the truth, I, too, was in bad shape. I tired easily, and often fell ill with anemia. At school, when morning assembly was prolonged even a little, everything would go black, and I would have to sit down right where I was. During physical education class and on sports days, I was an observer. After a while, I contracted infant tuberculosis and had to get streptomycin injections in my buttocks every day. Eventually, I dropped out of school for a year.

The only thing I always looked forward to was going to see my mother in Nagasaki. Usually once a month, my grandfather would take me from Isahaya by bus. We went up a small hill to the sanatorium, walking up a long slope from the bus stop. I was so happy and got so excited, thinking, "I'm going to see my mother!"

My mother was in a room with six female patients. I used to take walks with her in the woods on the sanatorium grounds. I sang her all the songs I learned at school. One day she laughed and said, "You're tone-deaf because I'm tone-deaf." I didn't feel offended at all. I was just happy to be like my mother.

Once, my grandmother patted me on the head, saying, "If only there'd been no war and no atomic bomb. . . If only your mother hadn't fallen so ill, the two of you wouldn't have ended up in such a pitiful state." She had tears in her eyes.

The meetings with my mother I enjoyed so much were often made impossible by bad health, either mine or my mother's. When that happened, I wrote letters. I wrote about my friends, my grandparents, anything that occurred to me, then sent the letter to my mother.

My mother would correct my writing and send it back to me. That made me so happy; I wrote again and again. Eventually, I started writing essays and sent those to her as well. This exchange of letters with my mother taught me the joy of writing. Because of those efforts and her training, I received many awards in essay contests.

Around 1960, Yasuko's mother decided to undergo a revolutionary operation to remove one of her lungs—the whole lung together with the ribs. The survival rate for this operation was estimated at 60 percent, but her mother was determined to gamble on a cure. The following year, her mother was finally able to return home, having survived the operation and living for 12 years in a sanatorium.

It was unbelievable to me. I still remember well the night I slept with my mother for the first time in my grandparents' house in Isahaya. I was a junior high student, and I was already as tall as my mother. We laid *futons* next to each other and just talked and talked endlessly.

I graduated from high school. Then, when I was 22, a few years after starting work for a local bank, my infant tuberculosis recurred, this time in the form of renal tuberculosis. I quit the bank job and had one of my kidneys removed.

In 1972, when I was 27, I met my future husband. We decided to marry, but my grandfather forcefully opposed our marriage. He said, "Yasuko, you are an only child. You should marry a man we can adopt who can succeed me in the Kunitake family!" He began looking for an appropriate son-in-law. However, my mother pushed back. "You can marry whomever you wish, as long as you're in love."

The next year we received a notice of marriage from my younger brother, who was taken from me when I was two. My father had remarried, and his new wife had suggested my brother should try meeting me before he got married. It was she who sent me the notice of marriage.

My mother rejected the idea, saying, "I'm not the one who raised him, so I have no right to see him." But I persuaded her. "If you don't see him now, you'll never see him at all." We decided to go and see my brother, who was living in Nagoya.

Using the excuse of visiting my grandfather, who was ill, we met my brother in a hospital in Nagasaki. I don't know why, but I have no memory of my mother's behavior or my brother's attitude at that time. However, I do definitely remember thinking that I was absolutely sure he was really my brother, even though I was meeting him for the first time in such a long time.

That was the only time Yasuko's mother ever saw her son. The next time they met was at her funeral. Yasuko feels it was a good thing she forced her to see him. She also met her father at her mother's funeral. There, Yasuko learned that her parents were six years apart in age and other details. She learned more from her brother. Her father had moved to Yokohama, thinking that it wasn't good for his children to live in a small city like Nagasaki. He had remarried in Yokohama.

My mother had started to compose *waka* poems in the sanatorium. She left a large collection of her *waka* written in smooth, beautiful characters. It was only when I read her diary and *waka* after she passed away that I learned it was not my father who left my mother. My mother had proposed, and insisted on, the divorce. I learned that from a *waka*:

> Looking at snows
> tossed about the sky
> from my bed
> I think about being
> a wife on my own.

In the postwar years, tuberculosis was said to be incurable. Everyone was afraid of it because it was so contagious. And patients absolutely had to find some way to get nutritious food. So families couldn't afford to have a tubercular patient, even if they were rich.

My father tried hard to feed my mother nutritious food. He was even willing to sell all his property. My mother knew her illness would require a long treatment, so she rejected his help and resolved to divorce him. She must have been thinking that she didn't want her disease to ruin his life. I am amazed by my mother's love for my father and her desire to spare him when she contracted a disease that would never heal.

The morning I put on
the lipstick I bought just in case
a letter arrived from my ex-husband.

There must have been many nights when she wept quietly in her bed. I am sure she hated being sick, but I believe she never regretted the divorce, which she willingly gave him.

My mother's last moment came in May 1978. Happily sipping a cup of tea I served her, she said, "I feel a bit tired, Yasuko. I'll go to the hospital tomorrow and stay there a few days." She was admitted to her regular hospital the next day.

The evening of May 30, my mother suddenly said, "I'd like to eat some watermelon." This was highly unusual. She was not the type to ask for something so outlandish. It was not watermelon season, but I went to look for one anyway.

I found a watermelon after some searching and brought it to her. She was overjoyed and held it in her mouth. "It's too early, isn't it? It's not very sweet." She screwed her eyebrows into wrinkles. Still, I felt relieved to see her eating a piece of watermelon.

"See you tomorrow!" I called out as I left the room. She said, "Good night," and put her hand up with a smile when I turned around at the door to look at her. That was the last time I saw her alive.

Coming back to my hometown
for the first time in years
I glimpsed my mother
in the motions of my children and their children

Yasuko

Hiroshi Baba

Joining the kamikaze when I was 17, I was prepared for death

Born in December 1925, Hiroshi Baba joined Army Unit 65 in Kumamoto as a volunteer when he was 17, dreaming of becoming a pilot. He was later transferred to the Army Aviation Academy, assigned to the Kamikaze Corps.

Hiroshi's home was at 235 Yamazatomachi, very close to the hypocenter. In a sports field near his home belonging to Nagasaki University, students practiced track and field or rugby. A big camphor tree near this field produced thousands of nuts every fall. Hiroshi would often climb that tree to gather nuts to use as bullets in his bamboo tube gun and be scolded by a security guard.

Because I was ready to die, I had nothing to say to anyone

My father died of tuberculosis when I was just a year old. My mother raised my sister (seven years older than me) and me all by herself. A widow at 33, she bought one of the first *futon* reconditioning machines. She began reconditioning *futons*, doing all the work herself. By the time I graduated from elementary school, my sister was already married with two daughters.

I graduated from Yamazato Elementary School in 1940 at age 14. I entered the Craft Technical School at Mitsubishi Ordnance Works and worked every day manufacturing the stabilizers designed to drop well-balanced torpedoes from fighter planes. We called it a school, but it was a precision machine shop that manufactured gun emplacements, course indicators and other similar devices. We had lessons only twice a week and spent most of the time making weapons.

I was making torpedo stabilizers for fighter planes, but what I really wanted to do was fly the planes. I took a field test offered by the naval preparatory course for student aviators. I failed the balance test, which involved sitting on a chair as it spun around, then walking a straight white line. I graduated from Craft Technical School in three years and was assigned to the Army Tank School in Chiba.

The Army Tank School was also called a school, but it was actually a kamikaze training facility. Half a year later, Hiroshi was assigned to Independent Tank Unit 1235 in Miyazaki, Kyushu. However, the war was going badly for Japan, and fighter pilots were in short supply. Thus, five soldiers, including Hiroshi, were sent to the Tachiarai Army Aviation Academy in Fukuoka to prepare for the Battle of Okinawa. All of a sudden, Hiroshi was being trained to fly an airplane after all.

The training for "instant fighter pilots" was merciless. To send us to Okinawa with a half-year of training, we were trained in quick takeoffs and nosedives from morning till night. We hardly spent any time in bed. Even after going to bed, we could be called without previous notice to "night flight exercises" at one or two in the morning. This was called "emergency training." If I made even the smallest error, I got a double slap on my face and was forced to run around the field all night until I collapsed. This was "basic training." Volunteers like me were destined to fly a suicide attack as soon as we enlisted, so we received no mercy. One comrade killed himself by cutting open his stomach because he couldn't bear the harshness of it.

After six months of this severe training, Hiroshi and two other comrades were sent to Chiran Kamikaze Base in Kagoshima. The day he was sent to Chiran he wrote a will to his mother, his sister and her husband in Nagasaki. He cut his nails and a lock of hair and sent those along with his will. By that time his flight was already scheduled, but he would not be informed until the evening before he was supposed to fly. He moved to the barracks at the Chiran Base on August 9, the day the atomic bomb destroyed Nagasaki.

The following day, the 10th, I woke up at dawn to go to the bathroom. I came back to my bed half asleep and had a dream that lasted until reveille. My mother, my sister, her husband and their two daughters were in a field of flowers with a stream running between us. The stream was small enough to get over in a single bound. I was just about to jump across when they stopped me. They were waving their hands at me, saying, "Don't come over here!" Perhaps, they might have all died around that time after the bombing.

The Kamikaze Corps barracks were small. Six or seven of us made them quite full. We lost contact with the outside world and spent our days waiting to fly.

To avoid making friends and getting attached to each other, we spent the time alone, and there was not much to do. I stayed in my room lying down, or went hiking up the hill behind the building. Because I was ready to die, I had nothing to say to anyone. I had nothing but my death to think about.

We sent out a sortie before daybreak. Three or four pilots took off at the same time. I woke up one morning and found that a few comrades had gone and replacements would be arriving soon. By then it was obvious that I would be the next to go. I was scheduled to leave on the 18th. My landmark was Kaimondake, a cone-shaped volcano on the southern tip of the Satsuma Peninsula in Kagoshima, so I would be flying straight toward the volcano to fly to Okinawa.

My superior officer called me in the afternoon of August 15 to say, "The war ended. The war is over!" He said it, but I couldn't take it in. It took a while to understand and accept. We had not been allowed to hear the broadcast in which the Emperor announced Japan's surrender, and because I had been waiting to die by flying into an enemy warship, the call just left me dazed.

I came back to myself when my superior officer yelled, "Take your insignia off!" At that instant, I finally realized that the war was over.

At that time, my strained nerves, which I had kept under such strict control for so long, suddenly failed me. I could hardly keep standing. Some stood with heads hung low. Others squatted down, their eyes staring vacantly at nothing.

The suddenly freed kamikaze pilots were told to return to their original units immediately. Hiroshi went back to Tank Unit 1235 in Miyazaki. Disarmament had begun, so he repaired or maintained tanks to be handed over to the US Army.

No trouble occurred at Chiran Base, but in his original unit in Miyazaki a young drafted soldier who had been abused brutally by his superior officers became violent, spraying bullets from a machine gun and shouting, "No more officers, no more privates!"

A few days later, an adjutant told Hiroshi that a new type of bomb had been dropped on Nagasaki and said, "Go home now."

By that time, the joy of being alive, as well as fond memories of my hometown had revived me at last. Human feelings welled up in me. From being a young man thinking of nothing but death, I suddenly recalled the faces of my mother, my sister, her husband and their daughters Mitsuko (aged four) and Teruko (two).

I had last seen them when I finished Craft Technical School and enrolled in the tank school in Chiba. The tank school was for soldier training, so, as a matter of form, I had to belong to a military unit. I had been assigned to Army Unit 65 in Kumamoto and went to tank school from there.

When I had told my mother I was going to Kumamoto as a volunteer soldier, she looked so sad and cried, "It's too early! Please wait two more years and pass your enlistment examination." I replied, "I'm going to protect you and my sister." She fell silent and looked down.

Because I was leaving, my sister's family hurriedly moved into my house to live with my mother. That's when I met Mitsuko and Teruko. The two girls seemed to regard me as the perfect playmate. They never left me alone, hanging around me like little sisters. I was with them only a few days, but taking them to Nagasaki University Sports Field and Ana Kobo Temple at the foot of Konpira Hill are good memories for me.

My mother saw me off at Urakami Station, wearing the Women's Patriotic Association sash and waving a Japanese flag. Thinking back on my life, I see that my entire boyhood was spent in wartime, from the Shanghai Incident to the Manchurian Incident and the Sino-Japanese War.

Now, the war had ended, and I was going back to Nagasaki. Speaking to my senior officer, I said, "My brother-in-law likes cigarettes, and I want to take him some." He said, "Take as many as you like," and he opened the commissary.

Because he said "as many as you like," I took about 500 cigarettes and put them in my pack. For Mitsuko and Teruko, I grabbed 20 chocolate bars that had been supplies for the tank unit and 10 bags of sweet dry bread with crunchy sugar balls in it. I packed as much as I could into my pack, thinking, "I haven't seen Mitsuko and Teruko for two and a half years. Girls at that age grow up fast, so they must be young ladies by now." I wondered if I would be able to recognize them. I imagined how excited they would be seeing the chocolate and sweet bread.

I also had an image of my brother-in-law smoking the cigarettes. I grinned just thinking how happy he would be.

It took three days for Hiroshi to reach Nagasaki from Miyazaki. Arriving at Urakami Station, his shock was indescribable. There was no station building. The station staff came out of a shabby shack with a galvanized tin roof.

More than a month had passed since the atomic bombing, but nobody was disposing of the corpses, and white skeletons were scattered all around. Maggots swarmed in decomposing bodies, looking like white spots. Hiroshi was overwhelmed by the stench. He felt too weak to walk.

I went looking for my house, of course. Since Yamazatomachi was close to the hypocenter, the whole area was a burnt plain. It had all disappeared to such an extent that I couldn't tell where I was. I found a grove of trees I had often played in, and followed the road that looked like the one I had used to get to school. I kept looking around and eventually found a well I knew. I also found the iron skeleton of a burnt *futon* reconditioning machine. In utter amazement, I realized that I was looking at the ruins of my house.

Where was my mother? Where were my sister and her husband? Where were Mitsuko and Teruko? I had assumed that I would find my family alive until I saw what had become of my house. I cannot express the horror and grief that spread through my heart.

Because I couldn't find any trace of my mother, I collected burnt earth near the spot I thought our Buddhist altar had been. I put the earth in my water bottle and took it with me as her remains.

I thought I would sleep under a bridge, but there were too many dead cows, horses and human bodies floating on the river. If I had to sleep beside dead bodies, I would rather sleep in a graveyard. I went to my family graveyard and slept there.

The first thing I thought was, "In order to eat, I have to work." The next day I showed up at Mitsubishi Ordnance Works. When I told them I had graduated from their Craft Technical School, they hired me immediately. However, the job they gave me was to dispose of the human remains abandoned in Nagasaki's "Big Four" Mitsubishi factories (the shipyard, steel works, electric and ordnance works). Almost all the men in Nagasaki were burnt or injured in some way. Those healthy enough to work were all ex-soldiers coming home, like me.

Searching for nametags or other identification, I examined the clothes of the rotten, melting corpses, classifying them as "corpses with names" and "corpses without names." Then, I incinerated them.

I worked for Mitsubishi Shipbuilding until retirement. I married a woman from Omura in Nagasaki Prefecture who was introduced to me by my mother's younger brother when I was 23. We had two daughters.

I built a grave for my parents in Omura in 1954. I mixed the earth I had kept as my mother's remains in with my father's ashes. This was the best I could do to show my devotion to my parents.

Part 4

Families Look at August 6, 1945
Ten Accounts to Pass Forward
Testimonies of families from Hiroshima

Keiko Oe
Masako Kosaka

The day my mother was bombed

Keiko Oe   *Masako Kosaka*

I will tell my mother's atomic bomb experience to the extent that I know it.

Her name is Masako Kosaka. On August 6, 1945, she was 15 years old and working for Toyo Industries (Mazda today). But for five days, starting that day, she and two friends were scheduled to help with building demolition.

My mother arrived at Mukainada Station to catch a train leaving at 7:50. One of her friends was late, so they missed that train. That was the moment that decided her fate.

My mother was exposed to the bombing while walking with her friends along the bank of the Kyobashi River from Hiroshima Station toward Tsurumi Bridge, 1.8 kilometers from the hypocenter.

An air-raid warning cleared as they approached the bridge. She took off her air-raid hood and looked up at the sky. Suddenly, an intense ray of light hit her from behind. The blast knocked her unconscious.

When she came to, she was covered in blood. She didn't feel any pain immediately, but, as she told me, "As time went by, the pain got worse."

I asked her, "What did you do then?" She said the entire city on the other side of the bridge was gone without a trace. "I didn't think about my body at all. I was simply stunned that the whole city had disappeared."

People around the bridge began jumping into the river. Her friends saw them and urged her to do that as well, but my mother said, "No, I don't want to go into the river. Let's go back to our workplace." So the three of them fled toward Hijiyama Hill.

Thousands of people took refuge on Hijiyama Hill. They met a Toyo Industries employee who took my mother and her friends to a dormitory. Many people exposed to the bombing were already there on the grounds of the dormitory. Many of them were dead, and the corpses were piled into what seemed like mountains.

My mother's hometown was Miyoshi City, but she had come to Hiroshima to earn money. She suffered bad burns on her head, the back of her neck, her elbow and below her knee. Still, she went home before long. She separated from the two friends who were with her at the time of the bombing and learned later that both of them died. When I asked how they died, she said she didn't know. Since all three were exposed at the same time and place, I'm sure she was afraid to find out.

At 27, my mother married my father, who was also an A-bomb survivor. They worked hard to bring us children up. The atomic bombing is lodged in my mother's mind even now. When August 6 approaches, she says, "I still have nightmares about the bombing."

My mother's most moving words were, "We didn't experience that bomb because we wanted to, you know." I want people around the world to know the horror of the bomb that made her have to say those painful words with such seriousness.

My thoughts as a second-generation *hibakusha*

As for myself, I was born 12 years after the bombing, on April 4, 1957. I grew up in Hiroshima and have heard about the atomic bombing often. It seems to me that I became aware of myself as a second-generation *hibakusha* when I entered junior high school, but I didn't willingly let anyone know.

I had a sad experience after graduating from high school and starting a new job. My friend reported that her acquaintance, someone I had never met, had said, "Is she from Hiroshima? Then her parents must be *hibakusha*, right?" She was talking about me, and if I had heard her, I would have been deeply hurt.

I keep many things in my mind as a second-generation *hibakusha*, but my feelings are quite complicated. For example, I sometimes wonder why Hiroshima, my parents' home, had to be targeted. But do I wish some other city had been targeted? How could I?

This is one of several conundrums to which I have never found good answers. The atomic bomb and the war keep torturing not only survivors but also their descendants, even after 70 years.

Prejudice and discrimination against survivors and second-generation survivors has diminished. We are slowly creating the conditions where all of us can think together about our problems. But do non-survivors know that survivors and second-generation survivors are still having regular medical examinations?

Hijiyama Hill, where my mother rested after the bombing, is now a nice park. In one corner of the park stands a facility called the Radiation Effects Research Foundation (RERF). RERF examines and studies survivors, looking for aftereffects. It takes about a month after each examination to get the results. While waiting for the results, I never feel fully alive. I keep thinking, "What if they found some A-bomb disease?"

I want so badly for people to hear the "raw voices" of survivors.

They are aging, and every year the chances to hear from them become fewer. When I showed this text to my mother, she cried, and August 6 appeared in her dream again that night. This is the "raw voice" of a *hibakusha*.

I hope everyone will listen to the heartrending cries of *hibakusha* and their children. In particular, I hope young people will listen and heed their cries as far into the future as possible.

Masaichi Egawa
My "double suffering"

Masaichi Egawa

I was born in Hikimi, Shimane Prefecture, in 1928. My father was a Korean who had come to Japan to make money eight years before I was born. My Korean name is Lee Jong-gun.

I honestly don't have much memory of Hikimi. I also don't remember much about my family moving to Yoshiwa in Hiroshima Prefecture. When we were forced to change our Korean names to Japanese, my name became Masaichi Egawa. I lived in Yoshiwa until the sixth grade. I was routinely called *"cho-sen"* (a derogatory name for Korean people) and discriminated against continually. I was miserable and suffered many bitter disappointments.

Because of our move to Hiroshima City, in addition to the discrimination I suffered as a Korean, I had the "double suffering" of becoming a *hibakusha*.

We moved to Sakamachi, Aki County, when I was in the second year of junior high school. I went to work with my father at a construction site to build a dock for Mitsubishi Shipbuilding. The construction workers were roughnecks, but, on the other hand, they didn't discriminate against me. I graduated from school when I was 16, while still working there. I decided to get a job at the National Railways. I studied hard and passed the examination.

I am able to admit something now. In the job application I was given by the school, someone had already entered my address and nationality. I erased and changed it before submitting the application to the National Railways. Hardly any companies in Japan would hire Koreans in those days, and the government-owned railways were particularly strict. But I loved trains and desperately wanted that job.

Once I was in the company, no one noticed that I was Korean. I was born in Japan so I spoke Japanese fluently. I lived like a normal Japanese in the dormitory. Still, I was beaten by senior workers frequently. They said, "We'll harden your spirit!" and they beat me every night. Two coworkers who joined the company with me ran away and went home. I wanted to quit, too, but I couldn't. I endured the beatings and finally left the dorm to commute from home.

Around that time, my family moved to Hera in Hatsukaichi. I went back and forth between Hatsukaichi and Hiroshima day after day. My workplace was the First Locomotive Yard. The locomotive depot was mainly for engines that transported military supplies to Shimonoseki and Okayama. People nowadays probably don't know that during the war there was a railroad track from Hiroshima Station to Ujina Port. The trains left from Platform Zero. I think scant traces of that track and platform can still be seen.

In the morning on August 6, 1945, I was preparing to go to work. I don't remember the cause, but I had a quarrel with my mother. I left home late and missed the train I usually took. That quarrel saved my life, and I'm grateful.

The atomic bomb was dropped at 8:15, just as I had got off a streetcar at Matoba and was crossing Kojin Bridge, 1.9 kilometers from the hypocenter. All of a sudden, I was enveloped by a brilliant flash. That August morning, the sun was already glaring off roofs and walls. The flash looked like another ray of yellow sunlight coming in on top of the glare. I still remember how unusual that light was. It was different from lightning: it wasn't that fast. I think it lasted two or three seconds, long enough for me to think, "What is that? This isn't normal."

I dropped my lunch box, took off my glasses and threw myself onto the ground covering my eyes, nose and ears. I had been trained in school and at work to do that if a bomb fell close by.

The blast came, and after a while I opened my eyes carefully and fearfully. The whole world was in darkness. I just lay there waiting until my eyes got used to the dark. As my sight gradually returned, I doubted my eyes. Whole buildings had completely disappeared. The scene was unbelievable.

My next action was to look for my lunch box. When something beyond comprehension happens, human beings turn their attention to something ordinary. I groped here and there in the dim light, and when I found my lunch box, which had flown 20 or 30 meters away, I felt a bit relieved.

I didn't know where to go. I couldn't think of any place to head for. I looked around and saw some space under a bridge. I went in. Some people who had taken refuge there before me were saying, "It's a new kind of bomb." Someone saw my face and said, "Your face is really red!" Then, for the first time I touched my face and felt pain. Or, maybe I just said, "It hurts." I don't know if I really felt pain or not. I had been burnt by the flash.

I started to walk toward the locomotive depot. On the way, I saw someone trapped under a collapsed house. A mother was crying, "My child is under this building! Please help us!" I heard her calling "Help us!" behind me, but I just kept going, pretending I didn't hear her. Every time I recall this, I get angry at myself. "Why didn't I help? I should have at least tried to pull out one child." This is an emotional conflict that will never be gone from my mind.

When I arrived at the locomotive depot, my colleagues said, "Egawa! Your face is burnt." They had been inside the building, so they didn't get burnt. Saying, "Oil is good for burns," they put oil for locomotive engine shafts on my face and hands. But that oil on my burns was so horribly painful that I jumped into the air. It was machine oil, which was crazy.

Around four in the afternoon, I went out to look for my company cap, part of my uniform. Passing the Eastern Drill Ground, I was shocked. Because I was a National Railways employee, my uniform was sturdily made, so I was protected. But others wore shirts that were normal for the season. People who had been exposed to the bombing had gathered in the drill ground. They were all blackish and looked like lumps of charcoal. Even the women were half naked. Their skin was swollen and sore. They didn't look like human beings at all. About eight hours after the bombing, I found I had an incredible blister on the back of my left foot.

I couldn't find my cap, so I walked back to Hera, where my home was. Fire was still smoldering all through the city. Walking by Hiroshima University, I saw another shocking sight: a dead horse, a big one. Its eyes had popped out. A fellow worker went part way home with me, and we were very scared. There were mountains of dead human bodies. A human being who has lost his normal mind is quite frightening, right? I came to feel nothing for dead bodies. I lost all resistance to simply walking right over a dead body on the road. Eventually, I didn't even feel guilty stepping on their hands or feet.

People swarmed around the foot of the bridge. Some said, "Please give me water." Some gazed intently right into our eyes. Maybe they thought we were family members. I will never forget the way they looked at us as if to say, "Please save me!"

It was probably after midnight when I arrived home. I entered the house, but my parents were gone. I asked my younger brother where they were. He said, "They went to Hiroshima to look for you." I had never told my parents where I worked. I was afraid if my parents showed up at work with their Korean accents, my Japanese colleagues would know I was Korean.

My mother saw terribly burnt people and was frightened, unable to keep going. She came home just before dawn. She was surprised to see me already home. She squeezed me, sobbing loudly. She stuck a needle into my blisters and discharged the liquid. She applied Mercurochrome. My father had gone to the station to look for me, and came home the next afternoon.

After a while, my burnt skin scabbed over. I peeled the scabs off and applied Mercurochrome every day. My mother took care of my back. When pus began oozing out, my wounds were soon infested with maggots. At first my mother picked them all out, but they were endless.

My mother started telling me, "Hurry up and die. Please, die quickly." I'm sure she thought that with my terribly burnt face and body, I would have a miserable life even if I lived. She kept saying things like that every day, crying as she did so.

About six months after the war ended, I went back to work. After about a year, I was asked to resubmit information for my family register. But that would reveal that I had previously submitted a document from which I had erased my nationality. If they discovered such a fraud, I would be fired immediately. That fear gradually made me reluctant to go to work. In the end, I quit the company without even sending a letter of resignation.

After that, I did many different jobs, including driving a truck, in order to support my younger brother and sister. My father was bedridden for a long time. I believe it was because he was exposed to radiation while looking for me in Hiroshima.

Despite having the "double suffering" of being Korean in Japan and a *hibakusha*, I decided to talk about the terrible things from my past because I don't want people to forget the misery of war. Any people who lose a war suffer miserably. Look at Korea, after losing to Japan. Then look at Japan, after being the victim of atomic bombing by the US, who were determined to win the war by any means necessary, testing their atomic bombs on the Japanese.

The Monument in Memory of the Korean Victims of the A-bomb in Hiroshima stands in the Peace Memorial Park. Thinking of my fellow Koreans, who suffered terrible racial discrimination and then were killed by the atomic bombing, I feel I have to pass my story on to future generations, even if I have to confront memories of which I am ashamed.

I hope young people will learn from my experience, at least part of it, so I can feel I survived like this for a purpose—to let as many people as possible know that all people are equal, their lives have equal worth, and how cruel and foolish war is.

Kozo Ikegami
Sumiyo Ikegami
Tetsuo Ikegami

Steadfast dialogue can strengthen peace

Kozo Ikegami

Sumiyo Ikegami

Tetsuo Ikegami

Reflections upon completing the written version of my father's story — Kozo Ikegami

I was in senior high school the first time my father, Tetsuo, told me about the atomic bombing. He responded to my request to interview him for an antiwar book our school was making. I remember that as I listened and wrote down the story of my father's A-bomb experience more than 40 years ago, I got very angry at the injustice of it.

He was born on August 5, 1930, so the bombing of Hiroshima happened the day after his 15th birthday.

I have never suffered discrimination or bullying as a second-generation *hibakusha*, and I have never suffered health effects. My life has been almost too normal.

My family took my Uncle Fumio (Fu-chan) to live with us in

Fukuyama. Fu-chan was born with Down syndrome caused by in utero exposure. He lived with us for 24 years. Fu-chan was a fine musician. His intellect was equivalent to that of a seven- or eight-year-old, but he loved classical music and had perfect pitch. Any melody he heard once, he could play on the accordion without sheet music.

In 2009, Fu-chan died at age 63. For our two children, I feel that growing up with Fu-chan was "peace education" in the truest sense.

I think my father, who had said little about his A-bomb experience, overcame his resistance to talk to us because he wants the peace we enjoy today to continue.

Peace is the most important thing. I feel keenly that we must do what we can to promote peace through steadfast dialogue.

Feeling anew the importance of conveying this tragic story to future generations, my wife and I collaborated to interview my father and bring you his words just as he spoke them.

Bombed the day after I turned 15
— Tetsuo Ikegami

When I was young, we lived on the streetcar route at Hondori 9-chome in Kure City. Because my father was a policeman, he was frequently transferred. We soon moved to Koi, and I went to Koi Elementary until I was in the second or third grade. Then we moved to Oshiba, and I went to Oshiba Elementary and Sotoku Junior High School.

By that time, enemy planes were regularly attacking the homeland. I think the bosses knew, "We're not going to win this." Students had to work outside as members of the air defense brigade—there wasn't much schoolwork going on. Every day, the ones living close by were mobilized for air-raid defense duty at school.

Prior to the atomic bombing, Hiroshima had hardly been hit,

while American planes were always flying over Kure because it was a key naval base. So people didn't take things seriously; they fooled themselves. "Okay, Hiroshima will be fine." Then, that day came...

It was the day after I turned 15.

We were out on the riverbank in front of the school waiting for class to start at 8:30—about a dozen of us, I guess. It was so hot, some boys jumped into the river—the Ota River.

The time was 8:15, but we only learned that later. I saw the plane that dropped it. It came after the air-raid warning cleared. It showed up so suddenly, I didn't think it was an enemy plane. I only saw one. It came over Ushita into the city skies and headed to Iwakuni...

Just when I thought, "Hey, this is weird!" my head suddenly heated up. The moment of explosion, for me, was the thought, "That's hot!" My student cap flew off, my hair caught fire. I had no idea what had happened. I could still hear the drone of the engine, so I was just getting ready to jump in the river, but then I saw my friends who were in the water—they were horribly burnt. The skin had cleanly peeled off some of them. No one died immediately, but some looked so bad you couldn't bear to look. Since I could move, I ran home.

My friends who'd been swimming naked mostly died in two or three days. Other classmates had been in the city helping demolish houses—most of them died too. If we hadn't been assigned to air-defense duty, we'd have been with them and died for sure. My grade had four classes of 40 students each. Three out of four of us died in the bombing.

Right after the explosion, you couldn't see a thing because of the smoke. Toward the hypocenter, the smoke was surging, up and up. I can never forget the unearthly sight of the people who came up from Kusunokicho, washing their blood off in the river.

Just after the bombing, the school building was still standing. But everything around it burned, until sparks got it and fire took it down. My home was damaged. At the time, we lived in staff housing for the driving school where my dad worked. The lights wouldn't come on. For some nights, I don't know how many, we slept in the air-raid shelter.

My mother worried awfully about my burns, but compared to what happened to others, mine were light. I was burnt from the back of my head down to my neck and upper back. I was wearing glasses, and it was summer. When I sweated, the burnt skin under the glasses hurt. Then it got infected and hurt more. It took a long time to heal.

There was a bank next to the Chugoku Newspaper Building in Kaminagarekawacho, and they turned the roof into a first-aid station. I went there for treatment for several days. Years later, I got prostate cancer, but the doctor said it wasn't related to the atomic bombing.

At the time of the bombing, our household consisted of my parents and four kids. But Mother was pregnant. My little brother Fumio (Fu-chan) was born after the war. He was exposed in the womb, and his brain was affected by Down syndrome. Whenever I saw my little brother, so far from me in age, and my mom struggling to raise us all, I remembered the atomic bombing. They were the main victims. My mother died of cancer at 74.

After the surrender, my father worked in Hiroshima. He died of old age at 92. I don't think our family suffered prejudice because we were *hibakusha*.

I used to be angry, really bitter about the bombing, but I let those feelings go.

Tatsuko Ota
My tragedy must never be repeated

Tatsuko Ota

Our family consisted of my mother, my father and eight children. My brother was the oldest; all the rest were girls. I was the youngest. By the time I was old enough to remember things, we were at war, and my brother had been sent to the front. One of my sisters was married, another had been evacuated to the countryside and a third had been adopted by a relative. Left in our house in Kobe were four daughters, my mother and my father, who had retired from military service to work for a company.

I had started elementary school, but the air raids became so intense that schoolwork was abandoned. I was in the first grade on June 6, 1945, when an air attack began at around 9 a.m., after my father had left for work.

Incendiary bombs thudded to the ground all around us and exploded. Bam! Bam! Around us swirled a sea of flame. I called out to my mother—no answer. My sixth-grade sister, who was near me, grabbed my hand. Through the sea of fire and smoke we ran, trying to get to the designated neighborhood evacuation place.

On the way, we encountered people who had been burnt, begging, "Give me water!" Injured people could not move, but we could do nothing—saving ourselves was all we could do. When we got to the refuge and did not see Mother and our other sisters, our fear grew. That night, I wailed and screamed, "Mother is dead!" which was very hard on my sister.

Two days later, my sister and I went home. The house had burnt down. As we dug through the wreckage, my sister said she could remember what Mother was wearing. All around us, people were using sticks to probe the ruins. The air was suffused with a strange smell. We never found the bodies of my mother or our sisters.

We stayed in the shelter for a week, wearing the same clothes. To stave off our hunger, we had packets of hard bread and water from kettles.

Our family's wartime tragedy was not over. My father, my two older sisters and I left Kobe for our mother's birthplace in Yachiyocho, Hiroshima Prefecture. My oldest remaining sister went to live in the dormitory of a spinning factory in Mihara.

When the bomb fell on Hiroshima, I could feel the impact out in Yachiyocho (about 30 kilometers away). Amazed, I ran out of the house and looked up to see a pitch-black cloud rising in the sky. That day, my father had gone to Hiroshima on business. My fourth-grade sister and I were supposed to watch the house, but we were so afraid for our father that we stayed outside to look out for him. While we sat by the roadside, we were rained on by black rain full of ash. We had no way of knowing it was radioactive rain.

Under the black rain, we waited for the trucks coming from Hiroshima. Trucks came by filled with badly injured people. We cried out to stop them. "Is Haruji Yamakado in there? If you're in there, please get off here!" But he was not in any truck.

Later, one of the neighbors came by to say, "Haru-san (our father) died. He was killed by the *pika-don* (flash-boom)." We wept and wept. Later, we went into the city. I remember walking through the ruins with my sister holding my hand, or carrying me on her back. I don't remember seeing bodies, so we must not have gone in the first day or two. Even so, a sharp smell pierced our noses. We could not find Father's corpse, just as we had not found Mother's.

During my first year of school, I had lost both my parents, and my brother was still off at war. Now my life consisted of being shuttled from place to place, dependent on relatives and friends. First I went to Imabari in Shikoku, where my sister had gone as a bride. My brother-in-law came to get me. To get to Shikoku, we had to change trains in Hiroshima. It must have been a week after the bombing, but the stench was still there. We slept outside in Hiroshima Station. The next morning, we went to Onomichi and learned that the war was over.

When my brother returned from the war, he took my sister, who was four years older, and me into his home. For a year, we lived together in Shioya in Kobe. But he couldn't earn enough to take care of two little sisters. It was decided that one of his war buddies would take me in. So I moved to live with that family in Hitoyoshi in Kumamoto Prefecture.

Meanwhile, my brother worked in a mine in Yamaguchi Prefecture. In September 1950 he was killed there, when Typhoon Kezia caused a landslide that buried him. My brother survived a war, returned to find his parents and two of his sisters dead; in the post-surrender climate of despair, he worked desperately hard, only to die in an accident. Whenever I think of him, my anger at war surges again.

I lived in Kumamoto until I was 18, when I moved back to Hiroshima, relying on help from my aunts. I lived in Nagarekawa for a month, then in Nagahara for about two years. In Nagahara, I did farming work all day. An acquaintance introduced me to the man I married. He was working in forestry at the time, but he later joined a company. He died at age 63. We had two sons, and I now live with the younger son.

At my older son's wedding, my brother-in-law in Shikoku talked with me about the time he came to get me, and asked, "Tatsuko, did you get an Atomic Bomb Survivor Health Book?"

I knew that I was an "entry victim." I had been hit by black rain and entered the city to look for my father's body. A week after the bombing, my brother-in-law and I walked through the city and slept outdoors at Hiroshima Station. I'd never applied for an Atomic Bomb Survivor Health Book because I had been healthy and because I couldn't write properly, not having graduated from school. I didn't feel I could fill out the application. But my husband said he would help me with the process, so I decided to do it.

In my three-page application, I listed the days I thought I had entered the city and the reasons I had entered. I submitted one copy to Hiroshima Prefectural Government Office and one more for my brother-in-law to Ehime Prefectural Government Office. I needed proof that I had attended elementary school, so we asked the Board of Education of Takata County to search through the lists of students for my name and asked for proof of my enrollment from Imabari Elementary School. We found someone who gave witness that I had been in Hiroshima on the days I indicated.

My application was accepted, and my Health Book was issued. My brother-in-law in Shikoku was also recognized as an entry victim, but he died two years later. My sister who had been rained on by the black rain at my side did not receive the Health Book because she had been officially evacuated in a group evacuation.

When I received the Health Book at age 48, I somehow felt it was a gift from my departed parents. We had not even found their remains, so this Health Book felt like my only keepsake from them.

When I was a child, my hair fell out easily, and I frequently suffered from nausea. I don't know if these were effects from the bomb or not. Ten years ago, I was operated on for thyroid cancer, but I don't know if that was related or not. Since I turned 70, my bones break easily, and I suffer from eye ailments. Various parts of my body are weakening. Maybe it is simply my age, but I often feel that my A-bomb exposure is affecting my health.

Though my sons are second-generation victims, and though people have advised them to apply for Health Books, they both refuse. They have their own ways of thinking about this that I must respect. I have had the good fortune to live with my sons without any recurrence of the tragedy that I suffered. These are good days, and I am happy.

Takashi Katsunori
Michiko Katsunori

"It's for the future." The past she wanted to forget

Takashi Katsunori   *Michiko Katsunori*

My mother's experience and her thoughts about war — Takashi Katsunori

When I was a child, I wondered why my mother's feet were cracked. Years later, she told me, "We got out of there running for our lives on bare feet... The river was full of dead bodies." On hearing her horrific story, I understood that the destructive power and impact of the bombing is absolutely cruel and inhumane.

In January 2014, my mother had a myocardial infarction; later, she suffered multiple fractures in her back. She had four compression fractures in her spine and one in her hip. Now that she is in her 70s, her body is weak; she has shrunk 16 centimeters.

Mother says, "Since it isn't clear whether the atomic bombing or my age is the cause, I'm not going to blame the bombing." Mother and I had argued in the past over the causes of her health problems, but we never discussed the bombing: I'm sure that she didn't want to recall it.

My mother first shared her A-bomb experience in 2007, when she began working as a Hiroshima Peace Volunteer (a guide in the Peace Memorial Museum). After she had her myocardial infarction, she could no longer do this work. This was so unfortunate, because it had given her something to look forward to. But as her son, I feel glad that we found this way to preserve her experience and her thoughts about war.

What follows is the account she struggled to write, to which I've added details that she has shared with me.

That day — Michiko Katsunori

I was born in Showamachi in Hiroshima City, and was exposed in the third grade, when I was eight. At the time, the government ordered children from the third grade to the sixth grade to evacuate to the countryside. Children went to stay with relatives if they could; otherwise, they went with their classes to stay somewhere as a group. My parents found distant relatives who were willing to take me in. I went to Fukugi in Asa County and attended Fukugi Elementary School. Many other children from Hiroshima who had evacuated with their classes were there too. Daily necessities were hard to come by, and we kids went to school barefoot.

On the night of August 5, 1945, my father came to pick me up and take me home to Hiroshima for a visit before taking me to a new evacuation site with my mother's family. That night, my father and I walked the 10 kilometers home to Showamachi. We arrived during the night; I was so exhausted I went right to sleep.

On the sixth, my parents, my five-year-old brother and I had breakfast and went back to our rooms. I was getting ready to return a book I had borrowed from a friend in the neighborhood. Just as I opened the sliding doors, they fell down onto me. I don't know how long I lay trapped under them. When I came to, I saw a faint light far away. I thought if I could get to it, I could get outside. So I struggled through the wreckage and finally made it out.

When I was hit, I heard nothing. Later, I heard people talk about the *pika* (flash) and the *don* (boom), but inside the house I saw nothing and heard nothing. I thought, "A bomb fell on our house!" Our two-story house had completely collapsed. From somewhere underneath, my mother was calling, "Help! I'm here! Help!" I saw my father crouching down, his left arm trapped between the threshold and the lintel. He couldn't move. Father cried, "Get someone to come help us!"

I walked around the area, but our neighbors were trapped under their houses, too. People who had been exposed outside were injured. I found no one to help us. I went back and said, "Daddy, there's no one to help!" He pointed to an iron shaft nearby and said, "Bring that to me." I handed it to him, and he inserted it between the threshold and the lintel. Fighting for his life must have given him superhuman strength. Even squatting, he was able to lift the weight enough to free his arm. Then he was out.

The two of us began looking for Mother and my little brother, but we had only their voices to go by. We couldn't tell where they were. Soon, flames licked up just as we stopped hearing Mother's voice. Sparks landed on me and ignited my clothes. Father quickly put out the fire. Then he found a *futon* and soaked it in the water cistern. Covered by the drenched *futon*, we ran for our lives, barefoot in the flames. My mother and little brother were burned alive.

At the time, every house had a cistern in front for putting out flames in the event of bombing. But when this bomb exploded, even those who were not making breakfast still had charcoal smoldering. The charcoal eventually ignited fires here and there. Apparently, the ferocious heat of the bomb shot ground temperatures up as high as

3,000-4,000 degrees Celsius, igniting anything flammable.

Weaving our way through collapsed houses and flaming wreckage, father and I aimed toward Hijiyama Hill.

The people who had been outside had all been blown down by the bomb blast. Those who had been inside were trapped in the rubble and burned to death. We heard people crying for help, but they screamed to no avail. When we got to Hijiyama Bridge, we saw many people in the river and many more jumping in. When I looked carefully, I saw bodies piled on bodies, all floating in the water. People were piled up on both sides of the bridge—their skin burnt black or peeling off.

Afraid to stay there, we crossed Hijiyama Bridge and found our way to a vineyard in Shinonomecho, four kilometers away. Many others took refuge there as well. We spent the night looking back at Hiroshima, where pillars of red flame shot up here and there.

The next day, the Shinonome Women's Association made rice balls and handed them out. The morning after that, Father and I were heading to Fukugi when he said, "I can't stand up anymore." It must have been an injury from being squashed under the collapsed house. He had to crawl on his knees. A truck picked us up and carried us, and finally we arrived at my grandmother's house in Fukugi.

Both Father and I came down with diarrhea and vomiting; our hair fell out. A doctor in the neighborhood said, "Could be dysentery, I don't know." We later understood that we were suffering acute effects of the bombing, but at the time we thought it might be dysentery. Lacking medicine, grandmother and my aunt went to the river to pick *dokudami* (saururaceae plants). We drank tea made from these plants in place of medicine. My aunt had evacuated to Fukugi after losing her home in the air raids in Kure.

After we were sufficiently recovered, my aunt, my father and I returned to Showamachi every day to look for the remains of Mother and my little brother. The first task was to identify our house within the mass of burnt ruins. All had been flattened, leaving nothing to serve as a marker. Because we had no idea where to start, Father later came back alone to search. A few days later, he brought home something that he called their bones. I have no way of knowing whether that was true or not.

Because people were saying that nothing would grow in Hiroshima for 70 years, my father was leaning toward abandoning Showamachi and building a little house in Fukugi. But when I was in the second semester of my sixth-grade year, he said, "Little by little, people are going back. Let's go back, too."

So we built a shack in the ruins of our home in Showamachi for my father, grandmother and me. Our school was not yet rebuilt, so I went to Senda Elementary School in the neighboring district. The auditorium was a buckled and twisted iron skeleton.

Together with my classmates or kids in the neighborhood, I'd go to a concrete structure with a tile floor in the ruins and play house. Whenever we dug, human bones would come up. In time we lost our repulsion or fear of human bones. Many air-raid shelters had been dug around the bottom of Hijiyama Hill, where we'd sometimes go to do group exercises to the radio. Many people were living in these shelters. Even two or three years after the bombing, people were still living there.

As a child, I never felt discriminated against for being a *hibakusha*. After all, everyone around me was one.

I got my Atomic Bomb Survivor Health Book in 1972, when I was 35. Survivors were often hurt by the way people reacted when they learned that we'd been in the bombing. Many of us were slow to apply for the status.

I was 22 when I married. The preceding two years, I worked for Daiichi Life Insurance in Motomachi. My father lived to be 93 without any particular ailments. I cared for him at home until the end.

When I started being a Hiroshima Peace Volunteer, I guided

elementary school children who came on class trips through the A-bomb Museum. When we were done, they'd share their impressions with me. A sixth-grade boy said, "What sticks with me is your saying, 'War makes people lose their humanity.' What do you think peace is?"

I countered, "What do you think it is?"

"Getting rid of the thoughts that make us want to hurt one another."

I was deeply moved, because I felt that he truly understood.

We who have experienced war believe that peace means the absolute refusal to make war. This is not hard to understand. We *hibakusha* don't enjoy sharing our experiences because we don't want to cry. The catastrophe was just too cruel, too horrible for words. It was a dark world utterly devoid of the light of human feelings, a living hell. We have no way to communicate this, so we remain silent. I believe that this feeling is common to all survivors.

While my father was alive, he never spoke of his experience. When I said this to another Peace Volunteer, she asked, "Why didn't you and your father speak to each other about what the two of you had been through?"

We did not—we could not—because we were parent and child. We were being considerate of each other's feelings. If we delved into it, questions would come up: "Why didn't we rescue them?" "We should have gone in, even if we burned up with them." If even I, a child at the time, blamed myself with such thoughts, how much more deeply must Father have felt them! All survivors bear these wounds of the heart. This is why I never talked to my son. If I did, the tears would come as I was forced to remember...

Now we have peace. To ensure that it continues, we must convey to people the horror of war. If that awareness takes root in the youth, when the rush to war arises, they will stand up and wave the flag that says: "No war."

Sachiko Nakanishi
My father's A-bomb story

Sachiko Nakanishi

My late father, Masato Watanabe, was born in Koimachi, Hiroshima City, in 1914. After graduating from higher elementary school, he worked until around 1941 on a government-owned ship, and then took a job at Tanaka Refrigeration in Koimachi.

When the bomb dropped, he was 32 years old. He had left his company on business and was walking near Hakushima Elementary School in the center of Hiroshima when suddenly everything was bathed in the bright light of the flash. He jumped into a ditch, pressing his fingers against his ears and eyes, as he'd been trained to do in bomb drills.

Immediately after came a huge roar and blast. When he regained consciousness, he found himself almost naked. He found a towel to cover himself and headed back toward his company. He ran into people whose skin was peeling and hanging from their fingertips.

"I was terrified." Behind my father's words I sensed anguish and despair at his powerlessness. When he got back to his company, he was given three cans of butter to apply to his burns. Then he headed home out of the city center to Hatsukaichi. He was burnt on his back, but his burns did not form keloids.

On the way home, he saw piteous sights, such as a mother who might or might not have known that the baby she carried on her back was dead. People were seeking water, jumping into the rivers. Through this hell, he walked to Hatsukaichi. He did not arrive until the next day, August 7.

In 1950, when I was two, our family moved to Minaga, on a hill in Itsukaichi. Our house was a converted storage building with a corrugated tin roof.

Around two years later, my father's lips began to fester. I remember the black vehicle of the Atomic Bomb Casualty Commission (ABCC) coming to our house every Friday to pick him up and then bring him back. I don't remember him ever telling us what happened to him at the ABCC, but I vaguely understood that it had to do with illness caused by the bombing.

Every morning, my mother applied hot water to my father's lips with a piece of gauze. Some time later, my father was finally able to move his lips.

My father's younger sisters also were exposed to the bombing. Shizuko, who was 17, died. She had been on her way to school. That evening, a neighbor carried her home in a cart. Her skin was melting off, but she could still speak. Nonetheless, in the middle of the night of the seventh, she passed away.

His other sister, Yasuko, who was 20, was exposed at the company where she worked as a telephone operator. When the bomb exploded at 8:15, she was on break in the waiting room, which saved her life. At the huge roar, she jumped up and ran to the air-raid shelter. After some time, she came out and entered the shell of the company building.

All the glass had shattered. The doors were barely standing, but the walls had crumbled, except for the posts.

Walking home, she was hit by black rain that stained her blouse black. Washing did not erase the stains.

"That was black hail, you know," Aunt Yasuko said.

This is what she had to say about her experience: "Lots of people lay where they'd fallen, their skin peeling as cleanly as a glove pulled back halfway off the hand.

"The roads were full of glass shards. Every evening, we smelled the stench from piles of corpses burning. We don't need any more war, that's for sure."

I was about 20 when my father spoke directly to me about his experience. I don't know where we were, but I believe we were alone when I asked him what happened. He died in 1979. My sister, who is six years older, was a "Hiroshima Maiden" (one of a group of young women badly scarred by the bombing who were taken to receive plastic surgery in the US). There was a period when we were forced to confront the bombing even if we hated to, but mostly I lived without feeling forced to talk about it. Even when I married, I did not mention that my father had been in the bombing, or that I was a second-generation *hibakusha*. Now I wonder: "Was it wrong not to admit that?"

As a child, I was weak. Riding buses gave me motion sickness. Twice, I could have toured the Hiroshima Peace Memorial Museum with my class, but I declined because I feared motion sickness on the bus journey.

My son said, "Mother, you live in Hiroshima, but you've never been to the Hiroshima Peace Memorial Museum. That's just wrong." When he was a child, he toured the museum on a class trip. When he got home, he told me, "I cried. I couldn't eat my lunch. Mom, you have to go there with me." That son is now 32 years old.

Two years ago, I underwent surgery for thyroid cancer. I'd lived free of health problems, so being a second-generation survivor had not felt real to me. Now it does.

Seventy years after the bombing, I bow my head to the young people who are becoming A-bomb storytellers to convey the experiences of survivors to coming generations. I'm not good at speaking. I lack the courage to do it myself, but it's critical that people step up to pass the stories forward.

Maintaining peace requires us to strengthen our resolve never to make war. It is deeply reassuring to know that so many young people understand this.

Tokutomo Hase
Tsuchio Hase

Each survivor has a different way of thinking

Tokutomo Hase

Tsuchio Hase

There's nothing like experience
— Tokutomo Hase

Hearing my father tell his story, I felt that he sees the atomic bombing in a way that is quite different from the thinking of most *hibakusha*. Rather than lamenting over the past, he concentrates on treasuring the happiness he enjoys now. Rather than talking about his atomic bombing experience, he wanted to convey to me his antiwar sentiment. I feel sure that's because he is focused on the present.

Each survivor has a different way of thinking, and second-generation survivors have still other ways of thinking. I had eczema as a child, and always wondered if it was a kind of A-bomb disease. But it subsided when I grew up. A long time has passed, so we can't say that all the illnesses of survivors and second-generation survivors are connected to the bomb. But we never know. Doctors can't tell if a disease is due to the atomic bomb or not.

One thing I can say for sure is that if there had been no war, there would have been no atomic bomb. Therefore, to avoid any repetition of the tragedy of Hiroshima, Japan should never again go to war. We should never glorify any kind of war.

After talking with him about this, I finally understood why my father was always saying, "This current peaceful state of Japan is precious. We have to take good care of this happiness."

I want to say, "Dad, there's nothing like experience, right?"

My father was exposed to the atomic bombing when he was 18. He had been mobilized to work for Mitsubishi Machinery, four kilometers from the hypocenter. He went home on August 5 because it was a Sunday. The next day, he took a streetcar from Hiroshima Station, getting off at Kanonmachi. He was walking toward his workplace when the atomic bomb exploded.

I will put down my father's words as he told them to me.

The tragic scenes I saw that day
— Tsuchio Hase

If I had left home even a little later, I would have been hit downtown in a streetcar, but I was already walking when I heard the huge boom. I fell immediately to the ground behind a ridge next to a rice field. I thought, "What was that? I wonder if they dropped some sort of light bomb."

When I cautiously looked up, I saw a grassy area already burning. The harvested rice drying in another field was also in flames. I looked toward my company and saw the roof of the building completely gone. Only the iron skeleton remained.

I decided not to go to work. I fled along Route 2, but felt like I was at the entrance to hell. I saw long lines of people with their skin blistered and peeling off. My skin was also peeling where it was bare.

As I was walking toward Itsukaichi, to the west, it started raining, black rain. I managed to get to an elementary school. I went to a person nursing the injured, but she said, "You're still young. Go away." So I headed back toward Hiroshima. In Hiroshima, the ties on the metal Enko Bridge were burning.

I was thinking I wouldn't tell you this, but a military officer suffering from burns was on the riverbank by Enko Bridge. He ordered me to carry a wooden door. An officer's order was an absolute command at that time, so I carried the door as ordered. But when he tried to make me help him carry dead bodies on it, I ran away.

Even the skin on the military horses was blistered. I felt sorry for them. When I got to the Enko River, it was low tide, so I waded across to the other side.

I heard that trains were running from Kaita, so I walked there. I was young and able to walk even though I hadn't eaten all day. The train was full. I clung to the wall of the coal car behind the locomotive and headed home.

I think I got home around 11:00 that night. My mother and brother said, "You smell! What a stink." They were right, because of the burns. I had burns on my exposed skin. A doctor nearby came to see me but found nothing special. I had a fever of about 40 degrees for a week, but after that I got better.

I don't know if it was an aftereffect of the bombing or not, but I had to have surgery for lower intestinal problems. I have macula lutea degeneration in my eyes. I go to a doctor in Hiroshima once every two months. I'm old, but I guess that means I'm supposed to live a bit more, so I'm grateful.

Our life after the war was truly miserable. War is wrong, no matter what happens. War is no good. It's especially terrible for women. We called those who lost their husbands "war widows." That makes me angry. No wives willingly send their husbands to the battlefield. That's why I feel so strongly that militarism is plain wrong. This is my opinion. And if Japan had won the war, Japan would be completely different from what we have today.

    I haven't told anyone about the atomic bombing or the war until today. I didn't tell your mother when I married her. When she found out I was a survivor, she just said, "So you're a *hibakusha* then, right?" She had no prejudice against me. To tell the truth, her attitude saved me. I wasn't trying to hide anything from her. I just never felt I wanted to or should tell her. She didn't care whether I was exposed or not. She didn't see it as a problem and had no sense of discrimination. Since my wife sees me that way, I don't care what other people think. I'm happy.

Teruo Tomita
Nuclear weapons are wrong, no matter what

Teruo Tomita

After graduating from higher elementary school at the age of 14, I got a job and left home in Akitakata City to live in a dormitory in Shinonome in Hiroshima City.

I had woken up twice the previous night because of air-raid warnings and yellow alerts. Each time I had headed to work. Whenever an air-raid warning sounded, I had to run to my workplace immediately. On August 6, after morning assembly at 8:00, I was scheduled to carry guns and other arms to a freight car waiting at a platform in Hiroshima Station where the ordnance workshop was located.

I was working with a female colleague, lifting up a box of guns. We grunted as we lifted it up, and we were just stepping forward when a dazzling flash filled the air. The atomic bomb exploded at 8:15, so it was right after we started working. Our supervisor shouted, "Take cover! Take cover! Take cover!" We were on our way to the shelter when I felt a shock. It was as if someone had knocked me down.

I fell face down on the ground with a thud. Because I fell on my face, I assume the impact came from behind me, but even now, I really don't know where that impact came from.

I came to quickly. Crawling forward, I took refuge in a temporary shelter. I was anxious about what had happened, but I just looked down at the ground as I headed for the shelter. I didn't look around or take in the general situation at all. I do remember it was dark, like during an evening shower.

Another man was in the temporary shelter, and the two of us filled it. We didn't exchange a single word. I guess both of us were stunned, at a complete loss.

Meanwhile, I started hearing noise outside the shelter. I went outside and saw black rain falling from the sky. People around me seemed to panic. Someone said, "Sky torpedo! It was a sky torpedo!"

Later, I fled with older workers away from the station, but explosions rang out everywhere, so we grew frightened and returned to the plant. By the time we got back, many injured people had gathered. Their skin hung from the tips of their fingers, and their faces were swollen like balloons. They looked like sleepwalkers, or more like ghosts. We couldn't just leave them, so we spread straw mats in the warehouse and laid them down. Some said, "Give me water." But we didn't give water to those we thought likely to die. Thinking back on that now, I regret it, but the whole scene was so cruel it would drive you insane to think about it.

I stayed at the plant until August 15. During that time I was ordered by my supervisor to go up to Hijiyama Hill to help dig a tunnel to hide weapons in. I slept in a car or the second floor of the warehouse. I stayed alive eating food stored in a dining room that had escaped total destruction.

I never again saw the female colleague with whom I had carried the box that morning.

On August 15, our supervisor said, "Gather around the radio."

It was then I found out that Japan had lost the war. It had honestly never occurred to me that we would lose the war. I stayed until August 31 to clear up some remaining tasks, and then went home to Akitakata in September.

My parents had been getting ready to go to Hiroshima to look for me two days after the bombing, but a colleague who happened to commute from Akitakata told them I was safe. Thanks to him, they were able to avoid entry exposure.

At home the morning after my first good sleep on a *futon* in a long time, I was shocked. My pillow was covered with hair. Because I had been sleeping in places I couldn't call a bed, I had not been aware of this phenomenon. I had no idea about the effects of the atomic bombing, so I just wondered in amazement why my hair was falling out. I drank *dokudami* (saururaceae) tea my mother made every day, and the hair loss stopped after six months.

I helped my parents with farm work, but when I was 19, I stepped on Hiroshima soil again for the first time in five years, to be apprenticed to a master plasterer. I got married in Hiroshima; we had our sons there. I had no aftereffects from my exposure. I suffered no discrimination or prejudice as a *hibakusha*, but even now, every time I go for my regular cancer exam, my anxiety level rises. "What if I have cancer?"

"War is wrong. The atomic bombing was wrong. We must never repeat such a tragedy." When I talk about my A-bomb experience, I picture the burnt victims walking along with their skin hanging down. I feel lost, wondering how I can describe such an unspeakable sight. But if I don't talk about it, I can't relate the horror of the atomic bomb.

I had a nephew who was my own age. He was killed by the bombing while working as a mobilized student. I went to where he had been working and found only scraps of his clothing.

Every year on August 6, I visit the Peace Memorial Park and

mourn the loss of my nephew and all other victims of war.

To tell the truth, I once stopped talking about my A-bomb experience for a while. Someone who heard my experience said, "You're just using your experience as a survivor to show off." That caused me to stop, and I feel sad about that comment even now. However, I am driven by my sense of mission, and feel I just have to tell the truth about war. I am not a good speaker, but I am able to tell my experience because I feel I must.

"No matter what, nuclear weapons are wrong." I absolutely have to keep saying this to the world.

Michiaki Fujii
Kazuko Fujii

"Your grandpa is a treasure"

Michiaki Fujii   Kazuko Fujii

I was an "entry victim" and didn't know it
— Michiaki Fujii

I worked for the Army Clothing Depot in Hiroshima City. I took leave and was in my parents' house in Fukuyama on August 6, the day of the atomic bombing.

In our factory, about 2,500 employees made shoes, shirts and other clothing for soldiers. It was quite difficult to get leave from work because of the war.

I had wetted a stamp and peeled it off an envelope I had received some time earlier. I wrote, "Father seriously ill; return immediately." I put the stamp I'd peeled off onto an envelope and made it look as if the letter had just been delivered. I showed it to my boss, and he let me go home.

I desperately wanted to go home, so I cheated. I was simply

overwhelmed by my desire to go home the day before the bombing. I don't know what drove me like that, but if I had not gone home, I would have gone to work and probably would have been killed in Hatchobori. My desire to go home saved my life.

I was at home when I heard that a new type of bomb had been dropped on Hiroshima. Immediately the faces of my friends and fellow workers appeared before my eyes. I was unable to sit still. I went back to Hiroshima on the seventh, but the train stopped at Kaitaichi, three stations before Hiroshima. I walked for three hours to get to the city. I was stunned. The cityscape I knew was completely gone.

Along the Motoyasu River running past the Industrial Promotion Hall (the A-bomb Dome), I saw long, high piles of corpses. So many had jumped into the river due to heat, pain and thirst. Some died standing up. Some were so burnt I couldn't tell if they were wearing clothes or not.

Inside a two-car tram stopped near Aioi Bridge I saw an especially cruel sight. The atomic bomb hit the streetcar at 8:15 a.m. It was morning rush hour, so the tram was full. People were still standing, as if holding onto straps, but the straps were burnt away. All those sitting had been burnt as well. The instant I looked into that streetcar, I felt dizzy. I knew I was looking at hell. Hiroshima lay in ruins, filled with a foul smell.

I was not exposed to the bombing directly, but I walked near the hypocenter the day after the bombing. Therefore, I'm an entry victim. At the time, of course, I had no idea of such a thing.

I somehow managed to get to my workplace on the evening of the seventh. In the warehouse, the injured lay on mats spread out on the earthen floor. There were victims in most of the 13 warehouses. Cries for water came constantly from here and there. The smell was terrible; I have no way to describe it.

I stayed there and helped care for the victims. There were all levels of injury. Some were unconscious. Others were pierced by hundreds of glass fragments. One whose clothes were just torn rags burnt black like a piece of paper. Some were burnt so badly their legs were fused together. Wounds were swarming with maggots. Such victims were carried in one after another.

There were three nurses from the Red Cross Hospital, and we offered treatment according to their instructions. There was not much we could do except put gauze with a yellow antiseptic called Rivanol on the wounds. When the gauze got dry, we took it off and put on a new one. The victims kept begging, "Please, give me some water." But the nurses said, "Don't give them water; they'll die if you do." I hated not giving them water.

When they died anyway without even a sip of water, we heaped their bodies on a cart and pushed them to Ujina, where they were cremated in mountains of corpses. I'm sure we carried more than one hundred. We would put six bodies side by side and on top of each other in the cart. Tall people would stick out over the end of the cart. Dead bodies are heavy.

It took 50 minutes to make one trip to Ujina. We brought back the ashes, put them in urns, wrote the names on the urns and put them out by the gate. When family members found those urns, they would take them home. Those who came looking but failed to find any loved ones left looking so dejected. I saw many such scenes. Day after day, night after night, we worked continuously until the war ended on August 15. During those nine days, my only thought was, "I have to cremate them as quickly as possible." That was the only thing in my mind. I had become desensitized.

After the war, I worked to tie up loose ends for supply management at the village office in Yasu, Numata County. An occupying US soldier came every day to check the books, put his signature and leave. I went back to Fukuyama in March 1947, when the job of clearing things up ended.

Fukuyama had also been reduced to a burnt plain by B-29 incendiary bombings. Many of my good friends were killed, and my desire to live faded. I lost my spirit, and was unable to find a job; I had no goal or direction. I started living a wild life that continued for more than 10 years. The strange feelings I developed during my nine days in Hiroshima continued for all those years. I had escaped direct exposure to the bomb in Hiroshima and the bombings in Fukuyama. I never suffered any obvious damage. Many entry survivors suffered aftereffects, but I have had no such problems.

I talked about my atomic bomb experience for the first time in front of an audience in 2013. I spoke for only 10 minutes, but everyone quietly listened to my story. To be honest, I don't want to talk about it. I haven't talked about it even to my family. If I speak about it, I remember. If I don't speak, I don't have to remember.

It doesn't happen anymore, but I used to see the bombing in my dreams—those tragic sights. I often thought, "Why do I have to suffer so much?"

I have to tell everything I know. I have made this my life's mission, so I intend to share my experience as much as I can.

I want to tell the truth to my grandson — Kazuko Fujii

One day someone from the municipal office contacted me to confirm my husband's personal history. That is how I came to know he was an entry victim. Until then I had heard fragments of his story, but, partly because of the difference in our ages, I couldn't quite comprehend what he said. He was unbelievably healthy, so I couldn't accept his story at first. He entered Hiroshima right after the bombing, the next day. "You had no aftereffects? Really?" I couldn't help being doubtful.

When my husband shared his A-bomb experience in public, I

listened to him speak. Then, at home, he said, "It was actually far, far worse than that. There were children in the audience. I'm afraid they would be terribly shocked if I really told them the way it was."

Some say it's better not to show tattered clothes or charred lunchboxes, but after I heard my husband's experience I came to believe we have to teach people the truth and pass the story on from generation to generation. My grandson in elementary school plays video games, never hesitating to say, "Kill them!" He has no real sense of the sanctity of life, or the fact that a living creature dies and never comes back. He plays games he can reset easily. His consciousness is completely different.

Living witnesses who experienced the misery of war must hand down their stories. I want to tell my grandson, "Your grandpa is a treasure."

Kazutoshi Nakamura

No time left to leave proof the survivors ever lived

Kazutoshi Nakamura

I was a first-year student at university when I heard my father's experience. His name was Yoshiharu Nakamura. I had a social studies assignment to interview my parents about the lives they had lived and write a report. I came home during summer vacation and heard my father's story. I had known he was in the atomic bombing, but this was the first time I heard details about his pain and suffering.

My father was 18. He was working in Hiroshima Station. He had an extraordinary experience, far beyond my imagination, when he was my age (at the time we talked), but he spoke as if it had happened to someone else. I understood why, when he said, "My senses were numb then." This made a powerful impression on me; it explained everything.

He had walked home stepping over dead bodies. He used the term "sensory paralysis" to express his ability to accept such surreal scenes as normal without realizing what he was doing. My guess is he was calling the war itself a time of sensory paralysis.

The father that I have known since my childhood always worked hard to raise his family, and enjoyed a drink with dinner at home. He never once scolded me. Therefore, when I heard his A-bomb story, I couldn't quite relate my gentle father to his tragic experience. What he told me lay heavy on my mind, but more than anything, I could not believe that the man before my eyes, my father, had experienced such things.

It may be that he himself found his experience impossible to believe. When Japan lost the war he had been convinced it would win, his whole world turned upside down. His values were suddenly reversed. At the age of 18, everything he had thought right suddenly turned out to be wrong. To survive, he had no choice but to push aside his war experience and call the whole thing sensory paralysis.

His gentleness was part of his nature. He was born with it, but it was also affected by having lived through that time, including both the war and the atomic bombing.

I became interested in how he lived from the time of the bombing through the postwar turmoil, but he passed away in August 2014 at the age of 87, leaving me with a lot of questions I wanted to ask.

After the bombing, he developed swollen lymph glands and underwent an operation. Whether or not it was an effect of the bombing was medically unclear. Several years ago, because he was exposed fairly near the hypocenter, he was officially recognized as a survivor by the City of Hiroshima. His cholesterol was abnormally high even though he was thin, and a doctor once told him, "Your thyroid is strange." He took medicine to control his cholesterol for a long time, again not knowing whether it was atomic bomb disease or not.

Thinking back now, I regret that I failed to ask him so many things. Was he discriminated against as a survivor? What did he feel during those postwar years?

He had encountered such a terrible thing when he was 18. He lost his job. He lived in a hut with no bath, no running water. How did he rebuild his status in society and get married from there? I take the A-bomb experience for granted, in a way, but day by day I feel more strongly that I have to pass on to future generations the way survivors lived after the war and the thoughts and feelings of the people who rebuilt Hiroshima from that plain of burnt ruins.

It's a matter of time before the chance to hear survivors' stories in person is gone. The generation that remembers that experience clearly and can share it with others is dwindling. We need to hurry. As a second-generation survivor, I want to hear the experiences of other family members. I want to leave proof that the first generation *hibakusha* lived.

Reference
Materials

Hiroshima

MAP showing areas destroyed by atomic bombing of Hiroshima

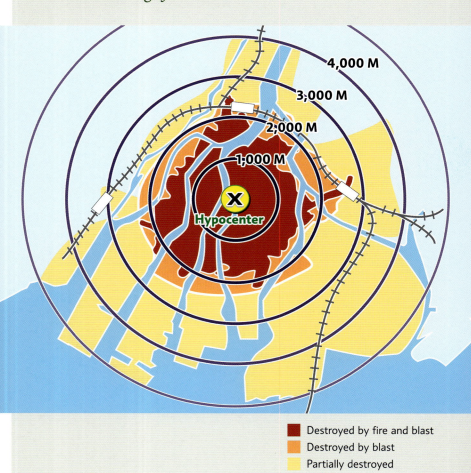

The first atomic bomb ever to be used in warfare in human history was dropped on Hiroshima at 8:15 a.m. on August 6, 1945. It detonated after 43 seconds at an altitude of approximately 600 meters with a blinding flash, creating a fireball that blazed like a small sun with a temperature of more than 1 million degrees Celsius at its center. The fireball expanded to a maximum radius of 280 m in just one second, and the temperature on the surface of the ground around the hypocenter reached 3,000 to 4,000 degrees Celsius. At the moment of detonation, fierce heat rays and radiation burst out in every direction, unleashing an ultra high pressure shockwave, compounded effects of which caused immense destruction.

Estimates place the number of dead by the end of December 1945 at roughly 140,000 out of a population of around 350,000.

— *Source: The City of Hiroshima*

The A-bomb Dome, remains of the former Hiroshima Prefectural Industrial Promotion Hall, stands as a symbol of the atomic bombing
Photo by US Army, courtesy of Hiroshima Peace Memorial Museum

Nagasaki

MAP
showing areas destroyed by atomic bombing of Nagasaki

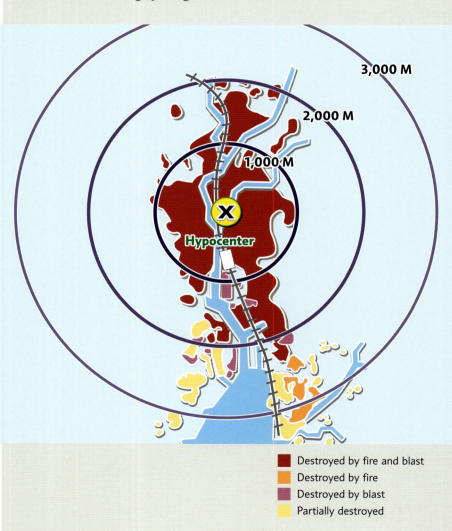

August 9, 1945, 11:02 a.m. Following Hiroshima, the second atomic bomb in the world destroyed the City of Nagasaki.

The plutonium type atomic bomb was dropped from a height of 9,000 meters by the American bomber, *Bockscar*. It exploded approximately 500 m above the ground. The enormous energy of the explosion sucked up matter from the earth, and propelled it into the air. This became a mushroom cloud, which was constantly evolving in color and shape as it steadily rose, until it reached a height of 9,000 m roughly 8.5 minutes later.

Nagasaki had a population of about 240,000. By the end of December 1945, 73,884 of its people had been killed, and 74,909 had been injured by the atomic bomb.

— *Source: Nagasaki Atomic Bomb Museum*

The remains of Shiroyama Elementary School in Nagasaki
Photo by unknown, courtesy of Nagasaki Atomic Bomb Museum

Nuclear weapons facts

The threat posed by nuclear weapons is not a thing of the past—it is a threat we face today.

Many states are developing nuclear energy capacities that would make it relatively easy for them to build nuclear weapons, should they decide to do so. The possibility that terrorist organizations will acquire such weapons is also real. The danger that these apocalyptic weapons will be used—by accident or deliberately in an act of madness—hangs over us all.

The nuclear-weapon states continue to place nuclear deterrence at the center of their national security strategies.

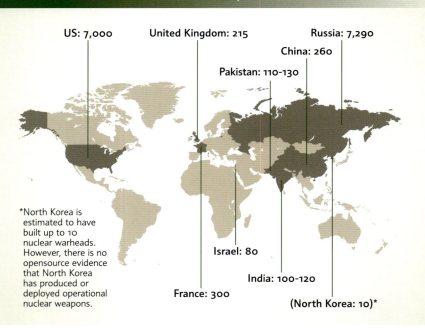

World Nuclear Forces: Total Inventory (2016)

US: 7,000
United Kingdom: 215
Russia: 7,290
China: 260
Pakistan: 110-130
Israel: 80
India: 100-120
France: 300
(North Korea: 10)*

*North Korea is estimated to have built up to 10 nuclear warheads. However, there is no opensource evidence that North Korea has produced or deployed operational nuclear weapons.

Figures and text from SIPRI (Stockholm International Peace Research Institute), 2016
(All figures are approximate)

IPPNW Campaign Kit

The Humanitarian Impact of Nuclear Weapons

— Text on pages vii–xiv excerpted from Campaign Kit created by International Physicians for the Prevention of Nuclear War (IPPNW)

Mushroom cloud over Hiroshima, one hour after the first atomic bombing in human history on August 6, 1945
Photo by US Army, courtesy of Hiroshima Peace Memorial Museum

NUCLEAR WEAPONS unleash the binding forces that power the stars to produce incinerating heat, powerful shock waves and overpressures and ionizing radiation.

Unlike conventional weapons or other weapons of mass destruction, nuclear weapons instantaneously wipe out entire populations, level cities and devastate the environment.

Moreover, they produce radioactive contamination that causes cancers and other illnesses that can persist across generations for millennia.

Nagasaki hypocenter and environs two days before the atomic bombing
Photo by US Army, courtesy of Nagasaki Atomic Bomb Museum

Nagasaki hypocenter and environs one month after the atomic bombing
Photo by US Army, courtesy of Nagasaki Atomic Bomb Museum

Incompatible with humanity

NO WEAPON ever invented can cause so much death and destruction so quickly, on such a catastrophic scale, or such widespread and persisting toxicity in the environment.

A single nuclear weapon can destroy a city and kill most of its people. A small number of nuclear explosions over modern cities would kill tens of millions of people. Casualties from a major nuclear war between the US and Russia would reach hundreds of millions in a matter of hours.

Around 800 meters south of the Nagasaki hypocenter
Photo by Torahiko Ogawa, courtesy of Nagasaki Atomic Bomb Museum

Physical trauma and burns

NUCLEAR WEAPONS have extreme blast and burn effects that kill people and destroy infrastructure on a scale and with an intensity that puts them in a class of their own compared with any other weapons.

The heat wave from a nuclear detonation incinerates everything combustible in its path, including human flesh.

Firestorms consume all remaining oxygen, suffocating everyone who might have managed to take refuge from the flames themselves.

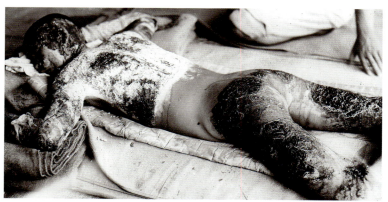

Man with burns over entire body, exposed within 1 km of Hiroshima hypocenter
Photo by Masami Onuka, courtesy of Hiroshima Peace Memorial Museum

Entrance to Sumitomo Bank, 260 m from Hiroshima hypocenter, imprinted with shadow of an atomic bomb victim, due to heat rays of up to 4,000 degrees Celsius
Chugoku Shimbun

- Explosive yields of the atomic bombs that destroyed Hiroshima and Nagasaki were 15,000 (15 kilotons, kt) to 21,000 tons of TNT equivalent.
- Modern nuclear weapons are typically 50,000 to 300,000, but up to 5,000,000 tons (5 megatons, Mt) of TNT equivalent.
- Ground temperatures from the 15-kt Hiroshima bomb reached about 7,000°F (3,800°C) = the sun's surface.
- Of the 76,000 buildings in the city, 92% were destroyed or damaged from the shock wave and blast.
- The 21-kt bomb detonated over Nagasaki three days later leveled 6.7 square kilometers (2.6 square miles).

Radiation

NUCLEAR WEAPONS produce ionizing radiation, which kills or sickens those exposed, contaminates the environment and has long-term health consequences for those who do not die right away.

Acute radiation sickness can cause death within hours, days or weeks; those who recover may remain ill for months or even years.

Lower doses of ionizing radiation can cause leukemia, thyroid cancer and many other cancers, even many years after exposure. Increased risk of cancer persists for the lifetime of those exposed.

Exposure to dangerous ionizing radiation has become a persistent global problem because of continuing fallout from atmospheric tests and contamination of land and water around the former test sites, nuclear weapons production facilities and radioactive waste storage sites.

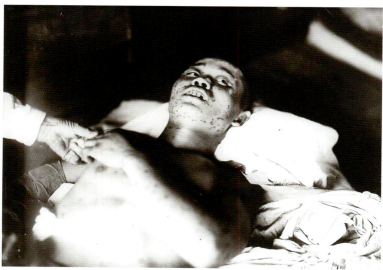

Soldier exposed within 1 km of the hypocenter in Hiroshima who died on Sept 3, 1945. Subcutaneous hemorrhage spots covered his face and upper body.
Photo by Gonichi Kimura, courtesy of Hiroshima Peace Memorial Museum

Inaccessible to doctors

PHYSICIANS AND first responders not themselves victims would be unable to work in the totally devastated, radioactively contaminated wastelands that would extend for kilometers beyond ground zero, making it impossible to reach and treat survivors.

- Of the 298 physicians in Hiroshima, 270 were killed or injured; of the 1,780 nurses, 1,564 were killed or injured.
- 80% of the hospitals were destroyed or seriously damaged; emergency rooms were set up in half-demolished buildings, without water, sanitation or medicines.
- Of the 70 doctors in Nagasaki, 40 were killed or injured; the University Medical Center was destroyed.

Emergency relief station, 1.1 km from the Hiroshima hypocenter, August 7, 1945
Photo by Yotsugi Kawahara, courtesy of Hiroshima Peace Memorial Museum

Nuclear famine and nuclear winter

LESS THAN one percent of the nuclear weapons in the world today could disrupt the global climate and cause nuclear famine.

A limited, regional nuclear conflict involving only 100 Hiroshima-size nuclear weapons would severely disrupt the global climate and agriculture for two decades or more.

The resulting food shortages would place at least two billion people at risk of starvation. The effects would hit hardest the people who are currently most affected by food insecurity, even if they are distant from the region of conflict; but no region would be spared.

The massive arsenals held by the US and Russia could destroy Earth's fundamental ecosystems, on which all life depends.

These findings have profound implications. Use of nuclear weapons by any nation, with uncontrollable risks of escalation, would be suicidal.

- Firestorms from 100 Hiroshima-size bombs used against modern cities would inject 5 teragrams of smoke and soot into the atmosphere, blocking sunlight from reaching the Earth.

- Average global surface temperatures drop by approximately -1 to -1.6°C for a decade.

- Rainfall decreases by 10% or more.

- Growing seasons are shorter by up to 40 days throughout the world's agricultural zones over years 2-6 after such a war.

- Drastic food shortages threaten at least two billion people with starvation.

IPPNW.ORG

Museums

HIROSHIMA
Peace Memorial Museum

http://hpmmuseum.jp/?lang=eng

NAGASAKI
Atomic Bomb Museum

http://nagasakipeace.jp/english/abm.html

» TO LEARN MORE
Visit Hiroshima and Nagasaki

Hibakusha Pok Soon-kwak shares her experience of the atomic bombing in Hiroshima
Seikyo Shimbun

There is no countervailing imperative
—whether of national security,
stability in international power relations,
or the difficulty of overcoming political inertia—
that justifies their continued existence,
much less their use.

Their catastrophic humanitarian consequences
demand that nuclear weapons never
be used again, under any circumstances.

Statement by Faith Communities Concerned about Nuclear Weapons to the First Session of the Preparatory Committee for the 2020 NPT Review Conference, Vienna, May 3, 2017